"*Once I started reading, I co* *page by page. It opened up a v.........*
Derek J., head of finance at a media company

"*The ABC of life has given me new perspectives and practical tools for interacting with not only my patients but also my friends, family, and colleagues. At my healthcare center, I now use the ABC as a best-practice guide for creating well-being and happiness for myself and my patients. Thank you, Marcus, for these amazing insights!*"
Lisa B., healthcare professional

"*This book has been an eye-opener for me. Marcus gave me a new perspective and fascinating insights on life. Now I know how to design my lifestyle for better health, more well-being, and success.*"
Naomi M., managing partner at a consulting company

"*The ABC of life has helped me to succeed at my workplace; better manage my personal relationships; and understand, monitor, and handle my emotions. Since first coming in contact with the ABC model, it has been in the back of my mind, effectively navigating me through my daily challenges.*"
Peter F., marketing manager at a fast-moving consumer goods company

"*This book is an awesome account of multiple science tracks translated into real life application. The ABC has become my guiding communication tool at home, at work, and with my friends. The tool has transformed my life. Thank you for sharing!*"
Andrea G., head of human resources at an industrial company

"*When I encountered the ABC of life, it immediately clicked. Finally I could understand people and—more importantly—myself and my children! For a single mother of three, the ABC represents the lighthouse guide for my daily routines, my life insurance in successfully managing my small 'family enterprise'.*"
Claudine K., single mother of three children

"I have been a teacher for over 30 years now. When I look at my students from an ABC perspective, I finally understand why they do what they do. As a result, I can better manage my feelings and steer students in the right directions. So in essence, for me, the ABC means a better life and a better education for my students."
Andrew C., high school teacher

"I have started to re-design my lifestyle according to the principles of the ABC of life. This book has fundamentally changed the way I look at life. I have already become a much happier and more energetic person now."
Patricia L., manager at an online platform

"Too bad the book is only available now. What a groundbreaking message! I wish I had known about the ABC during my professional life. It would have saved me from many failures. Now I understand what makes people tick. Looking at it from the bright side, the ABC gives me guidance on success and happiness for the rest of my life."
Francois G., retired senior executive

"I met Marcus a couple of years ago when he told me about the ABC of life. It all made sense to me in terms of my own performance as well as the team I played in at the time. The book has now become my bible in managing my day-to-day interactions with my family, my friends, and my coaches and teammates."
Connor W., professional football player

The ABC of Life

In recognition of
Ed and Rich,
for inspiring and leading a movement
that has been changing the world
for the better!

The ABC of Life

Success Has 3 Letters

Marcus B. Müller

Amsterdam University Press

Cover design: Eric Guémise, Freelance Motion Graphics
Lay-out: Crius Group, Hulshout

ISBN   978 90 4855 905 3
e-ISBN   978 90 4855 906 0
DOI   10.5117/9789048559053
NUR   801

The "Why" and "What" of This Book

Success has three letters: A, B, and C. Please do not immediately judge my spelling skills. I did pretty well learning my ABC's in primary school. At the time, my room was full of exciting spelling exercises such as "Annie Apple", "Bouncing Ben", and "Clever Cat". But then life happened and I realized that the ABC I learned in primary school would not be enough to be successful in life. On my mission to explore the secrets of success, I discovered the ABC of life. My journey was an all-engaging rollercoaster of trial and error that took a substantial amount of time as well as emotional and physical resources. In this book, I want to inspire you to shortcut your own route to success. Before jumping right into it, let me briefly share the story of the book's origin with you.

When I was 5 years old, all my parents' friends as well as our extended family panicked whenever they heard that I would be joining my parents for a visit. They knew that I would be running around their house again opening all sorts of drawers and closets. Maybe I was hyperactive. Fortunately, attention deficit hyperactivity disorder (ADHD) was not high on the agenda of pediatrics at the time, so I got away with my behavior without the side effects of today's common medical treatments. My parents were not so lucky: they lost quite a few friends and acquaintances due to my eccentric impulsiveness.

What I know today is that my behavior at the time was fueled by my insatiable curiosity. I was driven by the thrill of not knowing what was in that drawer—maybe there was a mouse or even a monster!—and the thrill of what further excitement would be waiting for me if I opened the closet door.

At age 14, I sticky-taped a world map above my bed. By that time, home and school had shaped my horizons. I believed that life was a battlefield. No pain, no gain. Good enough was never good enough. Another thing had also become clear to me by then: I would never be a polished stone. Instead, my activities had started to increasingly irritate the people around me. I had chopped up my grandfather's garden hose with an axe to explore the impact of water pressure, and for my actions I was promptly reprimanded and punished by my grandfather. One summer, I built a spray gun to find out how driving behavior changed when neighbors driving by in front of our house were suddenly hit by a water jet through their open windows. For this, I was questioned and penalized by my parents and our neighbors. Another time, I ignited a series of firecrackers at a group of pensioners strolling in a nearby forest to observe the scare this would cause them. This earned me a questioning by the police and some social work at a local kindergarten.

The reason I had put the world map over my bed was that my insatiable curiosity had found a new purpose: my quest to become a success in life. Neither garden hose, spray gun, nor firecrackers had done the job—quite the opposite. So each and every evening when I went to bed, I looked up at the world map and fantasized where success was waiting for me in a corner of a side street—in London, perhaps, or New York, Rio, Tokyo.

Since then, I have visited most continents, many countries, and even more major cities. My curiosity prompted me to search for success as an engineer, a software developer, a management consultant, an investment banker, an ironman triathlete, and as a monk in a Buddhist monastery. Family, friends, and colleagues may have looked upon my life as a success. But from my perspective, I had not found success anywhere or in anything.

At age 42, I drove out of the underground parking lot of the Frankfurt bank I was working at, and it was at that moment that I decided this would be my last day in the finance industry. I wanted to search for success elsewhere for the rest of my life. Six months later, I started my PhD in organizational psychology at the University of the Sunshine Coast in Australia. It was there that I finally discovered success, after over four decades of searching. Fortunately, due to my curiosity, I had never stopped searching for it. But to my surprise, there was nothing particularly magic about that place in Australia. Instead, my journey to success turned out to be a self-discovery. I had been carrying success and its building blocks around with me—inside of me—all my life. The secret code of success that unlocked my inner vault revealed itself to me when I first came in contact with the self-determination theory, which taught me that success had three letters: A, B, and C (for Autonomy, Belonging, and Competence).

Since then, I have been researching, practicing, teaching, and sharing what I have called "the ABC". It has changed my own life and inspired others to become successful ABC practitioners. Groups of friends and colleagues from all spheres of life have invited me to introduce them to the ABC approach over a cup of coffee, a meal, or a workshop. Organizational psychology is a course I teach at my business school based on the ABC. Individual and corporate clients have been energized by the ABC. As ABC practitioners, they have benefitted from the three letters through personal and organizational success stories. Many of them— friends, colleagues, students, and clients—have repeatedly asked me to write a book on the ABC of life to make it available to a wider audience.

I have finally responded to their request with this book. In the chapters that follow, I will share the ingredients of the ABC of life with you. The book's mission is to invite you to explore the ABC as an evolutionary approach to creating success in your own life as well as making a positive difference to the lives of others.

Part I (Chapters 1 through 4) will introduce you to three pillars of success and what propels them. I will show you how and why our feelings determine successful behavior. A closer look at the feelings of Autonomy, Belonging, and Competence will reveal the foundation of the ABC of life. You will discover that what makes the ABC so powerful is its grounding in our human nature.

Along the way, you will learn about and from scientists across the fields of social and evolutionary psychology, neuroscience, anthropology, and economics. You will find out why the ABC of life almost did not make it out of the pits of scientific research and into this book. I will show you how the results from research into the ABC in the 1970s had remained a mystery to conventional science for decades until more recent discoveries. I will share success and failure stories across life domains with you. Exploring how the ABC impacted an English soccer club, an investment bank, a hospital, and a coffee shop will give you an understanding of the practical side of the ABC of life. In further chapters, you will become familiar with the potentially devastating effects of a lack of ABC in people's lives. I will give you detailed insights into the role of ABC deficiency in failures spanning from a prominent Olympic Games disaster to a famous musician's suicide. You will also find out the crucial role that your brain's CEO and its bodyguard play in the success of your life.

In Part II (Chapters 5 through 9), the focus switches from the foundation of the ABC of life to its application in various life domains. An analysis of work environments sheds light on how the ABC can help create success for employees, teams, and organizations. There are substantial overlaps between the spheres of work and sports. The ABC will be showcased as a tool to enhance and sustain top performance in individuals and teams. For those of you who may not engage in physical exercise for performance but for well-being, another chapter will focus on health. Exploring how the ABC of life can be applied as a tool for the prevention and curing of illnesses, stress, and burnout will highlight the ABC's importance for individual and societal health. The Dalai Lama once said: "Happiness is the highest form of health", and this quote sets the agenda for a section on the relationship between the ABC and happiness. You will find out how the ABC can explain the pitfalls of episodic happiness, help achieve sustainable happiness, and clarify the difference between happiness and life satisfaction. In addition, you will discover the ABC's role in when and how money can buy happiness. Learning about the ABC as well as how to lead a happy life are just two aspects of what makes learning a central human survival mechanism. How we educate our children today determines how we will live tomorrow. The final section of Part II demonstrates how the ABC of life can serve as a guide to creating success for students, teachers, parents, school administrators, politicians, and societies based on more effective learning environments.

On your journey through Part II, you will be guided by the findings and experiences of leading-edge psychology researchers and neuroscientists, business leaders and employees, professional and amateur athletes, health professionals and patients, a Buddhist nun, and children caged in classrooms.

In Part III (Chapter 10), I unveil how you can apply the ABC to your own life and create success for yourself and others by managing your ABC as well as contributing to the levels of others. The ABC of life can be taught, trained, and learned. Chapter 10 will tell you how to diagnose your levels of A, B, and C. I will also show you how to adapt new habits related to the ABC. You will find out how to (re-)design your life according to the ABC principles and become the director of your life movie instead of feeling victimized by circumstances. And you will learn how to use tools and interventions of give and take to become an ABC practitioner and doer!

The final part of the book represents an epilogue reflecting on how the ABC can help resolve the most challenging and complex puzzle of survival in the history of humankind: overcoming the exploitation and pollution of our planet to prevent our species' mass suicide. You will figure out why apocalyptic scenarios of doom and gloom as well as overcontrol and bans will be counterproductive to sustainable innovation. I will show you why the solution needs to start with thinking differently and how the ABC of life can be an effective tool in releasing the power of human creativity to ensure our survival.

In this book, I want to inspire you to pay more attention to your feelings as a source of success and failure in your life. If you do not understand what drives people, including yourself, you do not understand what drives success. Feelings are usually not openly discussed. The following chapters will provide insights into a structured approach to feelings that you can apply to fuel yourself and others to achieve success and prevent failure. "ABC-ing" yourself and others is a skill that can be trained, taught, and learned. By practicing the ABC, you can design the very foundations of success in your life.

Thank you for your time and consideration.

Marcus

Table of Contents

Part I

1. Learning from Pygmalion

Knowledge of what is possible is the beginning of success.
– George Santayana

In the fall of 1963, the principal of Oak Elementary School in the South San Francisco Unified School District read an article in the journal *American Scientist* that changed her life. In the article, the German-born Harvard professor Robert Rosenthal summarized close to a dozen laboratory studies he and his colleagues had conducted on what is known as experimenter expectancy effects.

Before starting an experiment, scientists develop a hypothesis of the expected outcomes. Experimenter expectancy describes the unintended effect of researchers treating their research participants in such a way that they influence them to behave in line with the hypothesis or the expected outcomes. In more general terms, the lab studies demonstrated that one person's expectations for the behavior of another could affect that other person's behavior. Rosenthal concluded his article by suggesting further research into potentially reproducing the effect in other disciplines such as healthcare, organizations, or schools.

Lenore Jacobson was electrified when reading about Rosenthal's findings. She was a dedicated school principal focused on creating the best possible learning environments for her students. Based on her extensive experience as a teacher, Jacobson had long had a suspicion that teachers' expectations of individual students' performance had an impact on teachers' behavior and, in turn, on students' behavior and performance. However, until then she had had no credible evidence to support her theory.

On November 18, 1963, Lenore Jacobson wrote a letter to Robert Rosenthal highlighting her interest in the field of teacher expectations. She ended the letter with the following line: "If you ever 'graduate' to classroom children, please let me know whether I can be of assistance." When Rosenthal contacted her, she understood that this was a once-in-a-lifetime opportunity to make a difference to school environments beyond Oak Elementary. Over the next two months, Jacobson and Rosenthal worked out the details of their collaboration. In January 1964, Rosenthal travelled from Boston to San Francisco to settle on a final design for the study.

All 320 children at Jacobson's elementary school were given the non-verbal Harvard Test of Inflected Acquisition, which was promoted to teachers as a test that could predict future intellectual performance. Oak Elementary had 18 classrooms, or three classrooms per grade: one for children with above-average ability, one for average ability, and one for below-average ability. A quarter of the students from each classroom—65 of the 255 children in total—were randomly selected as the experimental group. At the beginning of the school year, each classroom teacher was given the names of the 65 randomly chosen children, their scores of the Harvard Test of Inflected Acquisition, and the feedback that the scores indicated that these 65 children would show extraordinary gains—that is, they would be "growth spurters" in intellectual performance over the coming eight months. However, in reality, the only difference between the experimental group of 65 and the control group of 255 children was in the minds of the teachers.

When the Harvard Test of Inflected Acquisition was administered again at the end of the school year, the children in the experimental group had gained an astonishing 12.22 points in intellectual performance compared to an increase of 8.42 points for the children in the control group. The results confirmed the hypothesis of an expectancy effect in teacher-student settings. However, there were two surprises. First, the almost 50% gains in performance by the growth spurters over the control group was unexpectedly high. And second, when teachers were interviewed about their experiences with children over the school year, they reported that the 65 experimental children were better equipped for becoming successful in the future—in the perception of their teachers!

The Oak Elementary School research study provided the basis for what has become known as the Pygmalion effect, named after the sculptor in Greek mythology who fell in love with a statue he had created. The phenomenon has been replicated in hundreds of scientific studies since then across various life domains such as organizations (e.g., executives' expectations impacting employees' performance), healthcare (e.g., care providers' expectations impacting patients' compliance and recovery), sports (e.g., coaches' expectations impacting players' performance), and courtrooms (e.g., judges' expectations influencing jurors' decisions). While academic scholars around the world were busy reproducing the expectancy effect in various disciplines globally, Rosenthal focused on extending his research by examining another burning question. If the effect of interpersonal expectancy was so powerful, what were its drivers? In practical terms, was there a magic formula people could use in their everyday lives to create the conditions for their own success as well as the success of those around them?

The Pillars of Success

The prevailing wisdom suggests that success is based on a formula combining three main elements of behavior—goals, skills, and persistence. Successful people have clear goals. They own, acquire, and apply the skills needed to reach their goals. And finally, they show persistence in using their skills in the pursuit of their goals.

GOALS + SKILLS + PERSISTENCE → SUCCESS

Rosenthal's discovery adds a further dimension to the success formula. Interactions between people generate the *fuel* that drives successful behavior, namely goal setting, skill application, and persistence. A Ferrari sports car needs fuel to move forward and unleash its power. The fuller the gas tank, the longer the sports car will perform at top speed. In the same way, people's interpersonal interactions generate the fuel for them to succeed in their daily races. In Rosenthal's studies, teachers somehow provided more or better fuel to some students who, in turn, were then substantially more successful in applying the goals-skills-persistence formula. What is this fuel? How does this mechanism work?

The Drivers of Success

I have been studying people across many different life domains around the globe for 30 years now—as a son, husband, father, friend, sports athlete, monk, and business executive. For the past 16 years, I have been exploring the drivers of success as a social psychologist, scientist, and professor of management at an American business school. Over 50 years of scientific work in the social sciences have yielded revolutionary findings. They show a clear pattern of how interpersonal interactions drive people's success. Let me introduce you to this compelling approach. I call it the *ABC of life*.

ABC stands for *Autonomy, Belonging,* and *Competence.* In a series of stunning, cutting-edge studies, social scientists have identified three basic human needs. We need *autonomy*, the feeling of having a say in what we do and how we do it, having discretion, options, and a degree of self-determination. Feelings of *belonging* give us a sense of being valued, appreciated, included, and supported. Finally, we need to feel *competence*, that is, we need to feel effective in mastering tasks and overcoming challenges as well as experiencing personal growth, facing new challenges, developing new skills, and extending our abilities. All three feelings originate from our interactions with people in our lives. The more "ABC" we feel in such encounters, the more fuel is generated to persistently use our skills effectively in the pursuit of our goals and, in turn, to drive our success.

In 1973, Rosenthal published the first results of his investigation into the drivers of the Pygmalion effect in schools. The so-called socio-emotional climate between a student and a teacher turned out to be by far the most important cause of a student's success in school. In non-scientific terms, this means that the amount of ABC generated in teacher-student interactions determined the student's academic success. Teachers were more open, more friendly, more trusting, more supportive, more encouraging, more empathetic, and more caring due to their experimentally designed expectations of student performance. They gave students the ABC they needed that fueled their performance. As a consequence, students felt more self-determined (Autonomy), more valued (Belonging), and more empowered (Competence), thereby turning into "growth spurters".

Sports Coach Scandal

Similar to teachers and their students, sports coaches form opinions on their athletes based on past achievements, physical appearance, or training impressions. How coaches' expectations are reflected in their communication patterns and their influence on athletes' motivation, performance, and successes has been well documented in academic literature.

A recent study by Malgorzata Siekanska, Jan Belcharz, and Agnieszka Woytowicz from the University of Cracow analyzed the Pygmalion effect from an athlete's point of view. They surveyed and interviewed 80 athletes competing at the national and international levels. When asked the question: "Do you think the coach's attitude towards an athlete with higher sports level differs from the one directed towards low achievers?", 90% of participants responded positively. As manifestations of such coach attitudes, participants described the coaches as "devoting more time", "being more lenient", or "showing post-training interest in the athlete". Asked for key coaching behaviors contributing to success in sports, "good coach-athlete interactions" were ranked as the top item by the athletes in this study. When cross-checking the results by exploring the factors that inhibited top athlete performance, "a lack of good spirit and interaction" was the most common response by far.

A lack of good spirit and interaction was clearly at play in the case of the English soccer club Fulham. When Fulham hired Felix Magath in February 2014 on an 18-month contract, he was the club's third coach of the 2013-2014 season after Martin Jol and Rene Meulensteen had been sacked. Fulham F.C. was dangerously close to being relegated from the English Premier League. Magath's mandate was to save the season for Fulham and keep the club among England's best. But this is not what happened.

One should not blame Fulham's owner Shahid Khan for hiring Magath based on his credentials as a former player and coach. After all, as a player, Magath had seen huge success. He won the European Cup (now the Champions League) with Hamburger SV, had 43 international caps for Germany, won the European Championship in 1980, and reached two consecutive World Cup finals. In the initial stages of his coaching career, he earned himself a reputation as a fireman after saving four clubs from relegation. More recently, he had won two doubles (championship and cup) with Bayern Munich and another German championship title with VfL Wolfsburg. However, in his coaching career, Magath had never completed a full three consecutive seasons at the same club. Shahid Khan and his team should have done more homework and background checking on Magath's coaching style and what he had left behind at previous clubs beyond his paper credentials.

Behind his back, Magath was known as "Saddam" at one of his former clubs. Another nickname for him from Germany was Quälix, a mix of his first name Felix and the German verb for torture (quälen). Magath had spent the most successful years of his career from 1980 to 1986 as a player under Ernst Happel at Hamburger SV, who had been known to be a strict and authoritarian coach. When Magath became coach himself, his style reflected what he may have perceived as keys to success under Happel. However, in perfecting his coaching style, he seems to have gone too far over the years. For example, English journalist Daniel Taylor argues that "there is a difference between being a coach who wants power and rule and one who is unreasonable and dictatorial to the point that it alienates everyone". Not surprisingly, his former player Bachirou Salou at Eintracht Frankfurt once called Magath "the last dictator of Europe". Jefferson Farfan of Schalke 04 once said about his former coach: "All the coaches at Schalke in the last few years gave something to the club. The only coach who did not leave anything positive behind was Magath. All he left behind were fines." That was the exact experience that the players at Fulham had with Magath—an extremely unpleasant man who left a trail of ill feelings.

Magath could not avoid relegation in the 2013/14 season but stayed on. However, the stories about his training methods became even more alarming. After one defeat, the players' day off was cancelled and everyone was brought in to play a full 90-minute match (Autonomy downer). On another occasion, players reported that they had to run three times a day until they dropped. When they went for their water bottles to refresh themselves, they discovered that the coach had emptied them all, for reasons only Magath understood (Autonomy and Belonging downers). One story of his coaching techniques emerged that he would call players into his office and then just stare at them for several minutes without saying a word (Autonomy, Belonging, and Competence downers). Reputable and experienced players like Bryan Ruiz or Fernando Amorebieta who openly opposed Magath's style were excluded from official training. They had to train on another field, and players were not permitted to talk to the outcasts (Belonging downer). In general, Magath was perceived as a sadistic control freak whose interaction with the players was nothing but punishing and primitive (Autonomy, Belonging, and Competence downers). When asked retrospectively, players reported that they had felt distressed, trapped, intimidated, and abused by Magath's style. As a result, they had felt deflated, tired, and exhausted before a match had even started.

It should not come as a surprise that Fulham lost six of the first seven games of the 2014/15 season in the lower division. After losing 3-5 to Nottingham Forest in September 2014, Magath was finally sacked by Khan. Players had been desperate to get out of the club and gave more details of a bewildering crazy world under madcap Magath. Former Wales international player Kit Symons then took over from Magath, and even though the team lost their first match under Symons, a few smiles on the players' faces were spotted. Success returned to Fulham shortly thereafter. The team won 10 of the next 20 games, with 3 draws. To quote *The Guardian*, Symons was working hard "to make Fulham a happy place again".

The case of Fulham F.C. shows how the dysfunctional communication style of a professional sports coach can negatively affect a team, a club, and its entire community of fans, friends, and families with only one way out—getting rid of the perpetrator. It may sound like a stretch to move from the world of professional sports to that of clinical health. However, the pattern of feelings that drive behavior was also at the core of a chain of events at a German hospital whose management arrived at similar conclusions to Fulham F.C. owner Shahid Khan.

Healthcare Hitch

It was Rosenthal himself who led a study in a nursing home with fellow researchers Lee Learman, Jerry Avorn, and Daniel Everitt. They conducted randomized experiments investigating the impact of raised expectations among healthcare workers regarding the health outcomes of patients on the actual conditions of their patients. As depression is a common phenomenon in nursing homes, Rosenthal and his colleagues wanted to see whether they could reduce the extent and occurrence of depression in a nursing home by giving caretakers bogus feedback on patient data, that is, optimistic predictions on the development of depression. Patient data six months later showed that depression levels in nursing homes residents had successfully been reduced.

Medical doctors' communication plays a significant role in their patients' health as well as in their own fortunes. There is a substantial amount of scientific evidence suggesting that it is not only what medical doctors say but also how they say it that can make a difference to their patients' lives as well as their own. For example, the physician's tone of voice has been associated with increased patient's compliance or successfully getting alcoholics to enter treatment. When another Rosenthal-led research team investigated the effects of the tone of voice used by primary care physicians and surgeons, they found that clinicians who came across as more bossy and less caring towards their patients based on their tone of voice were more likely to be sued.

The orthopedic surgeon Dr. Richard Hoffmann fell into that trap. As a university professor and head of a regional German hospital's orthopedic department, Hoffmann had developed a rather pushy, commanding, and authoritarian communication style with students, staff, and patients. When an ambulance delivered Sarah to the emergency room of Hoffmann's hospital after a horse riding accident in July 2012, nobody could have expected this case to bring about a big blow to the orthopedic surgeon's career. Sarah was a 45-year-old marketing and sales professional working for an international firm in Germany. She worked long hours and travelled extensively. Horse riding was her passion. Whenever possible, she spent time with her equine friend Calypso to maintain her work-life balance.

That late afternoon in July 2012, a sudden noise had made Calypso jump, causing Sarah to lose her balance and fall. When Sarah arrived at the emergency room, a junior doctor did the first check-up and had some X-rays taken. Neither the junior doctor nor his senior could see any damages on the pictures taken. It seemed that Sarah had been lucky and had gotten away with just some bruises. However, given that her back and left shoulder seemed to be hurting so much, the two doctors did not want to take any risks. They called the head of the orthopedic department to get his expert opinion. When Hoffmann arrived in the emergence room two hours later, he was in a rush. He had been operating all morning, visiting first-class patients in the afternoon, and now he was on his way to a management meeting where he would have to defend his department against budget cuts.

When Hoffmann entered the room, he did not pay any attention to Sarah on the stretcher. In his commanding style, he asked the two doctors "So, what is it?" When provided with the X-ray results, he spent some 30 seconds analyzing them before turning to Sarah. Hoffmann did not feel the need to introduce himself to Sarah. Instead, he went straight on to shooting questions—not at Sarah but at the doctors. What happened? How did she feel right now? Where did she feel the pain? He also inspected the areas on Sarah's back and left shoulder and concluded that there was nothing that could not be fixed with a couple of pain killers and some rest. When Hoffmann turned around to leave the room, Sarah stopped him to ask for some more tests, for example an MfRI. "Are we a little wimpy?" was Hoffmann's reply. This was actually the first time he had spoken to Sarah directly. "Do you know how many patients we have here with serious injuries and pains that need my attention? I cannot justify the cost of an MfRI in the context of what I see on your X-rays! Go home and if you are still in pain in 10 days' time, come back and my doctors will have another look," said Hoffmann and then left.

Sarah sued Dr. Hoffmann and the hospital one year later. It was not only the social interaction at that emergency room that had been a painful experience for Sarah. With a broken vertebrae and a ruptured tendon in her shoulder, she had been in a lot of physical pain for the past 12 months. In addition, she had been on sick leave for several weeks, as it was virtually impossible for her to travel in cars, trains, or planes. When I asked Sarah about her expectations of the outcome of her legal proceedings, she said,

> I did not feel like a human being in that emergency room [Belonging downer]. Dr. Hoffmann treated me like a thing [Belonging downer]. He did not care about me [Belonging downer]. He could not wait to get out of the room and move on to other things [Autonomy downer]. The way he talked down to me, I felt like a complete idiot, like a schoolgirl talking to

her master teacher [Autonomy, Belonging, and Competence downers]. The way he spoke to me hurt me more than the actual pain of my injuries. I felt like I was not taken seriously, at his mercy, worthless [Autonomy, Belonging, and Competence downers]. I want him to pay for that!

The interesting aspect of this incident is that Hoffmann's medical mistake only formed the basis for Sarah's legal case. However, her true motivation was to make Hoffmann and the hospital pay not for his medical mistake but rather for the way he made her feel in that situation by depleting her ABC in a matter of minutes. Sarah won the case and received financial compensation. Hoffmann's pristine success story as department head and university professor was now blemished due to the publicity surrounding the case. He was asked to leave his position at the hospital, and his university contract was not extended.

In both cases—Fulham F.C. and the hospital—we are assuming that Magath and Hoffmann were the causes of both failures due to their ABC-depleting interaction styles. But perhaps Fulham players were simply not up for it at the time, and maybe Sarah was a generally difficult person? To answer that question, we take a look at two other compelling cases. In each case, the same person acts in response to two different scenarios—one that is ABC-fueling, and one that is ABC-depleting.

Features from Finance

In 2000, Nicole Kierein from the University at Albany and Michael Gold from New York State University conducted a meta-analysis of 13 Pygmalion organizational studies examining adults in military, retail, and factory settings. They identified an even stronger relationship between leaders' expectations and subordinates' performance than Rosenthal had found in classrooms. Based on their analysis, Kierein and Gold suggested that the "inner workings of the Pygmalion effect" were due to a kind of special positive treatment of employees by their managers which, in turn, made employees feel better and increased their motivation, ultimately leading to better job performance. In the same year, Brian McNatt from the University of Iowa reviewed a further 17 research studies that had investigated the same effect in banking, manufacturing, engineering, and management. He arrived at the same conclusions and proposed that the strength of the effect was a matter of positive interpersonal interaction.

When I started my career in the financial industry as a member of a pool of associates in an investment bank in London, most of our supervising vice presidents (VP) were not very personable creatures. They were under a lot of pressure from the bank's directors and managing directors as well as the clients, and they passed the pressure on to us associates. More than once, vice presidents showed up at my cubicle after 8pm to dump a stack of material on my desk and demand that I turn the stack into a client presentation by the next morning. Upon leaving, the usual good-bye was something like: "DFU (don't f*ck up!) or you will not have a job tomorrow!" Needless to say, these words were not inspiring for the all-nighter ahead of me. I felt overwhelmed (Competence downer), exploited, and let down (Belonging downer). I also felt as though there was no way out (Autonomy downer) and that my life was under threat!

The situation was altogether different with Stephen Henderson, a second-year VP. He had an inspiring personality. Stephen would never order you to do something; instead, he would come to your desk and ask for your time, help, and expertise on a project (Belonging and Competence boosters). He always gave you the option to say no (Autonomy booster), but no one ever did. Every associate in the bank wanted to work for Stephen. If you were one of the chosen ones, you put in extra effort in terms of time and quality to support him. Stephen stuck around for a couple of more hours at nights. He often inquired whether there was anything I needed, often went to the copy machine himself, and gave me the feeling that we were in this together (Belonging booster). Stephen quickly rose through the ranks of the bank and finally became a member of management.

David, another second-year VP, often put pressure on me by suggesting he would have me fired, as I would never make it at the bank (Autonomy, Belonging, and Competence downers). One time, when David was under enormous pressure from his superiors to support a multi-billion dollar negotiation, he put so much pressure on me that I completely messed up my spreadsheet, which resulted in faulty valuation numbers. The transaction still closed, but I was told that David looked pretty stupid in front of everyone at the negotiation table. Obviously, I took a lot of heat from him for my mistake, which did not make much of a difference from his usual interaction style with me and the other associates around. However, he did not have me fired. Instead, David soon left and was never heard of again in the banking industry.

It took me a couple of years to realize what Stephen's career success was based on. People felt good in his presence. He energized people in his interactions by fueling their feelings of ABC. In turn, having people high on ABC around him helped him deliver superior results that supported his career success.

In this case, we can see how the same person (me!) responded differently to ABC-boosting and ABC-depleting interactions. I went the extra mile for Stephen, but I sabotaged David. Recently, I had coffee with Stephen at Caffè Nero in London. We discussed the ABC approach, which he confessed he had never applied consciously. In hindsight, his more than 30 years in banking had led him to conclude that "a lot of a*holes make it to the top". However, he was convinced that "in order for success to be sustainable, in business and in life, you have to understand people".

Coffee Shop Charisma

When I met Stephen for coffee that day, I also met Stacey, who was working at Caffè Nero. When I entered the coffee shop, the first thing I noticed was her charismatic, engaging smile. Stacey moved like a feather behind the counter, pouring coffee and delivering pastries. I listened to her subtle humming and singing as she served customers. Then it was my turn. Stacey stopped singing to address me with a sweet smile: "Good morning, my love, new to the neighborhood? What can I do for you?" After I placed my order, Stacey resumed singing. I said, "You're in a good mood today!" She replied that this was always the case when she was working here. I asked her "So, you like your job?" She promptly replied, "I love it here!" That was quite a statement. You often hear people say that they like their jobs, but referring to work in terms of love seemed quite extraordinary to me. I followed up. "So what do you love about working here?" Stacey immediately replied that they were working as a team, helping each other out, supporting each other (Belonging booster). She considered her co-workers as friends (Belonging booster). Her boss was not a typical boss. Instead of telling her what to do, she asked Stacey how she could best support her (Autonomy and Belonging boosters) so that she could keep up the good work she was doing (Competence booster). My reply was that maybe she was just happy to be here in London. "It has nothing to do with London, only with this particular shop," Stacey responded. "I only have a part-time contract here. So I also work at another coffee shop down the road. There, it's not fun at all. The boss there is always after you [Autonomy downer], criticizing you [Competence downer] and pointing out mistakes [Competence downer]. Singing there would get me fired immediately [Autonomy and Belonging downer]. That coffee shop is a dictatorship in the middle of London. I cannot wait to leave as soon as another opportunity comes along."

There is a dramatic difference in Stacey's feelings and behavior based on the two coffee shop environments. Once again, this is the same person with different outcomes. At Caffè Nero, her ABC is boosted, resulting in constructive, contributing, and positive behavior for herself, the team, and customers. If I lived in London, this would be my favorite coffee place to start the day. After my meeting with Stephen, I could not wait to check out the second coffee shop down the road where Stacey had her other part-time job. When entering the place, I sensed a tense atmosphere. Behind the counter, the facial expressions of the employees were rigid; there was no fun, no singing, no friendly interaction with customers. I could hear the shop manager talking in a commanding, military-like style. It did not feel like a coffee shop where people socialize and have a good time. It felt more like an industrial assembly line, an environment full of ABC downers. The following chapter will delve deeper into the dynamics of how feelings affect outcomes.

2.   Feelings: From Fiction to Facts

Your feelings attract your life into you.
– William James

Feelings are omnipresent. We all experience a constant flow of feelings triggered by the way your partner looks at you, the news you read on the internet about a plane crash, the high-five you received from your sports teammate, or a colleague's snappy comment at work. Feelings have been highlighted as the colors of the soul. Positive feelings like joy, enthusiasm, confidence, or love are bright and shiny. Negative feelings like fear, anger, sadness, or despair are dark and dull. We need to understand the basics around feelings to fully capture the power of the ABC of life.

Imagine your alarm is blaring at 6:00 in the morning. You are slowly gaining consciousness and trying to find the starting point for your new day. You feel disoriented, foggy, tired. Your inner voice tells you to get up and get going. Wait a minute, though— your bed feels extremely comfortable. You hit the snooze button and dose off into another nine minutes of coziness and warmth. And then—bang!—your alarm is blaring again. You feel even groggier and drowsier this time. There is no way that that was nine minutes! You start to feel angry at the alarm. The prospect of getting up now and facing the world outside gives you the shivers. The prospect of feeling much better after another nine minutes of snoozing makes you hit the button again, and again, and maybe again. There are those who claim that snooze buttons were an invention of the devil, given that it makes you experience the worst part of your day multiple times.

The ups and downs of feelings do not stop after getting up. You go to the bathroom to brush your teeth. Just the right amount of toothpaste on your brush, not too much mint bubbling in your mouth, just enough to wake you up slowly. Same in the shower, not too warm to make you feel like going back to bed again, just cold enough to energize you for the next step of your morning routine—coffee! Find the exact, right amounts of milk and sugar. Not too much, not too little, so that it feels like a natural extension of the extremely comfortable bed you had to leave behind.

Feelings keep changing moment by moment as we move through our lives. So do our feelings of autonomy, belonging, and competence. Humans tend to pursue pleasant feelings and try to avoid unpleasant feelings. But what about feeling neutral? How often have you received the response "neutral" when asking someone how they were?

The social sciences have been grappling with the question of neutral feelings for quite some time. Some scholars have suggested that people cannot feel neutral, as they are always feeling *something*. Others have postulated that neutral is not a feeling, as feelings are either positive or negative. A third group of scientists avoid the issue altogether by proposing that neutral feelings are not important, as they do not influence people's behavior.

Karen Gasper is an associate professor of psychology at Pennsylvania State University and the director of the Feeling, Behavior, and Information Processing Lab. One key focus of her lab research is the investigation of neutral feelings. Together with her colleagues Lauren Spencer and Danfei Hu, Gasper challenged all of the above theories in a groundbreaking 2019 article. In turn, she outlined a framework of her own. Gasper proposed that people cannot *not* feel. However, in sharp contrast to conventional theories, she defines neutral feelings as "feeling indifferent, nothing in particular, and a lack of preference one way or another". According to her work, neutral feelings were an important piece of people's experiences as they go through their daily rollercoaster of events. Instead of spending energy on keeping the ups and downs of your feelings under control, Gasper argues that neutral feelings are beneficial due to the flexibility they offer. The energy spent on managing your positive or negative feelings is better focused on interactions such as giving and taking ABC. For example, taking others' perspective requires energy, as we need to go outside our own frame of understanding. But when you are in a neutral state of feeling, you are more effectively able to take the other person's perspective than when dealing with your own positive or negative feelings.

Gasper's concept of neutral feelings resonates well with the avant-garde idea of mindfulness. The number of people engaging in mindfulness training in the West has been exploding in recent years. When you ask people why, they tell you that it makes them feel good. Mindfulness and meditation are two core ingredients of Buddhist philosophy. Any practice that trains your mind qualifies as meditation. Mindfulness is a technique that allows you to take a break from the craziness of daily life. It could be defined as open awareness of what is occurring in the moment. Let's use the analogy of a fish tank to describe mindfulness. In your daily life, you are interacting with all the other creatures in the fish tank. With mindfulness, you step outside the fish tank and observe it from the outside. That gives you two things: a clearer perspective on what is happening in the fish tank and a feeling of calmness as you are no longer directly involved in interactions. Buddhists often refer to the constant ups and down of feelings as your "yo-yo mind", and when that calms down and settles into a neutral state, you start feeling stable, composed, and peaceful. Gasper concluded in her article that neutral feelings were a source of mental well-being. No wonder so many people in the West have been subscribing to the technique of mindfulness as their meditation practice. If switching off by stepping outside the fish tank can play such an important role in feeling good, the question then becomes: what triggers our feelings, and who is responsible for them?

Causes of Feelings

Whenever we face a problem, its source as well as its solution seem to be outside of us. "S/he made me angry" is a household expression. But are we really hostage to our feelings? Are they imposed on us by others?

In one of the courses I teach, I start the first class by shaking hands with each student, welcoming them to the course. I ask them to rate this handshake in terms of how they felt about it, on a scale of 0 (= disgusting) to 100 (= ecstatic). They do so anonymously by writing down the number on a piece of paper and submitting it to the front of the class in bulk. Over the years, I have had the full array of responses from 0 to 100 over the years. But my handshake has been more or less the same all along.

This exercise demonstrates that our feelings are not at the mercy of factors external to us. If one simple handshake can prompt 100 different feelings in people, there seems to be an element of individual interpretation by each student. Deciphering the underlying algorithm of how we experience feelings has been a principal area of scientific research. Originally starting in the social sciences, today feelings are being studied from multiple perspectives, including biology, neuroscience, anthropology, and economics. What researchers have concluded is that feelings are at the very core of being human. Feelings are grounded in human evolution and represent the backbone of our human survival mechanism. Information can enter our brain through one of the five senses of sight, hearing, smell, taste, and touch. Scientists call this a stimulus or arousal. When such arousal occurs, one of the oldest parts of our brain—the so-called limbic system—starts processing the information. Incoming information is interpreted in terms of how positive, neutral, or negative the information is for our survival. This judgment is then translated into positive, neutral, or negative feelings that power our behavior in response to the situation we are facing.

Imagine a situation of intense feelings. You are calmly cruising down the street of your neighborhood when a parked car suddenly pulls out right in front of you, forcing you to slam on your brakes to avoid an accident. Your heart is pounding, your hands are shaking, and you are angry at the driver of the other car. In that situation, the arousal came from the other car pulling out. Your limbic system interpreted the incoming information as danger and immediately issued negative feelings of a threat to be avoided. You felt threatened by the sudden appearance of the other car and slammed on the brakes. This episode shows how information and its interpretation create our feelings which, in turn, drive our behavior.

INFORMATION + INTERPRETATION = FEELINGS ->
BEHAVIOR

The feelings formula was first derived by scientists Stanley Schachter and Jerome Singer in 1962 and has since been known as the two-factor theory of feelings. What Schachter and Singer indicated is that the intensity of the information plus the interpretation of the information determine our feelings. This means that it is not the information itself that determines our feelings but our interpretation of it. Let's take a look at the near-accident scenario again. One person's interpretation of the car pulling out all of a sudden could be: "That was close and could have injured me", leading to a feeling of fear or relief. Another person may think "What an idiot", which in turn might cause a feeling of anger or revenge. A third person may judge the situation as follows: "It was really hard for the driver to see me", and this would lead to feelings of empathy or compassion. This shows that our feelings are not based on the way things are, but rather on the way *we* are.

So what does all this mean for succeeding in our daily lives? Feelings are a choice. They change, from moment to moment, based on the choices we make, moment to moment. We are not victims of our environments. We can have a say in how we feel—if we choose to do so. By choosing the ABC of life, we can be the director of our life movie.

Are You a Doer or a Victim?

I often meet people who have chosen to be a victim as their role in life . Their interpretation of the information they receive through seeing, hearing, smelling, tasting, or touching reflects their belief that "it is out of my control", "there is nothing I can do about it anyway", and "it is happening to me again". As a result, these people feel constantly victimized—by their partners, colleagues, and even close friends. The victim role is a very convenient one. It transfers all responsibility for our own feelings to others. From the perspective of victims, the external world imposes all feelings on them. That is great for them, as there is no need to do anything or show any initiative themselves. It is always the others' fault. The only issue is that the victim role is not a very constructive choice for achieving success in life. Victims voluntarily surrender responsibility for their feelings—and in turn the drivers of success—to others. They are setting themselves up for failure, which is always someone else's fault.

What if you are not a victim but a doer? First, we can choose what we are paying attention to—that is, we can control the quality and quantity of the sources of information. In a world where we are constantly being bombarded with information, it is up to each one of us to be selective in terms of the information we allow to reach our limbic system. Less TV, less Facebook, or less smartphone time would mean fewer rollercoaster rides in our feelings. In that sense, it is not surprising that people have been flocking to meditation and mindfulness practice to take a break from their yo-yo minds. Mindfulness techniques limit incoming information, or the lefthand side of the feelings formula developed by Schachter and Singer. Therefore, mindfulness and meditation are powerful tools to calm down your feelings. As a result, you achieve more clarity and generate more energy to drive your success.

And even when you are not meditating but feeling overwhelmed by information at times, you can still do something about it by changing the other factor on the lefthand side of the feelings formula: your interpretation. As Shakespeare put it: "There is nothing either good or bad, but thinking makes it so." A question my students often put to me at this point is: "Why are most people then so negative in our world?". The answer is that being negative is part of who we are. Think back to the Stone Age when we were hunter-gatherers. If you were in a situation where you saw some mouth-watering berries in a field but you also knew that this was the territory of a saber-toothed tiger, the negative feeling of fear would override the positive feeling of good nutrition, and you would leave without attempting to get the berries. Those optimistic humans who did go for the berries and disregarded the tiger were more often than not killed and were therefore unable to pass on their genes, leaving us with a planet of humans who have more negative feelings than positive ones. This ensured the survival of our species during the Stone Age. But that does not mean that you have to accept that for yourself in today's world. We no longer live in the Stone Age, so you have the freedom to feel whatever you choose. And there is substantive evidence that feeling good and being successful are two sides of the same coin. So how exactly does the ABC of life drive outcomes?

Feelings and Outcomes

The upsides of feeling good are far more tangible than just being happy. Science has found that positive feelings are associated with better relationships, higher levels of resilience, better mental and physical health, as well as more successful careers. Traditionally, generations of people have subscribed to the chronology of working hard, achieving success, and becoming happy. Instead, modern research shows that positive feelings—as in "being happy"—provide the foundation for the hard work, which in turn results in success in life. If you feel positive, you have more self-esteem and self-confidence, and you are more outgoing, energetic, and creative. Who would you rather hang out with? A boring, depressed, suspicious slowpoke or an open-minded, dynamic, fun go-getter? It should come as no surprise that positive people have more friends, make more money, and live longer and healthier lives.

Remember how Felix Magath's negative approach to coaching was not sustainable beyond three seasons with the same team. The chief surgeon at the hospital lost his job and career due to his negativity toward Sarah. Both behaviors were ABC killers, ultimately leading to failure.

How negative feelings impact goal achievement was a core theme of a comprehensive review led by Jennifer Lerner of research studies in the field of decision-making in 2014. Lerner is a professor of public policy, decision science, and management at the Harvard Kennedy School and co-founder of the Harvard Decision Science Laboratory. As part of her work, she reviewed 35 years of scientific research on the link between feelings and decision-making. What she found was that negative feelings lead to short-term actions at the expense of long-term goal attainment as well as a lack of resilience in goal pursuit. The bottom line is that negative feelings are detrimental to goal achievement.

Conversely, the Caffè Nero coffee shop where Stacey was singing behind the counter was full of customers. Banker Stephen made it to the top by receiving support from people around him based on his positive approach. And students were much more successful academically when teachers showed positive concern for them. All three environments were ABC-supportive, which drove success.

A great example of how positive feelings generate positive outcomes is hope theory. Charles Snyder was an American psychologist who first proposed the concept of hope in 1994. He suggested that hope was the positive feeling of being able to find ways to achieve desired goals and to motivate oneself to pursue these goals. David Feldman from Santa Clara University and his colleagues Kevin Rand and Kristin Kahle-Wrobleski conducted a clever study on the impact of hope on goal attainment in 2009. The participants were 162 college students who were asked to complete surveys on hope and goal importance at the beginning of the semester (Time 1). Three months later (Time 2), they completed the survey on hope again as well as questions on goal attainment. The researchers found confirmation for their hypothesis that goal-specific hope predicted the achievement of that goal. Another finding was equally revealing to understanding the dynamics of success. Participants' hope levels at Time 2 had changed from Time 1 based on their level of goal achievement. The more students felt they had achieved specific goals, the more they had adjusted their hope levels upward, which in turn drove specific goal attainment yet again. The upward spiral effect that David Feldman and his colleagues found in their research on hope represents a key facet of success—its circular, self-reinforcing nature.

Feelings, Behavior, Success

Success is a process. What do Lady Gaga, Tom Brady, Oprah Winfrey, the coffee shop lady Stacey, and the banker Stephen have in common? Their successes are entirely based on how they make other people feel. They used their own behavior to inspire behavior in many others, ultimately leading to their own success. In a way, these people and their audiences have been "ABC-ing" each other. By performing music, winning Super Bowl trophies, conveying empathy and compassion, smiling contagiously and singing at work, and being human at the workplace, each of them unleashed positive feelings in others. In return, people bought their songs, sponsored them, boosted their TV ratings, preferred Caffè Nero over other coffee shops, and put in all-nighters to support them. All these are prime examples of the circular nature of the ABC of life.

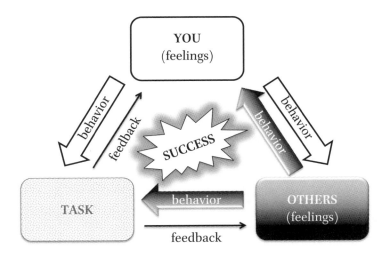

Feeling positive and inspiring positive feelings in others create success for yourself and others. But feeling good is only a first step. There is a crucial element translating positive feelings into success: your behavior!

Interpersonal Interactions

"No [hu]man is an island", wrote English scholar and poet John Donne. People interact with their environments either by engaging in a task, engaging with people, or a combination of both. You are impacting other people's lives through your behavior. Your actions provide information that is inputted into other people's brains through their five senses. Their interpretation of that information translates into how others feel about you and your behavior. This triggers a behavior in them in response to your behavior. The other's response inspires feelings in you in return, based on the information and your interpretation of that information. This process is what we call human interaction.

Task–Person Interactions

In our daily lives, we interact not only with people but also with tasks. Reading, gardening, or cooking are some of the many tasks we often do by ourselves. In that case, we are interacting with a task. Our behavior of picking up a book, clearing the garden beds of weed, or preparing a meal of spaghetti bolognaise prompts various feedback from the task at hand. The feedback information arouses our brain through the five senses. The interpretation of that information triggers how we feel and, in turn, our behavioral response. For example: we feel excited by the book and keep reading, we feel tired from clearing the weeds and sit down for a rest, or we feel hungry and plunge our fork into the spaghetti.

Collective Tasks

Collaborating with others on specific tasks is what most of us experience most of the time. In such cases, we are interacting with both the task and with the people involved in the task. When students work in teams on an assignment, each of them invests their individual behavior into the project. Each team member will interpret the task and the feedback differently. Therefore, each student will have different feelings about the task and how to accomplish it. For example, in a team of four, there may be four quite different task-person interactions regarding each person's views on the difficulty of the task, the task details, and how to structure the team report. But it becomes even more complicated. Each team member interacts with the other three, leading to interpersonal information, interpretations, and feelings overlaying the task-person interactions.

Success would take the form of many rounds through this process, inspiring an upward spiral of positive feelings in yourself and others. Now we can see why successful behavior includes persistence in addition to goals and skills. Success usually does not occur overnight. It is a journey in which you keep trying and make adjustments when others let go. When you feel deflated, depressed, down, and dispirited—the four D's of failure—your interactions enter a downward spiral. Your negative feelings suck up fuel. When your fuel reservoir begins to show signs of depletion, the process will start to suffer. Our interest in the tasks at hand diminishes and may ultimately prompt us to quit. We avoid human interactions or behave in anti-social ways that prompt other people to quit or avoid interacting with us. Both are typical signs of what modern civilization has come to know as burnout. Instead, success requires positive feelings such as enthusiasm, imagination, agility, trust, or hope, which provide the fuel that powers effective behavior at both ends of the loop. Now it may be clear to you why motivational speakers emphasize how successful people love what they do and surround themselves with people they love. Both give them feelings of Autonomy,

Belonging, and Competence and thus generate positive feelings and energy.

Meaning Fuels Success

Loving what you do and who you do it with energizes you by providing meaning to your life. This meaning conveys positive feelings that fuel the process loop. I have met many successful people in my life. For most of them, success was short-term, as they did not see any meaning in what they were doing. Their focus was mainly on money, fame, and power. Success without meaning is not sustainable and will ultimately lead to failure. Your process loop will simply run out of fuel.

Deepak Malhotra is a professor of negotiations at Harvard Business School. In 2012, he shared his quest for meaning in a speech to graduating students at Harvard Business School. He recounted to them how he changed his major five times in college, moving from computer science to psychology to education, English, math, and criminal justice. Finally he majored in economics after changing schools in the middle of his college journey. After graduating with a bachelor's degree from the University of Michigan, he was hired by a consulting firm. In the beginning, he was very enthusiastic about his job. Consulting can be a very fulfilling career for some people, but not for Deepak. He resigned after three months and decided to try high school teaching as a substitute teacher at a local school. While teaching, he came in contact with martial arts and decided that he wanted to start a martial arts school. When researching how to start a business, Deepak became sidetracked after he developed an interest in the tutoring business in education. To get such a business off the ground, he had to recruit clients for his business. How could Deepak convince clients to sign up for his service? To answer that question, he looked into how people made decisions. Game theory attracted his attention, so much so that Deepak decided to abandon his business idea and study game theory more formally.

He enrolled in a PhD program in economics at the Kellogg School of Management at Northwestern University. After completing his PhD, he worked as a game theorist. It was great for about half a year, but he realized that modelling, analysis, and hard core economics alone were not for him. He missed the human factor in his work. He transferred to the field of negotiations and decision-making. Finally, everything that had interested him started to come together, and he found his meaning in his work. Economics, business, teaching, consulting, research, analysis and the human factor were all individual colors of Deepak's soul that finally turned into a meaningful painting. He joined Harvard Business School in 2002, where he has been for 18 years. Deepak has become a globally recognized scholar and practitioner in negotiations and strategic decision-making. His professional career is a great example of success as a process. The feeling of not having found his true meaning in life drove his behavior of quitting all his previous activities until he felt he had arrived at his destination. At Harvard, he achieved the levels of Autonomy, Belonging, and Competence that subsequently energized and propelled his career. Once there, his success developed naturally, as he was doing what he loved.

The dramatic case of Tim Bergling shows how losing what you love doing can result in a lack of meaning. Tim was born in Sweden in 1989. At age 8, he started mixing music in his bedroom. Inspired by his brother who was a DJ, Tim started posting his remixes on electronic music forums at the age of 16. By 2011, he had become a prominent electronic musician and songwriter. In both 2012 and 2013, his nominations for a Grammy Award added to his global success. However, by that time, his passion for mixing music had turned into a toxic combination of money, fame, and commitments. His coping mechanism was alcohol and drug abuse. Tossed around by his fans and by the economic interests of his environment, Tim no longer felt that mixing music gave his life meaning. He stopped touring in 2016, as he felt emotionally overwhelmed by the superficial hype of gigs. He received a flood of hate mails by upset fans. His former sources of ABC turned into killers of his feelings of Autonomy, Belonging, and Competence. Back in 2011, he had started work on the House for Hunger, a charity dedicated to alleviating global hunger, in order to create new, alternative sources of ABC for himself. However, this initiative did not produce sufficient meaning quickly enough for him to fill the emptiness and lack of ABC resources in his life. Tim, whose artist name was Avicii, took his own life in 2018 in Muscat, Oman. Following his death, his family issued the following statement:

> Our beloved Tim was a seeker, a fragile artistic soul searching for answers to existential questions. An over-achieving perfectionist who travelled and worked hard at a pace that led to extreme stress. When he stopped touring, he wanted to find a balance in life to be able to be happy and to do what he loved most—music. He really struggled with thoughts about meaning, life and happiness. He could now not go on any longer.

A key difference between Deepak Malhotra and Tim Bergling seems to be that Deepak had enough ABC-based fuel in his tank to continue his search for meaning. Deepak had hope, while Tim was in despair, his ABC fuel tank empty. Both decided that quitting what they were doing was the answer, only Tim did not have the energy to start over again.

Feelings, Meaning, and Fuel

Both humans and sports cars need fuel. Ferraris consume fuel for their performance, which leads to depletion and the need to refuel from external sources such as a filling stations. Recent studies have yielded surprising findings when it comes to the fueling mechanism in humans. When Bob Vallerand and his social psychology laboratory at the University of Québec at Montréal examined energy levels of participants who engaged in activities they were passionate about, the team of researchers was astonished. What they found was that the study participants reported higher levels of energy *after* performing the activity then at the start. This means that passion generates more "fuel" for you than the energy that is needed to perform the activity. When you find meaning in what you do and who you do it with, you feel good about it, and this represents an internal source of fuel. This internal fuel-generating effect is what gives people the resilience to keep the process loop going. Moreover, the surplus energy generated from meaningful activities can be spent on other missions in your life.

In conclusion, there are two fuel sources powering success in life: one that is external and another that is internal. Both sources support feelings of Autonomy, Belonging, and Competence. When people focus on external fuel sources such as money, fame, and power, they make themselves dependent upon others. They turn from humans with a capacity for self-fueling into the equivalent of a sports car constantly in search of the next refill to prevent a burnout. A sense of meaning or purposes energizes you from the inside. It is an internal source of ABC that allows you to be independent of external factors. Success depends on your ability to go another round in the process of zooming in on your meaning. The closer you come to your spark, the more natural success will feel as your meaning starts energizing your actions directed at achieving your goals. Success will come as long as you never stop searching for meaning. In the next chapter, we will take a closer look at the role of the ABC of life in the energizing process.

Feelings as Push or Pull

There are two ways in which feelings drive behavior: (a) I feel, therefore I do, and (b) I do because I want to feel. Feelings can be enablers. They push and support our behavior, either positively or negatively. For example, Sarah sued Hoffman not because of his mistake but because of the way he made her feel in that situation in the hospital. Similarly, the Fulham players were unable to perform to the best of their ability on the soccer pitch because Coach Magath made them feel worthless. Conversely, when teachers made specific students feel good through their positive expectations in Rosenthal's studies, these students outperformed their peers academically. The positive feelings were enablers for student performance. Students felt good, and therefore they outperformed. In the same way, the banker Stephen's behavior inspired positive feelings in us junior bankers. We felt good about Stephen and therefore supported him. Our positive feelings pushed us toward multiple consecutive all-nighters and motivated us to go the extra mile for him. The supportive attitude of the coffee shop's management inspired positive feelings in Stacey, who in turn created a unique and pleasant atmosphere for Caffè Nero customers with her singing and smiling.

In the world of professional sports, there are many cases in which players change clubs and either show a surprising explosive performance boost or perform far below expectations. For example, when the German soccer player Lukas Podolski moved from FC Cologne to Bayern Munich in 2006 at the age of 20, he had spent his entire career at Cologne. Podolski stood for a new generation of German soccer players. Cologne fans loved him and nicknamed him "Prince Poldi"; he was one of them, which gave him a clear sense of Belonging. Also, he was the one and only star in the Cologne team, which boosted his Competence and gave him Autonomy in terms of his behavior both on and off the pitch. After his move to Munich, his performance deteriorated and he never lived up to expectations. At Bayern, he was just one of many stars. Munich was not his home. Fans did not fancy his contributions to the same extent as Cologne fans had done. All that drained his ABC. After three years without being able to claim a spot in Bayern's first eleven, he returned to Cologne. In retrospect, he commented on his move to Bayern Munich: "Cologne is my home, this is where I belong. Munich was not a catastrophe but obviously I did not feel the same way as in Cologne and that impacted my performance." Translating his comments into the language of the success loop model, Podolski did not feel the same levels of ABC in Munich as he did in Cologne. Consequently, he did not have the energy to perform at the same level as he did in Cologne. The enabler, the push, the actual feelings that boosted his successful behavior were missing in Munich.

When Feelings Pull

There is a second mechanism when it comes to feelings powering behavior. Instead of actual feelings pushing action, people can be pulled into specific behavior in a desire to experience certain feelings. That is, feelings become the motivation for behavior: I do because I want to feel. Customers return to Caffè Nero because they like the way Stacey makes them feel, for example in terms of Belonging. The reason all junior bankers put in extra effort for Stephen was that they wanted him to invite them to be part of his team again for the next project. Given the otherwise hostile ABC environment of the banking world, they were pulled toward the ABC that Stephen's behavior gave them.

The pull effect of feelings is a core technique in advertising. Buy this product or service, and this is how it will make you feel. Many years ago, the premium spirits company Diageo ran the following TV commercial. A guy dressed in a prime suit returns to his flat after work. The flat is in a high rise building, and you can see the illuminated skyline from the lounge. The flat is empty: he is alone, and there is no one waiting for him. At this point, the camera turns to a low white lounge table. You see a bottle of Johnny Walker and a whiskey glass with some whiskey in it. The guy sits down on the comfortable lounge sofa and takes a sip of whiskey while overlooking the skyline. A warm, smokey voice summarizes the experience for the audience: "The day goes, Johnny Walker comes!" If you want to experience this warm, hearty feeling with your good friend Johnny Walker in your flat the next evening, you go and buy a bottle the next day. The TV commercial pulls you into buying behavior because you want to feel Belonging and maybe also a bit of Autonomy. What makes the Johnny Walker commercial so effective is the way it links task-person interactions with interpersonal interactions: buy the bottle and you can spend time with a friend.

Another example of how pull feelings can lead to action is the desire to lose weight. "The Biggest Loser" is an American TV show that started in 2004. The reality TV format has overweight participants competing to lose the most amount of weight. The contestant losing the most amount of weight or highest percentage of weight is the "biggest loser" and wins a cash prize. The show started in Australia in 2006 and has now been taken to other countries around the world. Emma Duncan was 25 years old when she became the Biggest Loser Australia in 2011. In four months, she had lost 62 kilograms—the equivalent of 46% of her weight (136 kg) at the beginning of the show. "Love it, hot," commented her husband when she first emerged in black heels and a skin-tight, short black dress with only one sleeve on the final evening of the show.

Katie, a marketing professional from Brisbane, spent most of her life overweight. She was obese as a child. At age 36, she weighed 186 kilograms. "I told everyone that I was happy back then, but that was a lie", Katie recalls. When Emma Duncan transformed from an obese, inconspicuous person with no self-esteem into a hot, self-confident model in high heels, Katie was glued to the TV screen, passionately following each show. She wanted to be like Emma. She wanted to feel like Emma. And she took action because she wanted to feel. When the 2011 version of Biggest Loser Australia ended at the beginning of May, Katie went down to a local fitness club, signed up for a weight loss program, and hired a personal trainer. In the first 15 weeks, she lost a whopping 52 kilograms. "It was very hard at the beginning, but at some point it all felt downhill. Nutrition, exercising, special bootcamp sessions, it was all up to me. My weight was my choice and my dream of looking and feeling like Emma pulled me into that new lifestyle." Over the next six months, Katie lost another 56 kilograms. Now at 78 kilograms, she experiences the Autonomy of wearing whatever she wants to. She also has a sense of Belonging to a group of people who look hot and are adored, as well as a sense of Competence from having lost all those kilos, including the ability to control her weight in the future. She can now proudly wear the same hot skin-tight short black dress as Emma.

The pull effect of feelings does not require the prominence of a TV format. The ABC can manifest itself in much more subtle and hidden ways. Frank is a good illustration of how a desire for feeling can pull people into specific career choices. Today, he is a 46-year-old medical doctor working at a hospital in Hamburg. When he was 12, his mother Andrea died. It was not only her death itself that had a major impact on Frank's life, it was also the circumstances surrounding her death. In the summer of 1985, Andrea suffered from nausea and vomiting. Her general practitioner diagnosed a virus and prescribed medication for treating the symptoms. But because the symptoms persisted, she underwent several rounds of gastroenterological diagnostics such as an ultrasound and a colonoscopy. This all took time and did not produce any relevant results. By the end of 1985, Frank's mother was experiencing severe and frequent headaches. Doctors considered the headaches as symptoms of the assumed intestinal problems. At the beginning of the following year, Andrea felt like her vision was not completely intact. Again, when speaking to her doctors, they saw this as another sign of her potential intestinal sickness. Frank was Andrea's only child. He and his father Kurt had noticed some changes in Andrea's behavior over the past months. She had become more irritated, impatient, and even aggressive. Frank suffered from Andrea's behavior as his mom turned from a compassionate, warm, and loving person into a cold, self-focused sociopath. He felt lost, helpless and overwhelmed by the situation. Almost a year into this ordeal, in the summer of 1986, Andrea started having difficulties with balance, speech, and hearing. The problems were so significant that Andrea was hospitalized for detailed examinations. The results came as a shock to the family. Andrea was diagnosed with a brain tumor that was considered inoperable due to its size and location. Frank and his father did everything humanly possible to support Andrea while undergoing chemotherapy to save her life. In November 1986, six months after being diagnosed, Andrea died as a result of her brain tumor. Today, Frank has become a very successful, globally recognized brain surgeon. "I never made the conscious decision to enter the field of neuroscience. It all came together over time, naturally. However, the one thing I would say though is that I never wanted to feel as helpless again as I did when my mother died." In essence, Frank became a brain surgeon because he got pulled into wanting to feel Competence in diagnosing diseases (knowledge on curing), a sense of Belonging (care and support) with his patients, and Autonomy (a certain degree of control) in the sense of not being at the complete mercy of circumstances.

Feelings are a choice. Since feelings drive successful behavior, success becomes a choice. Having a meaning in life, feeling good, and inspiring positive feelings in others all fuel the process of persistently applying skills toward life goals. As a result, you create success for yourself and others. Sounds like a simple algorithm, right? Feel good, work hard, big success! But the "feel good" part in particular represents a key challenge in terms of implementation. According to conventional wisdom, feelings are abstract and we are all different in the way we feel. So how does one apply the algorithm? Since the late 1960s, a common denominator framework for feelings has evolved, somewhat unnoticed. Grounded in scholarly research, its application in practice has gained increasing momentum because it is intuitive and practical and delivers measurable results. Today, this progressive discovery has inspired a global movement, creating success for people in all spheres of our world. This framework forms the scientific foundation of the ABC of life.

3. The ABC Principles

We cannot predict the future, but we can create it.

– Alan Kay

Batman, Elektra, Spiderman, Wonder Woman, Asterix, or the Avengers—all superheroes have origin stories. They are backstories revealing how the characters turned into superheroes, how they gained their superpowers, and the circumstances under which they became protagonists. In this chapter I outline the origin story of the ABC of life, the superhero founders of the science behind it, and the sources of its superpower.

In 1960, at the Democratic National Convention held in Los Angeles, John F. Kennedy was nominated the Democratic presidential candidate. In his acceptance speech, he coined the term "New Frontier" as the Democrats' slogan to inspire Americans to support him. His postulate of "we stand today on the edge of a New Frontier—the frontier of the 1960s" would lead to an era of unprecedented change.

The period of reconstruction after World War II was coming to an end. A phase of challenging the status quo, revolutionizing social norms, and breaking societal taboos was about to begin. The only constant throughout the 1960s was progress. The Civil Rights movement progressively gained momentum. The Beatles progressed to become the world's most successful band. The Boston Celtics progressively claimed nine out of the decade's ten NBA titles. In fact, they won their last consecutive title in June 1969, a summer to remember.

In June 1969, an uprising of the gay community against a police raid of the Stonewall Inn in New York's Greenwich Village, later referred to as the Stonewall Riots, was the start of the gay liberation movement. In July 1969, the world watched as Neil Armstrong became the first (hu)man to walk on the moon. In August 1969, the Woodstock festival in Bethel, New York represented a pivotal moment for the counterculture revolution, which was to influence the lifestyles of generations to come.

The graduation of Alan Kay with a PhD in computer science from the University of Utah in the summer of 1969 went unnoticed by the public. He was offered a professorship at Carnegie Mellon University but decided to join Xerox's Palo Alto Research Center (PARC). When at Xerox, he developed the foundations of networked workstations, messaging, laptops, tablets, ebooks, and mobile learning. He also invented something that billions of people use countless times every day without ever having heard his name: the graphical user interface technology of overlapping windows on your computer screen.

If Alan had decided to accept the position at Carnegie Mellon, he may have bumped into a guy named Edward Deci on campus. Ed was studying for his PhD in social psychology at the time. No-one would have suspected that his experiments would provide the spark for a global movement.

"Why do we do what we do?" has been a fundamental question addressing the core of what makes us human. The summer of 1969 marked a new frontier in this line of inquiry. "People feel, therefore they do" is what we know today. Feelings determine our success, whether it be happy family lives, mental and physical health, organizational outperformance, winning Olympic gold medals or Nobel prizes.

In 1969, Ed had no idea that 50 years later, the ABC principles that he and his future colleagues were about to discover would change the world. As part of their self-determination theory (SDT), the ABC would empower people in all parts of life such as work, sports, healthcare, or education to create success for themselves, their families, their communities, and societies at large.

The Origins of ABC

Edward Deci was born on October 14, 1942 in Clifton Springs in upstate New York. His parents Charles and Janice were very proud of him when he graduated from Hamilton College with a Bachelor of Arts in mathematics in 1964. Mathematics is a core discipline of economics, which Ed had become interested in. He moved to the UK and enrolled in the London School of Economics as a postgraduate student. While studying in London, Ed realized that economics was only a small piece of a much bigger puzzle—business and finance. Therefore, he decided to return to the United States and enroll in the Wharton Master of Business Administration (MBA) program, which to this day is one of the most reputable business schools globally. After graduating from Wharton in 1967, something strange happened, something you do not see very often on a resumé. MBA programs are designed to give postgraduate students a broad overview of the various business disciplines such as strategy, marketing, accounting, finance, and operations and to teach their interconnectedness when managing businesses. That means that people enrolling in MBA programs are usually more interested in breadth and to a much lesser degree in depth. PhD programs, on the other hand, have a very narrow focus. PhD students investigate a phenomenon in depth in order to obtain new knowledge about a very specific area. Not many people have the personality to study both dimensions: breadth and depth. However, fortunately, this is what Ed decided to do after completing his MBA. Ed started his PhD at Carnegie Mellon University in late 1967, but not in business. While studying at Wharton, he had realized that business decisions were only as good as the motivation and behavior of the people behind them. Ed graduated in 1970 with a PhD in social psychology. His initial findings in the field of human motivation would remain controversial if not a mystery for several decades.

Since the beginning of the twentieth century, the social sciences has held an almost uniform view that human behavior is driven by external factors. So-called behaviorists such as Edward Thorndike, John Watson, and Burrhus Skinner advanced the theory—known as behaviorism—that people's actions could be controlled and manipulated by external consequences such as reward and punishment.

When performing a review of the literature during the first phase of his doctoral studies, Edward Deci stumbled across the work of Harry Harlow. As a professor of psychology at the University of Wisconsin, Harlow had conducted experiments with primates in 1949. The results had been quite controversial because they contradicted behaviorism. In fact, Harlow's studies seemed to indicate that monkeys' behavior was not driven by external incentives but some kind of internal mechanism. His findings were received with much skepticism. As a result, Harlow decided not to fight mainstream science at that time and turned to another field of research. But Edward Deci's curious mind was electrified by Harlow's work. Was human behavior driven by factors other than carrots and sticks? Were there internal resources propelling human actions? He decided to investigate the phenomenon in humans as part of his PhD studies.

The *Soma* Studies

Deci designed several laboratory and field experiments in which he asked two groups of participants—an intervention group and a control group—to solve different puzzles. For the intervention group, participants were promised monetary rewards contingent upon the speed with which they solved a puzzle. The monetary rewards were not offered in all rounds of the puzzle-solving, however; rather, they were alternated so that the incentive was offered in one round and omitted in the next round. For the control group, no incentives were provided in any round. The Soma cube was used as the puzzle to be solved.[1]

The results were astonishing. Participants in the intervention group showed less interest in the puzzle and were slower in solving the puzzle than the control group. At this point, Deci decided to add another experiment to his research design. He maintained

1   See https://www.youtube.com/watch?v=uaK5vSUQSQw). Invented in 1933, the puzzle remains popular to this day.

the original set-up, but instead of providing monetary incentives to the intervention group, he gave them encouraging feedback. This time, the intervention group performed significantly better than the control groups. Without realizing it at the time, Deci had discovered the superpower behind the ABC. In 1971, he published his findings in the highly reputable *Journal of Personality and Social Psychology*. Despite his work being recognized by the journal, the behaviorist establishment by and large ignored the findings. The mechanism behind his discovery should remain a mystery for another 30 years. Later in this chapter, we will find out how so-called MfRI technology, that is scanning a person's brain activity, finally validated Deci's findings at the beginning of the 21st century.

The Next Step

After completing his PhD, Deci joined the psychology department at the University of Rochester. In 1977, Deci met Richard Ryan, a philosophy undergraduate who had recently joined Rochester's clinical graduate program and was focused on psychotherapy and sustained behavior change. Deci and Ryan initially worked together co-leading Gestalt therapy retreats. In their evolving discussions, they discovered a mutual interest in human motivation, in particular the issue of human autonomy and freedom. The two explicitly agreed to join forces to develop a broader theory of human motivation that would rebut the skeptical behaviorists.

What followed was the establishment of the Human Motivation Research Group (HMRG) at the University of Rochester in 1978. Given that the intervention group and the control group in Deci's experiment exhibited different behaviors, the hypothesis was that there were inner resources at play that were driving behavior. HMRG's central mission at the time was to explore what these inner resources were.

After in-depth literature reviews, a series of experimental studies, never-ending brainstorming sessions, napkin scribblings at a local pub, and gatherings at Deci's property on Monhegan Island off the coast of Maine, Deci and Ryan came up with the following framework. The three basic feelings that our two protagonists identified as the drivers of behavior were autonomy, belonging, and competence. These three feelings are the sources of superpower and, in turn, success.

Autonomy

The word "autonomy" has its origins in ancient Greek and consists of two parts. The first part ("auto") translates into "self", while the second part ("nomos") means "law". Put together, the word could be interpreted as "living according to one's own law". Autonomous activities are those one endorses and willingly engages in. As a result, your behavior feels self-organized and you can wholeheartedly support it because it feels congruent with your values and interests. You do it because it is in line with your inner self. If you see meaning in what you are doing, you are able to draw on an endless reservoir of fuel. Your activities will produce more fuel than you invest in them. In contrast, if we focus on external incentives such as reward and punishment, we feel controlled by factors external to our self. The larger the gap between your inner self and the values surrounding external factors, the more energy you spend on managing that gap and the fewer fuel is available for your pursuit of success. At some point, that reservoir is depleted, and you either give up or burn out. That is why success without meaning is not sustainable.

As I write these lines, we are in the middle of a lockdown due to the corona pandemic. If I see meaning in staying at home and see it as a contribution to my own health and that of others, quarantine is an experience that is at the very least neutral if not positive for me. Alternatively, the more I believe that COVID-19 is a plot that is preventing me from getting ahead in my life, the more draining the experience will be for me.

Autonomy can easily be confused with individualism or independence. When I interviewed senior executives for one of my research projects, many of them made the remark at some point that they did not need anybody. This is not autonomy but rather individualistic thinking. The Dutch social scientist Geert Hofstede defines individualism as a low degree of interdependence between people. So people who feel they do not need anybody tend to feel highly independent of others. Autonomy has a different connotation. As per my interactions with Stephen Henderson during my time as a junior investment banker, I was as dependent on him as I was on the other vice presidents in my investment bank. All of them, together with the directors and the managing directors, determined my work, my promotion, my bonus—indeed, my life at the time. However, by asking instead of telling me, Stephen offered me a choice that boosted my feeling of Autonomy. As a consequence, I felt an inner urge to contribute and did not even mind spending all-nighters on his presentations, as I wanted to help him look good in front of his clients the next day.

Similarly, Deepak, Stacey, Katie, and Frank had found their "thing": Harvard Business School, Caffé Nero, working out to lose weight, and curing brain diseases are all examples of what we can find meaning in, giving us feelings of Autonomy. In turn, this shows how feeling autonomous contributes fuel to sustainable success.

Fulham players had quite a different experience with their coach Magath. With his authoritarian style, he tried to control every aspect of his players' lives up to how much water was in their water bottles. What followed was an exodus of established players who gave up, leaving behind many of Fulham's academy-produced players, many of whom were young, inexperienced, and had fewer options to escape. Observers have argued that these players were better suited to Magath's control-freakishness, as young players were less likely to speak up and did as they were told. Not surprisingly, feeling as if they had their backs against the wall produced a free fall in their Autonomy. This resulted in the players' underperformance and Magath's ultimate failure at Fulham.

The case of Avicii was more dramatic than a mere relegation to the next tier of the competition. He had reached a level of fame at which he could no longer be his true self, and the result was that he felt controlled by the world around him, a puppet performing what his management and fans expected of him. It seems that the gap between the two personas of Tim Bergeling and Avicii became so large that the musician saw taking his own life as the only way out of the dilemma.

When we feel controlled, constrained, and under pressure, our feelings of Autonomy suffer. This changes our behavior, leading to underperformance or other forms of failure. Alternatively, whenever we can express our ideas and opinions, pursue our interests, and have choices and opportunities consistent with our inner voices, our Autonomy is high. In such conditions, we are setting ourselves up for success.

Belonging

Investigating people's feelings of belonging has a long history in science. It has been researched and documented under various labels such as affection between people, positive regard from others, love, affiliation motivation, social connectedness, and relatedness. A theoretical foundation in the field was provided by academic scholars Roy Baumeister and Mark Leary when they reconciled over 300 individual research studies from the twentieth century in their seminal paper "The Need to Belong". In their 1995 article which has been referenced over 30,000 times to date, the authors suggest that the two fundamental ingredients of belonging are: frequent personal interaction, marked by stability and mutual affective concern. In 2009, my colleague Geoff Lovell and I conducted a series of research studies examining the phenomenon of belonging in the organizational context. The four constituents of belonging identified by the research participants were: 1) joint activity (the quality of interaction), 2) time (hours, days, years the people had known or interacted with each other), 3) continuity (the regular nature of interaction), and 4) common concern (the pursuit of common goals, including mutual care). In a second step, we asked participants to rank the four constituents in terms of their importance for their feeling of belonging. Common concern was named the top booster of feelings of belonging by far. This result did not surprise us, given that participants in a previous study had described belonging as synonymous with feeling supported. Other terms associated with the feeling of Belonging were feeling included, valued, understood, accepted, trusted, appreciated, recognized, and part of something.

This is how I felt when Stephen approached my cubicle in London. By asking for help, he made me feel like he valued my work, appreciated the effort I put in, and gave me the impression that, even though I was not invited to be present at the actual meeting, I was part of the project team that was about to talk to an important client the next morning. I worked with him on that presentation, and I was going to give it my best shot that night to support Stephen. I never worked "with" the other VPs in the bank, only "for" them. They made me feel exploited, worthless, and excluded—all in all, ultimate Belonging downers—by making use of their patronizing communication style, using the DFU term, and threatening to put my job on the line. In conclusion, I was disengaged. More than once, we associates played mind games imagining what it would be like to play a prank on a VP, making him look like a fool in front of our managing directors and clients. In a way, I subconsciously did precisely this by giving my VP David the incorrect valuation numbers.

Common concern and feeling supported and included were the last things that Felix Magath conveyed to his players by emptying their water bottles, staring at them without talking in his office, and excluding them from training. King Magath had continuously emptied his players' Belonging fuel tanks during his reign. Fulham was not a happy place anymore, as players felt excluded, devalued, and exploited.

Belonging fuels success. Deepak, Stacey, Katie, and Frank all felt like they were part of something—accepted, valued, appreciated, and supported members of a team (the faculty, Caffè Nero, the fitness center, and health community). Podolski did not feel the same sense of Belonging in Munich that he had felt in Cologne, as exemplified by his comment that he didn't feel at home in Munich. As a result, he never performed at the same level.

How can you feel Autonomy and Belonging at the same time, given that belonging implies a degree of collectivism that constrains individual freedom? Let's say you are invited to a party at a friend's house. The event is in full swing, and the owner asks you to go downstairs into the cellar to get a couple of more beers for the guests. Now, if you feel immersed in the situation and are having a good chat and a few laughs, you will feel accepted, valued, and appreciated—i.e., a sense of Belonging. As a result, the owner's request will be congruent with how you feel about the situation. You will be happy to help by going downstairs to pick up a couple of more beers. You will feel Autonomy, as there is no gap between the owner's request and your self. Alternatively, if you do not like the people at the party, you are likely to feel excluded and rejected. Faced with the owner's request, you might think, "Not only has he only invited idiots, now he even orders me downstairs to get some beers for them." You do not feel you belong, and therefore the request is a downer for your Autonomy. This might lead you to leave the party early.

Competence

There are very few terms as controversial and diffuse as Competence in our everyday language. Take a minute to reflect on a recent situation in which you felt competent. It is highly likely that your personal episode will be somewhat related to performance. In 1959, the American psychologist Robert W. White, who was director of Harvard University's psychological clinic at the time, mentioned Competence for the first time in an article as a coping mechanism for people. Since then, the concept has been predominantly picked up by organizations to improve performance. That is why the language associated with Competence has been dominated by organizational vocabulary. We talk about core competencies, management competencies, and competencies required for the implementation of business strategy as a basis for the recruitment, training and development, promotion, retention, and compensation of employees. However, even in the corporate world, there is no generally accepted definition of Competence. What we usually mean is a set of knowledge and skills to effectively perform a job. But Robert White was not an organizational psychologist. Instead, he suggested that Competence is a framework applicable to any form of human community including families and sports teams.

In order to better understand Competence, let's take a look at extremely competent people that are often referred to as experts in their fields. That means Competence could be defined as qualification for specific contexts or goals. Ask a plumber to fix your roof, an NBA player to play defense on a Major League soccer team, and a psychology professor to give a lecture on energy engineering. Or even better, ask the psychology professor to fix your roof, the NBA player to lecture on energy engineering, and the plumber to play defense on a Major League soccer team. They are unlikely to perform as effectively as they would in their respective fields of expertise. Actually, they are likely to feel completely out of their depths, overwhelmed, and possibly panicking when confronted with novice tasks. So what *does* make people feel competent and boost their Competence levels? Research shows that when people are given opportunities to learn and grow their capabilities, to contribute proven skills, to overcome challenges, and to experience constructive feedback, it adds to their Competence reservoir by conveying a feeling of "Yes, I can".

Stephen Henderson invited the bank's associates and analysts to contribute their time and knowledge to his projects. I felt pretty competent when asked to display my analytical and presentation writing skills. Also, I would look forward to Stephen's timely feedback after each meeting. He helped me become a better banker by allowing me to learn from his experiences and by discussing potential areas of improvement for the next presentation. Instead, Magath's message to his players was that he considered them a bunch of incompetent losers. By isolating many of the established players, he took away their opportunity to contribute by passing on their proven soccer skills. They could no longer help the team fight relegation or get back into the Premier League. The coach's feedback to players in general was everything but constructive, given his communication style and repertoire of punishments. The players' experience was therefore not too dissimilar to us banking associates dealing with our VPs. The most important thing for both of us was to survive our superiors proving our incompetence to us, and the only way to do this was to run or work until you dropped! Fulham players' Competence levels were probably below the base level of the soccer teams they were competing against back then, contributing to the team's underperformance under the German coach.

Deepak, Stacey, Katie, and Frank had become experts in their respective fields of negotiations, serving clients, losing weight, and brain surgery. They had gained Competence levels that enabled them to contribute, develop, learn, and grow. In contrast, Tim's expertise in mixing music was by far outweighed by his feelings of incompetence in coping with the complexities of his fame. When we feel overwhelmed and downgraded, when we lack opportunities to contribute our knowledge and skills and feel deprived of the chance to grow our capabilities, these experiences drain our Competence levels, ultimately leading to failure.

The ABC of life shows how we can be successful in all parts of our lives by paying attention to three basic feelings. Autonomy, Belonging and Competence can explain why we do the things we do. So far, so good. The next challenging question for the two founders was related to the mechanism by which the ABC powered, drove, and fueled successful behavior.

Energized for Success

Right from the start of their collaboration, Deci and Ryan had hypothesized that the three basic feelings of ABC provided some kind of energy to people. Most of us think of energy in terms of its physical sense. Energy is required for the body to perform the task of walking, sitting, speaking, working, or exercising, for example. It was Sigmund Freud who suggested that we also had a reservoir of psychic energy. In his view, when people were free from "repression" and "conflict", they were more alive. After this idea had floated around in the twentieth century, Mark Muravan at the University of Albany and Roy Baumeister at Case Western University picked up the topic. In 2000, the scholars suggested that psychic energy was required for coping with unfavorable or unpleasant situations. Once the reservoir was depleted, they argued, people engaged in anti-social and self-defeating behavior such as aggression or unhealthy eating. They concluded that psychic energy determines success, while its depletion leads to failure.

Freud was not the first to reflect on a potential psychological component of energy. In fact, the idea of psychic energy has a long history. Qi is a source of life, creativity, and harmony in China. Ki provides physical, mental, and spiritual health in Japan. In Bali, vital spiritual and physical power is based on Bayu. Loong (in Tibet), Pneuma (in Greece), Prana (in India), and Mana (among Native Americans) are all thought to underlie, empower, and regulate physical and mental phenomena in people. What all the traditions have in common is their psychosomatic view on energy, a relatively new concept for the modern world. Up until the early 2000s, psychosomatics, which proposes that body and mind are related, was still considered a pseudo-science in Western countries. A simple self-test can help us to verify the link between body and mind. Imagine a large, juicy lemon in front of you on the kitchen table. Your partner takes a knife and cuts the lemon in half. The lemon is so juicy that the juice runs all over the kitchen table. Your partner grabs one of the two lemons halves and takes a big bite, sucking the remaining juice out of the lemon half. What is your body's response? Is saliva filling your mouth all over? This is how your body reacts to your mental, psychological experience. Or consider another example. This of the last time you were in a pressure situation—an exam, an important presentation, or a job interview? Take a minute and close your eyes to immerse yourself in that situation again. If your mind is truly in that situation again, you are likely to feel an increase in your heart rate. If you were to measure your blood pressure, it will have gone up as well.

ABC drives psychosomatic energy. It powers both physical and psychological behavior. In a series of groundbreaking studies in the late 1990s, Ryan and Christina Frederick validated the use of "vitality" as a scientific and practical tool for capturing both aspects of psychosomatic energy. Since then, ABC has been shown to power behavior in the pursuit of success through the mechanism of vitality.

Glen Nix and John Manly worked alongside Deci and Ryan in a series of experiments exploring the impact of ABC on vitality. They divided undergraduate students into two groups. They gave each group different instructions for sorting a deck of cards. For group 1, Autonomy was manipulated downward by providing extremely rigid guidelines. By providing the immediate feedback of "right" or "wrong" after each card, the researchers created a controlling environment. The opposite design was applied to group 2, where the student participants were given options and feedback was provided only after sorting through the entire deck of cards, which meant that Autonomy was manipulated upward. Vitality was measured before (Time 1) and after (Time 2) each experiment. There was no difference in vitality between the two groups at Time 1. After their Autonomy feelings were manipulated, vitality for group 1 had plummeted at Time 2, while it had shot up for group 2.

The power of ABC applies not only to young college students. Virginia Kasser interviewed and surveyed residents of nursing homes over time, correlating their levels of ABC with their vitality as well as their physical and psychological symptoms. She found that the higher the residents' levels of ABC, the higher their reported vitality was. In turn, vitality was positively associated with physical health and mental well-being and negatively linked with cardiovascular problems, depression, and anxiety. Over time, Kasser showed that higher levels of ABC also predicted lower mortality rates for the nursing home residents.

Vitality has also been shown to be a key driver of organizational performance. When I was recently asked by a global organization to help them with a cultural transformation project, we used a survey as a first diagnostic tool. Employees' ABC levels and vitality levels were measured. In addition, we collected physical and mental health data as well as information on employees' behavioral performance indicators. We found that ABC levels predicted vitality. In turn, vitality was highly correlated with employees' job satisfaction, physical health, psychological well-being, physical performance, mental capabilities such as creativity and resilience, and social skills such as empathy.

Across life domains, ABC levels determine success by providing people with vitality, the superpower energy for action. This goes far beyond the conclusions reached by Muravan and Baumeister. Not only do Autonomy, Belonging, and Competence help one cope with adversity, they also refuel the reservoir of psychosomatic energy to allow one to move on to further rounds in the pursuit of success. Success is based on interactions in which people ABC each other. The more Autonomy, Belonging, and Competence you feel, the more energized you will be to interact with people. Also, the more ABC you give—and the more ABC others perceive—in your interactions, the more likely people will come back for more. This mechanism applies in all domains of life, including in politics (government–citizens), in organizations (leaders–followers), in families (parents–children), in schools (teachers–students), in sports (coaches–athletes and athletes–teammates), and in healthcare (caretakers–patients). The same is true for individuals engaging in a task. If the task enhances your ABC levels, it provides the energy to keep you going. Otherwise, you stop performing the task due to energy depletion.

A Short History of SDT

ABC and its energizing effects form the core of the self-determination theory (SDT), which was coined by Deci based on the first basic feeling he identified after his initial experiments in 1969. He theorized that the external incentives provided had compromised participants' feelings of self-determination. When the basic feelings of Belonging and Competence were discovered later, Deci and Ryan decided to rename the feeling of self-determination into autonomy but did not change the name of the theory.

From its formulation by Deci and Ryan in the late 1970s, SDT has evolved in several development stages. Up until the mid-1980s, it was largely ignored by mainstream psychology. Following a 1985 book in which Deci and Ryan outlined the theory and its supporting evidence in more detail, SDT received more attention. Many behaviorists now considered SDT a fundamental threat to their concept. In a 1990 book, Edwin Locke and Gary Latham from the Universities of Maryland and Toronto suggested that if SDT seriously called into question the positive impact of rewards on motivation, "it is doubtful that it has much application to real life". In fact, Deci and Ryan never alleged that external incentives did not affect performance. However, they made an important distinction in terms of the task at hand.

The early 1900s up until the 1980s were still marked by the second industrial revolution with its assembly lines, the division of labor, simple tasks, and everything following an algorithmic plan controlled by managers. In his 1911 book *The Principles of Scientific Management*, Frederick Winslow Taylor sought to perfect Adams Smith's idea of the division of labor by arguing that maximum prosperity was achieved on the basis of maximum efficiency. As a result, he proposed to separate the headwork from the physical work and to install "managers" to systematically control, observe, measure, and optimize workers' physical performance. At the center of Taylor's scientific management was the belief that the human factor represents the biggest obstacle to achieving maximum efficiency. This implies that "In the past, the man has been first; in the future, the system has to be first". In Taylor's view, workers were an easily replaceable resource whose shortcomings as human beings had to be managed. Ideally, workers should be managed to perform as noiseless, unthinking machine parts in a sophisticated system geared toward maximizing output.

In such a world, external incentives such as money or keeping your job can drive human behavior, but such incentives can only provide a shallow and short-term effect. Let's take a minute to perform a thought experiment on external incentives. If you are sitting on a chair and I would like to motivate you to get up from your chair, behaviorism prescribes two options. I can throw a $100 bill to the ground in front of your feet as a reward for rising up from your chair to pick it up. Alternatively, I can punish you by setting your chair on fire to make you jump off your seat. Both strategies work initially. But there are two problems with these strategic options. First, every time I want *you* to do something, *I* have to do something. Second, both options have detrimental consequences. Over time, the $100 will no longer be enough, as the effect wears off. This means I need to increase the amount or I will achieve less of an effect. Repeatedly setting your seat on fire will cause you substantial stress, fear, and anxiety, which will reduce your productivity.

Now, in an algorithmic world where humans are just another resource performing donkey work, the above plot may not scare you. If an individual no longer gets off a chair for $100 or dies from a heart attack due to fire, you simply replace the person with another one. However, in an unpredictable world of increasing speed, complexity, and ambiguity, people make all the difference. Attributes such as self-starting, creativity, and mindfulness provide the foundation for creating success for yourself and others.

For example, in a knowledge economy, people's social-emotional skills such as creativity, innovation, and communication are the last sustainable competitive advantage that an organization can have. Technology performs the donkey work. Humans are no longer easily replaceable resources. Today, people make the difference in every part of life. Each individual counts.

By the late 1990, the ideas of SDT had spread across Lake Ontario into Canada and further up the St. Lawrence river into Quebec. Therefore, Deci and Ryan's Human Motivation Research Group decided to bring researchers together for the first SDT conference, held at Rochester University in 1999. Around 40 faculty, mainly from the United States and Canada, gathered for two days of discussion and debates in order to brainstorm and design directions for future research. Since then, the SDT has turned from an academic theory into a global movement. After Rochester, SDT conferences have been held on a triennial basis in Ottawa, Toronto, Ghent (Belgium), Rochester (again), Vancouver, and Amsterdam. At its most recent five-day SDT conference—its seventh since 1999—over 800 scholars from almost 50 countries attended. Over the last decade, GoogleScholar has registered over 30,000 SDT publications, which brings the total to over 50,000 since Deci's initial experiments. The Center for Self-Determination Theory (CSDT), founded in 2000 in Florida, has become a think tank that challenges the frontiers of human motivation by enabling people to lead healthy, fulfilled, and productive lives. CSDT supports a global network of SDT research labs with over 100 registered international scholars and well over 10,000 SDT researchers. They have been creating, translating, promoting, and applying cutting-edge knowledge based on SDT. The findings have been implemented across life domains including education, parenting, healthcare, sports, and even video games, virtual worlds, and space travel. In the business world, companies like Google, Apple, and Warner Brothers have been applying SDT to gain a competitive edge through highly motivated organizational cultures.

Since the turn of the century, the SDT movement has experienced explosive growth. After being ignored until the mid-1980s

Number of SDT publications

1970-1980	1981-1990	1991-2000	2001-2010	2011-2020
26	71	797	15,243	29,878

Source: GoogleScholar

and ridiculed until around 2000, SDT today is recognized for its superpowers and has become the leading approach to human motivation. While an ever-growing amount of psychology research has added to SDT's credibility since its beginnings, another scientific field has now begun conducting research that strongly supports SDT: neuroscience!

New Perspectives through Neuroscience

If You Could Read My Mind is a popular song by Canadian folk-rock legend Gordon Lightfoot that topped the US music charts in 1970. Due to a series of fascinating twentieth-century inventions, today we have the means to "read" minds by showing physical brain activity associated with psychological phenomena.

Neuroscience is the science of the nervous system. It addresses the question of how neurons and neural circuits work. Over 20 Nobel prizes for medicine were awarded for neuro-scientific discoveries in the previous century. One of them was awarded in 1979 to Allan Cormack and Godfrey Hounsfield, who had developed a technology to produce detailed anatomic images of the most prominent neural circuit in humans—our brain. They called it computerized axial tomography, known as CT, which, based on X-rays, delivered amazing insights for diagnostics and research. The discovery electrified scientists around the globe, leading to a significant increase in research activity in the field. In the early 1980s, Peter Mansfield and Paul Lauterbur started experiments on mapping the brain with magnetic fields instead of X-rays. After a decade of explosive technological refinements, magnetic functional resonance imaging (MfRI) became the dominant approach to brain imaging due to its low radiation exposure, high-quality results, easy implementation, and high availability. Mansfield and Lauterbur received the Nobel Prize for Medicine in 2003 for their discovery.

One of the most stunning areas of research using MfRI is the visualization of information processing in the brain as it happens. Brain activity causes metabolism to increase in those parts of the brain that are being used, which causes these areas to "light up" on the scan. This enables us to see the various functions of respective areas of the brain. What can also be measured is the "strength" of the brain activity via the amplitude of neural signals.

SDT research findings were doubted and ignored from the start. But by the early 2000s, the sheer number of research studies and resulting publications on SDT began to provide it with a certain degree of scientific credibility. The invention of MfRI was an exciting opportunity to add another layer to the validation of the theory. Researchers hoped to detect the physical manifestations of brain activity that would clarify the previously discovered psychological effects of ABC. It was thought that neural imaging might even help to resolve the mystery around Deci's first experiment in the summer of 1969.

To examine the effects of ABC on brain activity, SDT researchers asked participants to perform the same tasks under different conditions. In one scenario, feelings of Autonomy, Belonging, and Competence were manipulated upward. In another, participants were confronted with an ABC-neutral or ABC-adverse scenario. So let me first explain how Autonomy, Belonging and Competence can be manipulated in experiments before revealing the neural manifestations of ABC manipulations.

Manipulating Autonomy

For example, Kou Murayama and his team at the Motivation Science Lab at the University of Reading used a stopwatch task to manipulate participants' Autonomy in a choice/no choice setting. Scientists asked 35 university students to accurately push a stopwatch button displayed on a computer screen that displayed two buttons: one in the shape of a soccer ball and the other in the shape of a star. In scenario 1, participants were given no choice: they had to use the soccer ball. In contrast, scenario 2 fueled participants' feeling of Autonomy by giving them a choice between the soccer ball and the star. Accuracy meant stopping the watch within a 50-millisecond interval of the five-second time point. Here is the specific design of Murayama's experiment:

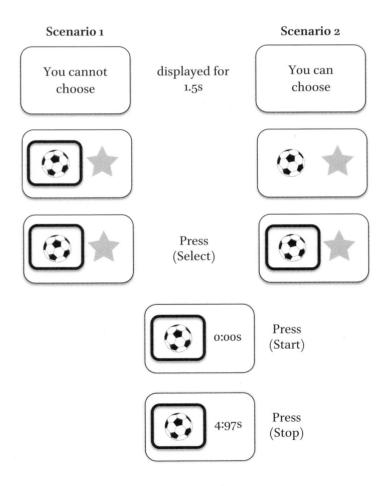

Manipulating Belonging

Some researchers have studied brain activity in relation to feelings of Belonging. In a series of studies, the neuroscientists Andreas Bartels and Semir Zeki examined the neuroscientific effects of viewing pictures of close relationships and compared them with the neuroscientific effects of the same people viewing pictures of those with whom they were less close to. They found that the first pictures boosted the participants' feelings of Belonging much more than the second pictures. For example, in one study, participants were first shown pictures of their partners and then pictures of friends. In another research project, mothers were shown pictures of their own children and then pictures of other children.

Manipulating Competence

In many neuroscientific experiments, participants are asked to perform tasks and then receive performance feedback designed to prompt a change in their feelings of Competence. For example, Woogul Lee and Johnmarshall Reeve asked participants in their study to solve anagrams. Sometimes, these anagrams were optimally challenging to give them a feeling of discovery, curiosity, and accomplishment. At other times, they worked on very easy anagrams designed to make them feel bored, disinterested, and pointless.

Findings of ABC Manipulations

What all of the above research experiments had in common was that each participant's brain activity was monitored under a scanner while performing the same task under different ABC manipulated scenarios. The results were staggering.

Scientists identified similar effects in all ABC-supportive scenarios. The more Autonomy, Belonging, and Competence

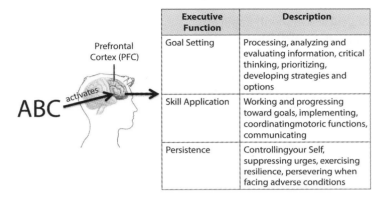

Executive Function	Description
Goal Setting	Processing, analyzing and evaluating information, critical thinking, prioritizing, developing strategies and options
Skill Application	Working and progressing toward goals, implementing, coordinatingmotoric functions, communicating
Persistence	Controllingyour Self, suppressing urges, exercising resilience, persevering when facing adverse conditions

the participants felt, the higher their neural activity in areas that ultimately drive the prefrontal cortex (PFC) in the human brain. The PFC is a big chunk of brain matter right behind our forehead. Some people call it the CEO of the brain. Throughout evolution, the PFC has grown more substantially in humans than in any other species. One could argue that it is this part of the brain that distinguishes Homo Sapiens from its predecessors. As the executive center, the PFC is running our daily lives. It is responsible for powering the three key components of success: goal setting, skill application, and persistence.

ABC Drives Behavior

Once you have boosted Autonomy, Belonging, and Competence levels in study participants by manipulation, you can go beyond scanning their brains for neural activity. In fact, SDT researchers around the globe have extensively studied the link between ABC levels and resulting behavior across life domains. The findings of over 50 years and several thousands of cutting-edge scientific studies in the areas of organizations, sports, healthcare, education, families, technology, and the environment have consistently confirmed that higher ABC levels power your executive functions of goal setting, skill application, and persistence. In turn, this translates into better:

- Physical performance
- Cognitive performance
- Creativity
- Interpersonal skills
- Social responsibility
- Empathy
- Loyalty
- Resilience
- Physical health
- Mental health

These are the 10 resources of success. Now you understand the mechanism behind the ABC driving your success. What makes the ABC so powerful is that boosting Autonomy, Belonging, and Competence in your life will enable and activate all your physical and mental resources. In turn, the ABC will superpower you to higher levels in each of the above 10 behaviors of success.

The Role of Neuroplasticity

There has been a further and equally compelling finding from neuroimaging in relation to the ABC. Neuroplasticity is a relatively new scientific field. Up until recently, science suspected that the brain and its neural circuits were hard-wired, fixed, and static over the lifespan of an individual. However, since the advent of scanning technology, researchers have found that the brain can in fact change continuously throughout an individual's life. As a result of a brain's activity, a given function can be transferred to a different location, the volume of gray matter can change, and neural connections can strengthen or weaken over time. Think of the brain as a muscle that can be trained. If you do the same curls over and over again, your biceps will strengthen and grow.

The same is true of your brain. If you have the same feelings again and again, the gray matter of your brain will grow in the region that is activated by such feelings.

This is what Gary Lewis, Ryota Kanai, Geraint Rees, and Timothy Bates found in their 2014 research study. ABC not only activates the prefrontal cortex in your brain; as a result of continuous activation, the strength of the ABC impact grows due to volume growth in brain matter. The higher the levels of study participants' psychological well-being, driven by feelings of Autonomy, Belonging and Competence, the greater the volume of gray matter in the regions powering the prefrontal cortex. This means that the ABC not only provides the fuel for the engine but also grows its capacity. The more you practice ABC in your life, the bigger the momentum and the more likely your chances of sustainable success are. In other words, success becomes a habit.

The new technology also sheds light on the old mystery of Deci's initial 1969 study. Murayama's team at the University of Reading replicated the experiment using the neuroimaging methodology. Participants were randomly assigned to a reward group and a control group. Each of them was asked to perform a game task while being scanned. The reward group received performance-based monetary rewards, while the control group played the game for fun. When analyzing data, the research team found that the reward group participants showed less interest in the task as reflected by decreased brain activation. In a follow-up study, Murayama investigated this "undermining effect" by examining interesting versus boring trivia question tasks. The results showed that while performance was better when working on trivia questions for reward compared to a non-reward control group, this effect was reversed in the case of the interesting task: rewards decreased performance compared to a non-reward control group. In fact, what Murayama and his colleagues found was that participants considered the rewards "external" to the self, which decreased activation in that part of the brain dealing with the self, the prefrontal cortex. Unfortunately, the prefrontal cortex also drives cognitive performance. As a result, attention and complex problem-solving skills were powered down, leading to a reduction in interest and performance. In essence, this new line of inquiry based on neuroscience provided an explanation for Deci's "mystery" findings. Using the SOMA puzzle was an interesting, complex task for participants. Interest and performance decreased when participants were incentivized by external rewards due to the deactivation of the prefrontal cortex. In summary, there are two contributors to the undermining effect: external (contingent) rewards and our perception of the task (as complex).

Features of ABC

When dealing with ABC in practice, a number of questions arise. Do basic feelings apply to all of us? Can the need for ABC be controlled? Is one basic feeling more important than another?

Universality

You may find it surprising that the ABC is persistent across age, gender, activities, life domains, and cultures. But every human needs water to survive. Water enables us to perform physical and mental activities. It is the *push* dimension of our feelings. At the same time, we go looking for water because we either know we need it or an inner urge drives us to search for it. That is the *pull* dimension of feelings. In the same way, as water drives our behavior through push and pull, feelings energize human behavior globally.

I can see the frown appearing at this very moment on your face. But aren't people very different across the world? Yes, they are! But all humans need water to survive. The difference between people is not in their need of water; it is in how they satisfy that need. In some parts of the world, people go to a well; in other parts, they go to a supermarket. Some may buy water in plastic bottles, others in glass bottles. Some buy them in gallons, others in liters. Translating that into the language of the ABC framework means that some people may feel autonomy in a situation that others won't. In academic language, scholars would say that ABC is context-specific, which means it depends on the circumstances. Remember my in-class exercise of having people rate my handshake on a scale of 0 to 100? Western students may rate my handshake an 80 or a 90 due to the sense of belonging they feel. A Japanese student, however, may rate it a mere 20, given that in Japan, people are used to bowing to each other instead of shaking hands. So while we all need ABC—and the more the better—each of us will feel different levels of ABC depending on the situation. Even though we may be aroused by the same information, each of us will interpret this information differently, leading to different feelings and, in turn, different levels of ABC. You may be asking yourself right now: "What is ABC for me?". This is a question we will turn to in Chapter 10.

ABC is a so-called "human universal". The term is based on a book by Donald Brown that made it into the *MIT Encyclopedia of the Cognitive Sciences*. He proposes that human universals "comprise those features of culture, society, language, behavior, and psyche for which there are no known exceptions". Examples of human universals include personal names, living in groups, tools, weapons, music, dance, conflict, language, trade, territory—and the ABC.

In two compelling research projects, Beiwen Chen and his colleagues from several SDT research labs around the world investigated the ABC as a human universal. In one project, they wanted to find out whether the ABC contributed to the well-being of people in high need of safety. The research question they investigated was: when people are looking for safety, do feelings of Autonomy, Belonging, and Competence matter? Does ABC add anything to well-being independent of people's feelings of safety? Researchers collected data from two participant groups. In group 1, they investigated environmental safety in a sample of young adults (N = 224) in South Africa, a country that ranks low in terms of public safety. In group 2, they focused on financial safety within a socio-economically deprived adult Chinese sample (N = 357). Feeling safe—either in their environment or financially—had a positive relation to well-being. However, in both studies, ABC contributed to participants' well-being independent of their need of safety. In a second project, the research team studied the impact of ABC on the well-being of participants from four culturally diverse nations (Belgium, China, USA, and Peru; total N = 1,051; mean age = 20 years). The effects were found to be equivalent across the four countries, underscoring SDT's proposition of ABC as a human universal.

Intention

The ABC is not intentional. You can set the intention for yourself that you do not need water but your physical condition will tell you otherwise pretty soon. In the same way, Autonomy, Belonging, and Competence are basic feelings that are essential for fueling your actions, regardless of your intentions. When I interviewed 124 executives as part of a research study, 61% of them said at some point in the interview "I do not need anybody". When surveying the participants later, this 61% showed a substantially higher rate of negative physical and psychological symptoms. The bottom line is that you can choose to ignore your basic feelings, but it will negatively impact the 10 behaviors of success. Failure is as much your choice as success is.

No Hierarchy of Needs

Maslow's hierarchy of needs is a popular framework. That is why many ABC practitioners wonder whether there is a similar concept embedded in the three basic feelings. What research has found is that all three feelings are equally important. It is like a series circuit: the weakest battery of the series determines the power of the entire circuit. Let's assume you are working alone

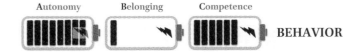
on a task. You feel highly autonomous and competent but you feel alone and excluded due to the lack of interaction with other people. The low level of Belonging will negatively impact your behavior and performance, despite the high levels of A and C.

Ken Sheldon runs the SDT lab at the University of Missouri. He and his colleagues conducted two insightful studies on the balance of individual ABC levels. In an experimental study in a game-learning setting, Sheldon's team were able to show that each of the three basic feelings—Autonomy, Belonging, and Competence—predicted objective performance independently. When surveying students at the University of Missouri, the research team discovered that the ABC's contribution to successful outcomes was higher when the levels of A, B, and C were higher and, more importantly, when they were more balanced. The higher the better, but the more balanced better still!

Cross-subsidization

Sheldon's work showed that basic feelings of autonomy, belonging, and competence cannot substitute each other. In other words, increasing your sense of Belonging does not make up for a lack of Autonomy or Competence. However, spillover effects between individual feelings and psychosomatic energy have been detected between life domains. A classic example of such an effect is the concept of work-life balance.

Many of us feel Competence at work, but we may not feel a lot of Autonomy due to a lack of control over what we do and how we do it. At the same time, we may not consider the people at work as friends. The lack of A at work can be offset by more Autonomy when we go out exercising or partying with friends. Our family life at home as well as our friends can potentially supply the B to make up for the shortfall of Belonging at work.

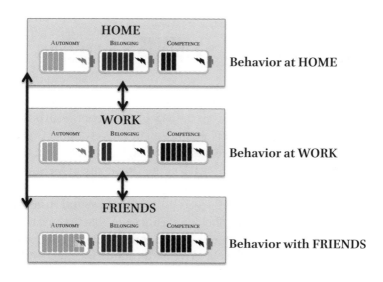

What this shows is that our different life domains impact each other. When people suffer at work, there may not be enough ABC in the other life domains to cover the black hole of outflowing energy from their job. Alternatively, enough ABC at work can energize a person's psychosomatic reservoir instead of depleting it. Energizing work could in turn even supply additional energy for activities in your private life. What matters is the gap between ABC from home and ABC from work. I collaborated with a European airline company on a research project examining company employees' ABC from both spheres. We found that work ABCs and home ABCs pointed in opposite directions: higher ABC at home correlated with lower ABC at work and vice versa, indicating a compensation effect. When we looked at the gap between both ABCs, it showed an impact on work engagement. The larger the difference between home and work, the lower the engagement at work was. Thus, if the home ABC was higher, employees concentrated on building and maintaining it at the expense of work behavior. Even if the work ABC was higher, the low home ABC seemed to drag down work engagement. Engagement was highest when ABCs from both spheres were high and balanced—that is, when A, B, and C were high at both home and the workplace.

ABC Deficiency

Just like flowers need soil, water, and sunshine to grow and blossom, people need feelings of Autonomy, Belonging, and Competence to thrive and succeed. When one component is missing, flowers die and people fail. What does failure due to ABC deficiency look like?

Let's first take a moment to reflect on how we feel when we lack A, B, or C. When Autonomy is deficient, people feel controlled; they feel they are being resisted and that they have no options or no way out, no say in what they do or how they do it. There is an incongruence between their self and their actions. An absence of a sense of Belonging leads to feeling excluded, rejected, ostracized, left out, neglected, unsupported, not accepted, not appreciated, or not recognized. The opposite of feeling Competence is when one feels overwhelmed, helpless, useless, and inadequate. People who are deficient in C begin to believe that they cannot do the task at hand, that they are a loser, or that the task is too difficult, and therefore they give up.

Similar to manipulating ABC levels upward, one can apply the same technique to find out how people behave under ABC deficiency by creating the conditions for it in a lab environment and observing the effects on behavior. Such experiments have evolved into a fertile line of inquiry since the 1990s. A superb group of social and neuroscientists have dedicated their work to manipulating participants' feelings of either Autonomy, Belonging, or Competence downward to monitor the resulting behaviors.

For example, Baumeister and colleagues designed an experiment in which they engaged university students in a get-acquainted task. After filling out a questionnaire on healthy eating behavior, the participants get to know each other. In a further step, they were asked to rate which people they would like to work with individually. The researchers disregarded these answers in order to manipulate feelings of ABC downward. By random assignment, half the group was told that no one had expressed an interest in working with them. The intervention was designed to instill feelings of social rejection in participants, immediately and negatively impacting their feelings of Belonging. The rest of the group was told that everyone had chosen them as desirable partners. The selected behavior to be monitored after the manipulation was eating cookies, which participants had previously rated as "fattening, undesirable, unhealthy eating behavior" in the questionnaire. In the ten minutes following the bogus feedback by researchers, socially rejected participants ate an average of 8.9 cookies compared to 4.4 in the control group. The effect of social rejection causing unhealthy eating was independent of participants' mood and the time that had lapsed since their last meal. An even more astonishing finding was that the socially rejected participants did not rate the cookies as better tasting than the other participants. Nonetheless, they ate more than double. The researchers concluded that socially rejected participants' self-control suffered when faced with a situation of social exclusion.

An increasing number of studies have applied methods similar to Baumeister and his team. For example, Autonomy has been manipulated downward by giving study participants rigid instructions or no options. A lack of Belonging is achieved by excluding people from tasks or assuring them of future loneliness. And researchers have simulated a deficiency in Competence in participants by providing them with bogus negative feedback on their task performance or giving them unsolvable puzzles. Following the manipulations, the participants' behavior was monitored and measured while engaging them in specific tasks. Social scientists have invested an impressive amount of analytical work and creative design into studying the psychological consequences of ABC deficiency. Three broad categories of behavior have emerged when people were deprived of feelings of Autonomy, Belonging, or Competence: 1) distorted goal setting, 2) destructive skill application, and 3) degraded persistence. All

ABC Deficient Behavior	Impacted Executive Function	Specific Behavior
Distorted	Goal Setting	– Cognitive impairment – Inappropriate and risky goals beyond capability – Seeking short-term benefits outweighed by long-term cost – Foolish, disproportional risk-taking
Destructive	Skill Application	– Aggression and violence – Revenge – Unhealthy food choices – Addiction – Increased spending – Violation of rules
Degraded	Persistence	– Retreat – Physical and mental lethargy – Reduced social and physical activity – Lack of self-awareness – Depression – Giving up

three dimensions can be directly linked to a breakdown in the brain's executive functions.

Distorted Goal Setting

Robert Wilson and a team of researchers decided to investigate a group of ageing people, as many of them suffer from worsening ABC deficiency. They often feel constrained by increasing physical limitations, which can lead to a decrease in Autonomy. Belonging is negatively impacted by a decline in social interactions. And as work has been found to be a key driver of Competence, ageing people often suffer from a lack of a sense of Competence due to retirement.

Wilson's team followed a group of some 500 older study participants with an average age of 66. None of the participants had cognitive impairments at the onset of the study. Over five years, the researchers monitored the participants' ABC levels. They also performed annual cognitive tests. The results showed a correlation between ABC deficiency and cognitive impairment over the term of the research project. Impaired judgment due to a lack of ABC is not exclusive to older people. In studies across all age groups, low levels of ABC have been found to correlate with poor decision-making, the pursuit of short-term benefits outweighed by long-term cost, foolish and disproportional risk-taking, and the pursuit of inappropriate and risky goals beyond performance and capability.

Franco was my classmate in primary school. His parents were Italian and had migrated to Germany in the early 1960s to help rebuild the country after World War II. Even though he was born in Germany, Franco never felt quite at home. He always thought he had to prove something, to do something special to become a part of the community. One time he jumped from a second-floor window to grab the attention of his classmates, breaking his arm. Another time, he took a broken chair and assembled it in front of the teacher's desk to make it seem like it was not broken. When the teacher sat on it, it collapsed and the teacher broke his arm. One morning at school, Franco told me and the rest of the class to come to the local train station after school. "Come and I will show you and the others what I am made of. After that, they will no longer call me 'The Italian'". I arrived at the train station along with another seven students from my class. Franco bragged that he could climb and ride the train to the next station and back. Franco climbed up the first wagon of the next train that arrived, and right when he made it all the way to the top, the train set off. He lost his balance and grabbed the first thing he could find in order not to fall off, which was the overhead electrical line. He died from the electric shock. Looking back on the incident now, I realize that it is a prime example of a lack of a sense of Belonging leading to foolish and disproportional risk-taking.

The business world is a fruitful context for further illustrations of distorted goal setting. Many employees who lack feelings of Autonomy, Belonging, or Competence at work consider the workplace as their source for office supplies. Staplers, copy paper, highlighters, sticky tape, scissors, pens, or notebooks are simply taken home without a thought. When you talk to employees who do this, it becomes immediately apparent that they would never consider this as stealing from the company. Impaired cognition prevents them from seeing the monetary values behind the items. Instead, the office supplies are just "immaterial things" for them.

Moving up the hierarchy from employees to executives, decisions that favor short-term results and disregard longer-term consequences have become par for the course. The toxic combination of pressure from shareholders, research analysts, banks, and competitors and short-term performance-related incentives leads to executives feeling stressed, lonely, and overwhelmed—all downers of Autonomy, Belonging, and Competence feelings and in turn, cognition. At the same time, managers are offered external rewards for short-term goals, which only reinforces the undermining effect, thereby accelerating the cognitive impairment process. How can we expect executives to make sensible decisions given such psychologically challenging contexts?

Richard Fuld was the longest-tenured CEO on Wall Street when his company Lehman Brothers collapsed in 2008. He had been nicknamed the Gorilla due to his aura of competitiveness and aggression. There had been early signs of a potential pattern of ABC deficiency in his life when he displayed destructive skill application, namely a loss of self-control. In his first career as an Air Force pilot, Fuld got into a fistfight with his commanding officer and was told to leave. On Wall Street, his aggressive attitude propelled his career. He quickly rose through the ranks and became CEO of Lehman in 1994. His tenure was marked by his obsessive suspicion that Lehman was being ostracized, not recognized, and pushed around by clients, competitors, the financial markets, and politics. Once, in a speech to Lehman employees, he claimed that he wanted to rip out his competitors' hearts and eat them while they were dying. In essence, Fuld himself lacked Autonomy, Belonging, and Competence and therefore tried everything to project these feelings onto the

Lehman organization. The ingredients of his questionable success brought him and Lehman down in 2008. In a series of highly speculative decisions, Lehman took on disproportional financial risks in an attempt to overreach its competitors. When the so-called sub-prime bubble burst in 2008, it only confirmed Fuld's delusion that the entire financial industry had been against them. In a hearing before the Financial Crisis Inquiry Commission in August 2010, Fuld insisted that nothing about Lehman's profile had indicated the bankruptcy of the firm, that the financial world had simply lost confidence in the bank, and that the government had failed to effectively intervene. Distorted goal setting due to ABC deficiency had caused the largest bankruptcy in American history.

Destructive Skill Application

When people suffer from ABC deficiency, they can try to squeeze it out of existing settings or find other sources. For example, aggression, violence, revenge, and the violation of rules have been found to be compensatory behavior in terms of fighting back at potential sources that have caused ABC deficiency. People dealing with ABC deficiency lose self-control, and as a consequence, they show anti-social or self-defeating behavior. When Sarah sued Dr Hoffman, she did not do so for his medical mistake. Sarah felt incompetent, alone, and trapped in that emergency room, depriving her of Competence, Belonging, and Autonomy. She retaliated as a consequence. During the COVID-19 lockdowns, there was a sharp increase in domestic violence. Feeling trapped in their homes and physically separated from their friends and from work, some people compensated by lashing out at their partners and families.

A second behavioral pattern of compensation, while perhaps less detrimental to the people around them, is not any less self-defeating. When we lack ABC from social interactions, we often turn to alternative sources of ABC such as food, alcohol, drugs,

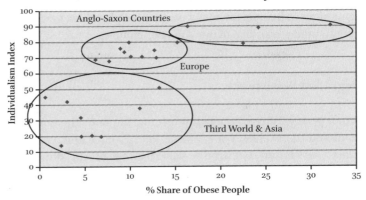

Individualism and Obesity

Individualism index extracted form Hofstede Cultural Dimensions (Tilburg University)

and shopping. Indeed, domestic violence was not the only thing that increased during the pandemic; the consumption of alcohol and cigarettes also went through the roof. Eating is often a kind of compensation for people. When my colleague Geoff Lovell and I prepared a grant application to Diabetes Australia, we plotted obesity rates per country over Hofstede's cultural dimension index of individualism. Our underlying assumption was that the more individualistic people feel, the lower their feelings of Belonging will be, and that people would then engage in more compensatory behavior such as unhealthy eating. What we found was that the most individualistic societies such as the United States, Canada, the United Kingdom, and Australia also had the highest obesity rates. It underscores what Baumeister and his colleagues found in their cookie study: people will try to "eat" Belonging if they feel a lack of it.

The advertising industry has been playing the compensation card very successfully. The consumer is encouraged to "buy this product or service" in order to immediately obtain a feeling of Autonomy ("Come to Marlboro Land" for Marlboro cigarettes), Belonging ("Together we can" for Adidas running shoes), or Competence ("Absolute power corrupts. Enjoy." for Apple computers). The Johnny Walker TV commercial I mentioned earlier where the drink gives the person a sense of Belonging in compensation for being alone in his apartment is a prime example of how marketing tries to take advantage of our ABC deficiencies.

Degraded Persistence

When people retreat, they stop interacting with the environment and their selves. For example, Jean Twenge and a team of researchers found that driving basic feelings of ABC down can lead to a "deconstruction of the Self", a pre-suicidal state. In a sequence of experiments, the scientists gave half the participants false feedback after a group interaction suggesting that no one wanted to engage with them. In a second step, they conducted a test comparing the false feedback group to the control group. The participants who thought they had been socially rejected were disoriented about time, feeling that time was lapsing substantially slower than it actually did. Time almost seemed to stand still for people when faced with a blow to their feeling of Belonging. The researchers further found feelings of numbness in rejected individuals. They did not want to talk about the future, goals, or dreams but were instead focused on the present moment's rejection and more likely to agree with the statement "my life is meaningless". These participants were also more lethargic and more likely to give up and withdraw from social interaction. They were also less effective in communication and produced significantly fewer words in a word puzzle task.

Perhaps the most fascinating aspect of the study was the outcome of a mirror experiment. Participants from both the manipulated group and the control group were invited into a room with two chairs, one facing a mirror and the other facing a wall. They were asked to take a seat while the researcher left the room to ostensibly search for another experimenter. Ninety percent of the rejected individuals avoided the mirror, while only 40 percent of the control group chose the chair facing the wall instead of the mirror. The scientists concluded that social rejection prompted a tendency to avoid not only the environment but also the self.

ABC deficiency can drive people toward withdrawal from reality. When this happens, they are less receptive to signals from the environment and retreat into their own world. They become socially inactive, communicate less and less effectively, and avoid interaction. Above all, they avoid their selves, leading to decreased levels of self-awareness and meaning in life. The withdrawal symptoms of social rejection could be categorized as a pre-suicidal state.

Avicii had stopped touring in 2016. He had retreated into his own world in an attempt to find meaning in his life. Instead, he received hate emails from his fans and was put under pressure from his management. As a result, his pre-suicide condition deteriorated and he took his own life. The Fulham players under Magath did not die physically, but mentally they flatlined. Magath's continuous humiliations made them so tired that they felt more lethargic before a game than they had ever felt after a game before Magath had taken over. When a former Fulham player was asked how he had coped with the situation under Magath, he said, "my mind just went elsewhere".

Another prominent example of retreat as a psychological consequence of a lack of ABC deficiency is the case of Australian rower Sally Robbins. Originally from Perth, Robbins had represented Australia in the women's four at the 2000 Sydney Olympics. For the 2004 Athens Olympics, she was one of 22 girls to be considered for the women's eight. The coach was German Harald Jahrling, a two-time Olympic gold medalist. He was ruthless, commanding, and known for his short temper. All in all, he was not an ABC-supportive person. Instead, when rowers were performing below expectations, he often did not talk to them for several days, which sounds somewhat like the psychological game-playing that Felix Magath employed. Competition amongst the 22 girls for the eight spots was fierce. Right from the start of the selection process, Sally was put into the stroke seat, the leadership position of the boat due to her incomparable strength and rhythm. However, she also had a reputation for being psychologically fragile. In numerous races before, she had stopped rowing and laid down in her boat under extreme pressure. Jahrling did not care about psychology. In his book, feelings were for wimps. When Sally underperformed in a preparation race before the 2004 Olympics, Jahrling moved her out of the leader seat into another position in the boat.

Let's take a moment to review the situation just before the 2004 Olympics. We had an experienced but not very resilient rower who had undergone a draining selection process competing against young, ambitious, envious athletes, only to be criticized for her performance and demoted from the leader seat into a follower position. Autonomy? Down! Belonging? Down! Competence? Down! All that in addition to a notably low ABC pre-condition. What would you expect? Top performance? In the final, the Australian women's eight were leading by 200 meters, second to the United States at 500 meters and still in competition for a medal at 1,000 meters. At around the 1,500-meter mark, Sally stopped rowing and laid down in the boat, preventing the rest of the crew from rowing. She had done it again! It was a scandal that would keep the Australian press busy for many months. The pressure of circumstances had pushed Sally over the edge. She laid down in the boat to disappear from the scene. She had switched off her attention, shutting down information processing and behavior. There was nothing left in her energy reservoir to keep any action or interaction going. Her ABC reservoir had reached rock bottom.

Physiological Consequences

The above examples showcase how ABC deficiency can lead to failure due to a breakdown of individual executive functions in the brain. But there are further physiological consequences when we lack Autonomy, Belonging, or Competence.

The link between physiology and psychology has long been downplayed by science. But in recent years, neuroscientific methods have enabled new ways of collecting data to support the credibility of psychosomatics. As a doctoral student at the University of California, Los Angeles (UCLA), Naomi Eisenberger was intrigued by the way in which people described social rejection in terms of physical pain: "My heart was broken", "I felt crushed", "It hurt my feelings", "It was like a slap in the face". She decided to study these physical manifestations of psychological phenomena.

In a landmark experiment, Eisenberger and her colleagues scanned test participants while playing a virtual ball-tossing game using virtual-reality (VR) headsets. Study participants could see their own hand and a ball, plus two avatars of fellow participants in another room. By pressing a button, each player could throw the ball to another player while the research team measured their brain activity using MfRI scans. In the first round of CyberBall, as the game became known, the ball flew back and forth just as you'd expect, but pretty soon the players in the second room started making passes only to each other, completely ignoring the player in the first room. In reality, there were no other players; it was just a computer program designed to make the participant feel rejected so that the scientists could see how a lack of Belonging—what they called "social pain"—affects the brain. After exclusion, the neuroimaging showed greater activity in participants' neural alarm system suggesting that "something is wrong!". When the results were compared to neural studies in the field of physical pain, Eisenberger realized that both social and physical pain activated the same circuits of the brain.

Another research project compared the experiences of social exclusion and specific physical pain. In the study, Ethan Kross and his team recruited participants who had recently gone through an "unwanted romantic break-up", an experience that would have caused a big blow to their ABC levels. During the MfRI sessions, the participants were asked to look at a photo of their ex and recall specific feelings of rejection. They were also asked to look at a photo of a friend and, somewhat later, someone of the same gender as their ex-partner. The same participants underwent two tests of physical pain to their left forearm: a "hot trial" with enough heat to cause discomfort and a "warm trial", which was hot enough to produce sensation but no discomfort. The same areas of the brain were activated to the same extent in both the hot trial and when they were told to recall their feeling of rejection while looking at a photo of their ex—i.e., both sounded the brain's alarm bells loud and clear.

The physiological consequences of psychological experiences have been found to go far beyond neural activity. The effects of an alarm situation do not stop at the brain. ABC deficiencies can trigger further biological reactions, commonly referred to as *stress*. Under normal conditions, all living organisms are in balance. Stress causes a shock to the system, for example by signaling a life-threatening situation, which the organism must respond to in order to get back into balance. In humans, the extent of the shock can be measured by levels of so-called biomarkers that enable the body to fight or flee the situation. Stress has been known to cause short-term increases in blood pressure, the heart rate, blood sugar levels, cortisol, and immunological proteins. It also has longer-term consequences such as obesity, diabetes, cardiovascular and skeletal diseases, and even DNA damage. Autonomy, Belonging, and Competence have been found to bolster people against stress. In contrast, ABC deficiency has been associated with increases in stress biomarkers.

Geoff Macdonald and Mark Leary suggested in a 2005 article that the association between social and physical pain was an evolutionary development. If the ABC plays a role in that mechanism, Autonomy, Belonging, and Competence could originate from our evolutionary roots. In fact, when I first came in contact with SDT in 2007, it prompted that exact question in my curious mind. Why did Deci, Ryan, and their colleagues at the Human Motivational Research Group identify A, B, and C as basic feelings driving human behavior and success? In a 2008 publication, Deci and Ryan also described ABC as an outcome of our evolutionary history, stating that Autonomy, Belonging, and Competence were a "common architecture of human nature". While searching for answers in fields such as sociology or anthropology, I stumbled across a relatively new scientific area: evolutionary psychology. It introduced me to a new way of understanding human behavior—and to the ABC of life as human nature's universal superpower driving success.

4. From the Stone Age to Apple© Stage

It has become appallingly obvious that our technology
has exceeded our humanity.
– Albert Einstein

Philosophers, social scientists, and anthropologists have all lamented the increasing gap between who we are and what we do. This was recently underscored by the statement by London Business School professor Nigel Nicholson: "You can take the person out of the Stone Age but you can't take the Stone Age out of the person." Let's take a minute to see how such academic claims may apply to everyday life, which will allow us to uncover the evolutionary origins of the ABC's superpower.

Brian Wansink designed a groundbreaking experiment. Participants were invited to eat soup out of bowls in groups of four at a restaurant-style table. What the scientists did not tell participants was that two of the four bowls slowly and impercepti-bly refilled as soup was consumed. The researchers wanted to see whether there would be a difference between the two groups in terms of actual intake of soup. The results were astonishing. Over a 20-minute period, participants eating from self-refilling bowls consumed a whopping 73% more soup! Moreover, these people did not believe they had consumed more and did not feel more sated than those eating from normal bowls. Wansink's experiment is a perfect example of what social scientists have portrayed as our modern skulls housing a Stone Age mind. What they mean is that despite all our modern gimmicks, we still have an ancestral mental program running in the background influencing our daily behavior. Our instincts have helped us humans survive over millions of years. However, what helped us to survive back then can kill us today. When confronted with information, our instincts function as "IF-THEN" interpretation filters that trigger human feelings and behavior. Assuming that the information was "food found in nature", the Stone Age interpretation of that would have been "IF you find food, THEN eat as much as you can", leading to maximized calories intake. Who knows when the individual will find another source of food? I guess we can all see how the "IF you find food, THEN eat as much as you can" mechanism has worked against us in our modern world of plenty. The abundance and ready availability of burgers, sweets, and soft drinks in our modern societies have led to unprecedented levels of obesity and associated cardiovascular diseases, osteoarthritis, and diabetes.

Human Universals

Instincts are human universals: the tendency to maximize food intake, for example, applies across cultures. The only difference may be in the quantity and quality of food available in certain regions. This effect is not limited to food; humans exhibit similar behavior towards other items in their endeavor to "provision for survival". This was made evident during the recent COVID-19 crisis: as soon as people understood the potential implications of the pandemic, they started hoarding or provisioning. Cultural differences did account for the difference in items that were stockpiled: masks in China, water in the United States, toilet paper in Germany, red wine in France, and champagne in Luxembourg. The drive to survive was so great that people started fighting over the last items in the shops. For most of the items, it was not that the supply chains had been affected, but it was the sudden and sharp rise in demand that led to shops running out of stock.

In the context of actual data, the behavior exhibited in the soup study and during the COVID-19 crisis could be described as irrational. This assessment changes when we switch the circumstances in which we analyze such behavior. I invite you to travel with me back in time to 100,000 years B.C. to get a firsthand experience of the ABC as the fundamental, universal "IF-THEN" survival instinct.

The Stone Age

The human species can be traced back to the upright apes who lived about 2.5 million years ago. Over time, these apes evolved into a variety of specialized and well-adapted hominid species. Approximately 100,000 years ago, there were three distinct groups of hominids separated by geography: Homo Neanderthal in Europe, Homo Erectus in Asia, and Homo Sapiens in Africa. Even though they had evolved differently based on their respective environments, they shared one fundamental challenge: their weak physical condition. There were some big and dangerous organisms out there such as mammoths, saber-toothed tigers, and toxic plants. How could a furless, clawless, armorless, soft-skinned biped whose children had to remain under their parents' wing for a decade survive under such circumstances?

Living together in groups was the answer. Given that there was no police, no national guard, and no hospitals to protect or cure them, our ancestors decided to join forces in packs. Survival in numbers. Our ancestors were hunter-gatherers at the time, which meant that survival under such conditions required superb physical, technical, mental, and social skills.

Physical Skills

Climbing trees, throwing spears, carrying loads, and running away from danger were some of the physical prerequisites. When hunting reindeer, foxes, wolves, wild boars, buffalos, bears, or even mammoths, our ancestors had to cover large distances, which required stamina. But meat was limited, so herbs, berries, mushrooms, nuts, edible roots, and beans were gathered on extended walks through the savannah.

Technical Skills

They also needed technical skills to build camps or shelter, develop tools like stone knives and spears, prepare traps, make clothes, light fires, and cook.

Mental Skills

As they were nomads, they had to develop detailed maps of changing territories with trees, wells, stones, animals, and plants. This required substantial mental abilities.

No one individual had all the above skills, which is why humans decided to pool together their individual skills. They hunted and gathered together, ate together, and stuck together at night when they slept. They were thus the first to engage in the division of labor, to use Adam Smith's term. Some were better runners, others better toolmakers, and still others better at navigating the terrain. Every member of the group had to pull its weight for the group to survive. Such concerted effort requires co-ordination. Therefore, social and communication skills were another key survival factor.

Social and Communication Skills

According to Robin Dunbar, professor of psychology at Oxford University, the groups that our ancestors formed had somewhere between five to ten members. But even such groups could not have survived without additional support. They joined a number of other groups to travel the savannah plain in clans of up to 150 people. Organizing such a clan construct involves mental and social skills such as remembering people, forging alliances, keeping promises, performing rituals as well as caring for and raising children. Communication was key. This is when Homo Sapiens got the upper hand over its Asian and European cousins. The evolutionary development of a complex language, known as the cognitive revolution, enabled Sapiens to manage social

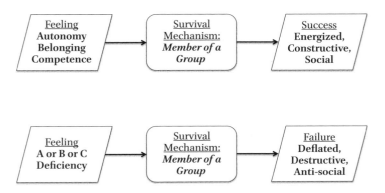

structures such as groups and clans more effectively than Homo Neanderthal or Homo Erectus. As a result, 10,000 years ago, Homo Sapiens was the only human species left on the planet.

The evolutionary lessons learned during the above period were programmed as an instinct: IF you want to survive, THEN you need to be part of a group. Or conversely: IF you are not part of a group, THEN you will not survive. In order to be an accepted member of a group, you had to contribute a set of skills. Incompetence or free-riding were not options, as this would have put the entire group at risk. Ineffective group members were excluded or left behind. They either found another group or died. We are all descendants of humans who survived on and reproduced due to this "IF-THEN" instinct throughout evolution.

To this day, we are social beings who need other social beings to survive. This psychological pattern of our evolutionary instinct is what Ed Deci started to uncover in the summer of 1969. The ABC of life is an approach grounded in our evolution. The reason it is so effective is that it is congruent with our human nature.

The ABC-Based Survival Mechanism

Why did Deci and Ryan identify Autonomy, Belonging, and Competence as basic feelings? Given the survival mechanism identified above, Competence is a requirement to be a member of a group. When we feel competent, we have something to add, something other people need and value. In exchange, others will contribute their skills and help and support us. They give us a feeling of Belonging. It is an exchange. You help the group, and the group helps you. This ensured survival for our ancestors and remains today a recipe for success. If people feel Competence and Belonging, it energizes them because it makes them feel safe. They can invest their energy for the benefit of the group to create success for themselves and others.

But what about Autonomy?

To understand why Autonomy is so important to us, we need to look at the evolutionary development of the human brain. What grew along with our ancestral abilities was our brain. In fact, the part that outgrew all other areas was the prefrontal cortex. The PFC is not only the CEO of the brain but also home to what we describe as our 'Self'. It is the PFC that enables us to recognize our Self and to have self-awareness and engage in self-reflection. What comes with it is what the German philosopher Arthur Schopenhauer once described as the porcupine problem:

> A number of porcupines huddled together for warmth on a cold day in winter; but, as they began to prick one another with their quills, they were obliged to disperse. However, the cold drove them together again, when just the same thing happened... In the same way, the need of society drives the human porcupines together, only to be mutually repelled by the many prickly and disagreeable qualities of their nature.

Humans need to have varying degrees of physical and mental space or freedom. Despite the existence of human universals, we all differ culturally but also individually in terms of the way we interpret incoming information. When individuals form groups, they undergo a process of setting norms and rules about how they want to live together. In this process, individuals must compromise on their preferences for the benefit of the group to ensure mutual survival. The feeling of Autonomy expresses the degree to which I feel that my Self is reflected in group conventions. The less I need to go out of my way to live within the framework of any given group, the less energy I need to spend on managing my discomfort. Instead, I can contribute the energy to striving for survival or success for myself and others.

ABC is thus the language of human nature. Autonomy, Belonging, and Competence were the foundation of our ancestors' survival mechanism. As part of our nature, it is as relevant for humans today as it was for our ancestors. Indeed, the ABC of life is a very effective tool for creating success in modern times.

Evolutionary Psychology

Scientists have been trying to figure out why we humans do what we do from various perspectives. Instead of drilling deeper within their own disciplines to answer this question, scholars have started collaborating across disciplines on multidisciplinary projects. Emerging in the 1990s, the relatively new scientific field of evolutionary psychology is just such a multidisciplinary approach to human behavior. It integrates diverse perspectives such as economics, anthropology, biology, psychology, technology, literature, marketing, and neuroscience. In newly created fields such as behavioral economics, researchers are exploring the impact of our ancestral nature on today's behavior, trying to explain what we consider irrational behavior today by looking at the circumstances faced by humans some 50,000 years ago.

The Big Mismatch

The core idea underlying the field of evolutionary psychology is that an increasing gap has emerged between evolution and innovation. What may have helped humans solve a problem in the evolutionary past may or may not be so useful today. For example, a physical fight over a field of berries between two band leaders cheered on by their crowds may have been a suitable way to resolve the situation in the Stone Age. But in today's world, two department heads getting into a violent exchange over a marketing budget in a meeting room would be seen as irrational. Modern life is so different in countless ways from the conditions that characterized the world of our ancestors. Industrial revolutions, digitalization, and globalization were extremely disruptive developments from an evolutionary standpoint. Even monthly software updates of our iPhones are far more disruptive to our environment than the gradual adaptations of our genetic code have been to our body and mind.

Genetic adaptations never happen swiftly, as such rapid change would kill our organism. Instead, genetics change under evolutionary pressure, or as Charles Darwin described it, by natural selection over hundreds of thousands or even millions of years. The genetic code that was better suited to the environment was the one that survived and was reproduced over generations. For example, about two million years ago, humans started losing a specific gene that enabled them to excel at hunting. At the time, hunting involved chasing prey over long distances and over a long period of time in the heat of the savannah. The more successful hunters therefore had less body hair, more sweat glands, and higher blood pressure, and so it was these features that were passed on to their offspring. The process of losing this specific gene is estimated to have taken about a million years. But today, we are no longer chasing deer in the savannah but sitting in front of our computers for survival. The combination of this lack of physical activity and the lost gene no longer regulating high blood pressure has now been found to be accountable for increased risk of cardiovascular diseases. The more we sit, the earlier we die. How long will it take for this feature of our genetic code to naturally die out?

Evolutionary psychology has uncovered countless examples that confirm what it calls the "mismatch theory"—the idea that our genes have not evolved quickly enough, leading to a significant mismatch between certain biological, emotional, and behavioral traits that have been passed down over many generations and our current environment. Below, I examine some more examples to reveal the extent to which our evolutionary interpretation of modern information can lead our feelings and behaviors astray.

Food

Perhaps the most fundamental and conspicuous mismatch between our genetic code and our modern lifestyle is our diet. Our ancestors, who were foragers, often had to endure droughts and famine and rarely had access to foods rich in sugar and fat. Moreover, as hunter-gatherers, they moved around a lot. When they came across a tree of ripe fruit, the smart thing to do was to eat as much of it as quickly as possible, as the savannah offered very little food with sugar in it other than fruit. In addition, because they had no way to preserve the fruit, eating the fruit right away was the only reliable option. Lacking refrigerators, the fruit would have either rotten or been eaten by a local baboon group the next day. People who were skilled at finding and eating large amounts of sweet things, extracting maximum nutritional value from them, had a better chance of survival. Over tens of thousands of years, our genetic code was perfected to survive in an environment of limited supplies.

Today, we buy our food in supermarkets. Back at home, we open the refrigerator door and serve ourselves. Our genes, however, do not know that we live in the twenty-first century. As far as they are concerned, we are still stuck in the savannah 50,000 years ago. Our instincts have not had the time to update to our modern living conditions. Evolution prompted our ancestors to develop a taste preference for foods high in sugar and fat because they were so rare and because they had maximum nutritious value. These taste preferences are why our lives today are filled with highly processed foods full of sugar and fat. This is a gross mismatch with our modern way of life.

Hunter-gatherers are estimated to have consumed somewhere between 30 teaspoons to three kilograms of sugar a year, depending on the vegetation in the area. Today, people eat on average 20 to 30 teaspoons of sugar *per day*, which is the equivalent of 40 to 60 kilograms a year. Pre-made or processed food makes it easier for our stomachs to digest, leaving room for more food. Not only that, chemicals are added to our food to make it tastier. Led by our instincts, we overeat the wrong things. What helped us survive 50,000 years ago is killing us today: obesity and all its related health issues are the main causes of death in Western societies. And there is a second mismatch that has substantially added to the detrimental effects of our diet: the lack of physical activity.

Physical Activity

In 1991, I experienced a health scare that convinced me that I was going to die. My heart felt as though it was pumping inside my head; I felt nauseous; my fingers were tingling; and I could not feel my legs anymore. What an athlete experiences in the last mile of an Ironman triathlon was what I felt like after climbing 48 steps to the third floor of an office building. What had happened to me?

Before starting my first fulltime job, I had led a very active lifestyle. I was a local and regional champion in athletics, and I played in regional tennis competitions. When I graduated from university at age 23, I was 183 centimeters tall and weighed 67 kilograms, which corresponded with a healthy body mass index of 20. In my first permanent position in the business world, I worked 80 to 100 hours a week. To keep up the hard work, I ate four warm meals: I had breakfast, lunch, dinner, and a late-night meal, ordering in some pizza or Asian food. In between, I kept my energy up by having candy bars, soft drinks, and lots of coffee. However, to keep my candle burning at both ends, I had no time for exercise from the first day of my employment. Instead of engaging in two to three hours of physical activity on average every day, which was my usual routine before the start of my professional career, my only exercise now was walking from my flat to my car; from my desk to the printer, toilet, or restaurant area at work; and around the shelves of a supermarket to collect provisions for my extravagant diet.

By the time I was three years into my first job, I had gained an amazing 41 kilograms. My healthy BMI of 20 had skyrocketed to a life-threatening obesity level of 32.

The average hunter-gatherer walked 10 to 15 kilometers per day. Most ancient foragers were as fit as Olympic marathon runners. Constant body activity such as climbing, chasing, and fleeing predators gave our ancestors a level of physical fitness that only professional athletes achieve today. Only those who were extremely active and agile were able to survive and procreate. Our genetic code and biological setting still accounts for physical fitness as a key survival mechanism. But it is no longer required. We no longer use it. Due to our modern-day innovations, there is no longer any need for us to walk anywhere because we can drive. In fact, we don't even have to drive. We can go online and select any item to have it delivered to our doorstep. Most of the work we do does not require physical activity but instead involves mostly brainwork that calls for us to sit in front of an electronic device.

This physical inactivity has had shocking consequences. A typical person in a Western country walks less than one kilometer per day, while the recommended amount is seven to eight kilometers (10,000 steps). The World Health Organization reckons that 85% of the world population do not manage to walk 10,000 steps. Their metabolism suffers as a consequence. Cardiovascular diseases have overtaken cancer and smoking to become the prime cause of death in all areas of the world except for Africa. Clearly, inactivity kills. The rate of metabolism that aided our hunter-gatherer ancestors 50,000 years ago in their survival is now downright deadly for the inactive office worker.

But the downside of making a living by sitting in front of a computer is not limited to physical inactivity. There is another detrimental dimension to our use of the computer: the over-stimulation of our brains.

Information Overload

In the amount of time it takes you to read this sentence, millions of megabytes of data are uploaded to social networks. Daniel Levitin, a professor of psychology at McGill University, reckons that more information has been created over the last ten years than in all of human history. The internet, smartphones, tablets, smart TVs, and social media applications have grown exponentially. The growth in the amount of data being distributed is simply mind-boggling. The final destination of all that data is our brain—the human data processing unit—which has not changed fundamentally over thousands of years. The mismatch could not be more conspicuous.

Imagine that 15 people are sitting around a fireplace. Some are keeping the fire going, while others are preparing food. Some are talking about the terrain they covered on their walks today. Others are working on some tools. Children are playing in the background. The atmosphere is intimate, calm, and peaceful. What may sound like a holiday camp is what life was like for our ancestors. It was simple, with few close relationships and information processing that was mostly limited to their group and their territory. That is what our brains are designed for.

A typical city person sees more strangers on the way to work in the morning than the average forager did in a lifetime. Worse still, while having a coffee—on the go, in the office, or at home—we are flooding our brains with information through various electronic devices. Billions and billions of bytes in the form of letters, words, pictures, or colors race through our brains as we consume the news, check our social networks, play games, and watch movies and advertisements. An average of 100,000 tweets are sent out each minute, 58 photos are added to Instagram each second, and 20 million emails are written in the time it took to read this sentence. The average social network user receives 285 pieces of content each day, containing 54,000 words and 443 minutes of video. Americans invest 60 hours a week in consuming content. In short, the modern human is suffering from information overload.

Scientists and practitioners are sounding the alarm bell. Infobesity, infoxication, and information anxiety are just a few of the terms being used to describe the effects of brain inputs far exceeding our processing capacity. The increasing gap between who we are and what we do has been driving stress levels through the roof. The mental and physical health issues generated by 'infostress' are consequential. Cognitive impairments such as apathy, attention deficit disorders, and memory disorders have been identified in relation to information overload. High blood pressure, cardiovascular symptoms, trouble sleeping, and depression have also been linked to infostress. With respect to its economic impact, information contamination has been estimated to cost employers billions of dollars each year due to reduced productivity, lower innovation, and ineffective decision-making.

The mismatch between the amount of information we are inputting into our brain and what our brains can cope with can put so much stress on our physical and mental systems that it kills what it was designed to protect. Ironically, stress itself represents an ancestral survival mechanism, as it is the body's response to a change that requires our attention or some kind of action. In our modern society, however, this mechanism has gone awry, as I explain below.

Stress

When an organism experiences stress, it reacts to the stressor. Causes of stress, which are called stressors, can be a deadline at work, worries about your children, a health issue, a near accident with your car, or a sports competition. Stress itself is neither positive nor negative. The extent and frequency of the stress as well as individual coping mechanisms determine the outcome. When stressors disappear, so does the stress, and the system goes into recovery mode.

Endurance training for running is a good example of how stress works. A typical interval training session that professional marathon runners may perform in the weeks leading up to a marathon involves running 400m at maximum speed 15 times in a row. After completing one session, the body goes into recovery mode and overcompensates physiologically. That means that it fixes more than was broken and thereby boosts running performance to a higher level. But timing is the critical issue here. This higher performance level cannot be sustained. After recovery, the body returns to its original equilibrium. Therefore, another training session is needed to continue building one's running form. If the next training session comes too early, however, and the athlete has not recovered enough from the previous session, the body either remains at the same level or even enters a downward spiral. Stressing the body again at the peak of the recovery creates an upward spiral in terms of running performance.

A marathon runner's success depends on applying the right length, intensity, and frequency of stress attuned to their actual abilities, and the same can be said about success in life. Traced back to its evolutionary roots, stress is nothing but a highly sophisticated and well-orchestrated survival mechanism. Stress is good: it switches on our goal setting, our skill application, and our persistence. Being alert helps the surgeon to perform a heart transplant, the soccer player to score a penalty, and the business executive to speak at an annual general meeting. But we all know the story about too much of a good thing.

It is here that we find the most substantial mismatch and prime cause of failure of our time. Feelings of Autonomy, Belonging, and Competence signaled safety and survival to our ancestors. This mechanism still determines our human nature. Therefore, any blow to our A, B, or C levels still represents a stressor, which triggers a response leading to the three big D's of failure: *distorted* goal setting, *destructive* skill application, and *degraded* persistence.

The CEO and Its Bodyguard

Did you know that each of us has a subconscious program running in the background of our conscious daily activities?

It constantly scans situations for potential danger. As soon as a potential threat to life is spotted, the program immediately switches to stress mode, which activates essential body functions needed to overcome the situation. The two core instincts for handling danger are fight or flight. To survive, our ancestors had the options of either fighting the danger—a saber-toothed tiger, an enemy tribe, or a natural disaster—or running away. A closer look at this evolutionary legacy provides some pivotal insights into how stress drives success and failure in our modern world.

The part of the brain that houses this subconscious program, which continuously scans all information collected through our senses for signs of danger, is called the *amygdala*. You might think of it as a bodyguard checking anything and everyone for your personal security. The amygdala has a direct reporting line to the brain's CEO, our prefrontal cortex. You may recall that the prefrontal cortex is home to the executive functions of goal setting, skill application, and persistence. As with any good subordinate, the amygdala reports any potentially threatening information to the CEO for decision-making, planning, and coordination of a response. The prefrontal cortex and the amygdala enter into a negotiation over how to best address the concerns signaled by the amygdala.

Here is an example of what the interaction between the amygdala and the prefrontal cortex might look like. It is a Friday night and you are out with friends. The club is packed. You are at the bar ordering beers when you are almost knocked over by someone jostling you. Your amygdala immediately signals potential danger to your prefrontal cortex. The stress caused by the danger causes you to want to immediately hit the guy over the head in return for his disrespectful behavior. Now you are in a situation in which the amygdala and the prefrontal cortex are wrestling over the response you should give. Acting as your instinctive brain, the amygdala tells the prefrontal cortex to activate the upper body, the arms, and the fist to hit the guy to prevent further harm. Acting as your rational brain, the prefrontal cortex assesses the situation. The guy is a hunky football-player type who is two meters tall with a grim face. In this situation, I would hope that your prefrontal cortex overrules your amygdala and apologizes to the guy for getting in the way. If so, you would have to thank your prefrontal cortex for having chosen rational behavior over the instinct to fight. For if the amygdala had convinced your prefrontal cortex to fight, it is likely you would have ended up in the hospital. This demonstrates how stress management determines our success and failure. The physiological processes around this episode add another enlightening dimension to stress. What used to be our ancestors' bodyguard—the amygdala—is now a kind of bloodthirsty killer.

A recent publication on stress by Harvard Medical School outlines a whole array of near-instantaneous, involuntary changes in our metabolism when the amygdala signals danger. Blood is immediately directed away from the center of our body to our muscles and our brain. "It [stress] is like a gas pedal in a car triggering the fight-or-flight response," according to the Harvard report. All such physiological changes happen well before the prefrontal cortex can intervene and slam on the brakes. Higher liver glucose levels supply additional energy, and one's heart rate, blood pressure, and breathing are increased for better oxygen supply. Enhanced cortisol production supports the transport of glucose by narrowing the arteries for the blood to flow faster. Adrenalin floods the body to increase blood clotting in preparation for repairing major wounds. Imagine these processes being set in motion in your body every time the amygdala picks up on a potential threat.

It is no wonder that participants in ABC deficiency studies engage in instinctive behavior. By manipulating Autonomy, Belonging, or Competence downward, the researchers stressed participants' amygdalas, signaling a life-threatening event. Their instincts for survival kicked in, and the executive functions of the prefrontal cortex were compromised. As a consequence, the resulting fight-or-flight behavior give rise to the three D's of failure—distortion, destruction, and degradation.

While our ancestors found themselves in a life-or-death situation every once in a while, in our modern society our amygdala activates this mechanism countless times a day. The American Institute of Stress (AIS) highlights job issues, money, and relationships as the top three stressors in everyday life. According to the institute's statistics, almost 80% of people experience constant stress. Social media was ranked fourth on the institute's list of stressors. A compelling study by Andrew Przybylski's team of scientists on the fear of missing out (FOMO) demonstrated how our daily internet activities constantly trigger stress through the ABC mechanism.

How often do you check your various social media accounts for news? The fear or regret of missing opportunities for social interactions, satisfying events, profitable investments, or any other kind of rewarding experience operates as a constant, nagging thought in the back of your mind. FOMO gives us the feeling that we have made the wrong decision in terms of how to spend our time, as potentially more rewarding experiences may be just a fingertip away. The Przybylski study revealed that FOMO negatively impacted one's ABC. Instead of enjoying the current social media interaction, participants felt excluded from alternative experiences, which was a big downer for their feeling of Belonging. One can also see how FOMO might compromise feelings of Autonomy and Competence. Too many options of social media decrease people's levels of Autonomy. And going out for drinks with friends to an actual event may even represent an additional option beyond the virtual world. By missing out on important content—for example, stock market information—people could also incur lower levels of Competence. What this means is that FOMO puts people in a no-win situation. Whatever you do, wherever you are, you are always wondering whether the grass may be greener on a different window of your screen. FOMO acts as a stressor that is constantly alerting our amygdala due to ABC deficiency. In other words, our levels of ABC represent an effective indicator of stress in our everyday lives.

Being a member of a group enabled our ancestors to significantly increase their chances of survival. In modern times, feeling a sense of Autonomy, Belonging, and Competence makes us feel safe. If our Autonomy is compromised by a traffic jam on the highway, or our sense of Belonging is lowered by an argument with our partner at home, or our feeling of Competence is diminished by negative feedback at work, we feel stressed. In our world of ever-increasing speed, complexity, uncertainty, and ambiguity, how much Autonomy, Belonging, and Competence do you think we actually feel? The answer is: very little. As a result of this ABC deficiency, people in Western societies suffer from continuous stress.

I am often asked how *real* this subconscious threat to life resulting from ABC deficiency actually is. How harmful can low levels of ABC really be? From an ethical point of view, it would be difficult to run experimental designs involving potentially life-threatening experiences in order to compare the impact of real danger with the impact of ABC deficiencies. However, there is a field of research that helps bridge that gap, namely, the experiments being conducted on people with post-traumatic stress disorder.

ABC and Post-Traumatic Stress Disorder

Post-traumatic stress disorder (PTSD) is a mental disorder that can develop after a person is exposed to a traumatic event such as sexual assault, warfare, serious injury, or other potential threats of imminent death. The disorder may develop after a delay. According to statistics, 3.5% of the United States population develop PTSD in any given year, and 9% suffer from some form of PTSD at some point in their life. The risk of post-traumatic stress varies by trauma type. The most common events triggering PTSD are combat (25%), sexual violence (11%), rape (19%), traffic accidents (20%), and the unexpected death of a loved one (20%). A high prevalence of PTSD cases has also been detected in refugee populations. The American Psychiatry Association shares the following PTSD-related patient story:

> Jared was a 36-year old married veteran who had returned from Afghanistan, where he had served as an officer. He went to the Veterans Affairs outpatient mental health clinic complaining

of having "a short fuse" and being "easily triggered." Jared's symptoms involved out-of-control rage when startled, constant thoughts and memories of death-related events, weekly vivid nightmares of combat that caused trouble sleeping, anxiety and a loss of interest in hobbies he once enjoyed with friends. Although all of these symptoms were very distressing, Jared was most worried about his extreme anger. His "hair-trigger temper" caused fights with drivers who cut him off, cursing at strangers who stood too close in checkout lines, and shifts into "attack mode" when coworkers startled him by accident. In a recent visit to the doctor, he was drifting off to sleep in the exam table. A nurse brushed by his foot, and he leapt up, cursing and threatening her—scaring both the nurse and himself.

These moments reminded him of a time in the military when he was on guard at the front gate. While he was dozing, an enemy mortar round stunned him into action.

Jared was raised in a loving family that struggled to make ends meet as Midwestern farmers. At age 20 he joined the U.S. Army and was deployed to Afghanistan. He described himself as having been upbeat and happy before his army service. He said he enjoyed basic training and his first few weeks in Afghanistan, until one of his comrades got killed. At that point, all he cared about was getting his best friend and himself home alive, even if it meant killing others. His personality changed, he said, from that of a happy-go-lucky farm boy to a frightened, overprotective soldier.

Jared was diagnosed with post-traumatic stress disorder. His main concerns were due to his symptoms of fear, and his aggression when startled by someone. Jared was jittery and always on the lookout for danger. He also had intrusive memories, nightmares and flashbacks.

The core symptoms of PTSD have been summarized as hyperarousal (aggression), avoidance (loss of interest in people and activities), and re-experiencing (memories, nightmares, flashbacks), as Jared's case demonstrates. They are in alignment with experimental results based on ABC deficiency including aggression, lethargy, and cognitive impairments. When neuroscientists used MfRI scanning to display PTSD on a screen, they found the same neural mechanism that SDT researchers had spotted in ABC deficiency experiments, where the amygdala had hijacked the prefrontal cortex. An article by Rachel Yehuda and Joseph LeDoux in the reputable academic journal *Neuron* demonstrated that PTSD patients showed attenuated activation of the prefrontal cortex which was then overwhelmed by chronic amygdala impulses. Similar to the way that traumatized patients experience threats of life on a continuous basis, people in everyday life feel threatened by chronic stressors to their ABC levels. The same mechanism of the amygdala overpowering the prefrontal cortex leads to instinctive responses in both cases. In conclusion, Yehuda and LeDoux suggest that prolonged stress alters the wiring of the prefrontal cortex and the amygdala, increasing the likelihood that the brain will go into survival mode.

From Failure to Success

Overstimulation of the amygdala leads to physiological and psychological malfunctions. At the physiological level, our organs become overworked, as reflected in the most common health issues in our modern societies. Diverting blood to our muscles and limbs causes digestive and immune system problems. Higher glucose levels and cortisol can lead to obesity and diabetes. Increases in heart rate, blood pressure, cortisol, and adrenalin trigger cardiovascular problems such as coronary heart disease.

The psychological effects are equally dramatic. When the prefrontal cortex is overwhelmed by the amygdala's chronic impulses, rational behavior suffers. Instinctive fight-or-flight reactions lead to anti-social and self-defeating behavior. The ABC plays a dual role in this process. First, the amygdala continuously

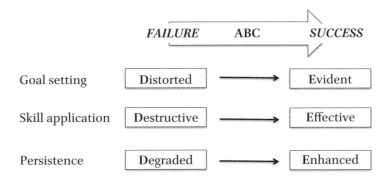

	FAILURE	ABC	SUCCESS
Goal setting	Distorted	→	Evident
Skill application	Destructive	→	Effective
Persistence	Degraded	→	Enhanced

monitors a person's ABC levels as a signal for potential threats to life. Second, the prefrontal cortex is powered by the energy reservoir fueled by the ABC. Both aspects together show the crucial role of ABC for success in life. The higher your ABC levels, the more power available to the prefrontal cortex to control the chronic activation by the amygdala. Your goal setting will be *evident* instead of *distorted*, your skill application *effective* instead of *destructive*, and your persistence *enhanced* instead of *degraded*.

The ABC of life is an evolutionary approach to success. We cannot change our instincts. But we can use the insights into our ancestral nature to create today's success. Achieving and maintaining high levels of Autonomy, Belonging, and Competence enable us to avoid evolutionary traps. As a result, the ABC empowers us to overcome the three D's of failure—which are triggered by our instincts—and to thrive on the three E's of success.

This concludes Part I, which focused on the foundations of the ABC of life. We now move on to Part II to discover what role the ABC plays in various life domains such as work, sports, health, and education. We will also explore how the ABC is related to something we are all concerned about—our happiness!

Part II

5. The ABC of Work

Companies are paying employees for their HANDS.
The same employees will give them their HEADS and
HEARTS for free if only companies knew how to ask.
– Bob Gorman, Chairman & CEO of Barry-Wehmiller

We begin our journey through the ABC of life domains in the workplace. Work is the dominating domain of our adult lives. Between the ages of 20 and 65, we spend an average of 15 years at work. The remaining two-thirds of that time are spent on family, friends, leisure, and sleep. If we spend the bulk of our adult lifetime at work, should we not feel fulfilled by it? Yet the increasingly popular term "work-life balance" indicates quite the opposite. It portrays work and life as mutually exclusive. Either you are at work or you have a life. If work does not qualify as life, we are all investing one-third of our adult lives in an activity that requires some kind of cross-subsidization.

According to institutions such as the World Health Organization (WHO), the International Labour Organization (ILO), and the European Agency for Safety and Health at Work (EU-OSHA), stress levels have been skyrocketing among workers and employees. Over half of us perceive our jobs as very stressful. More than 65% of us believe our work negatively impacts the other parts of our lives. Close to 15% have experienced physical violence in their workplace, and over 50% work in an atmosphere where yelling and other verbal abuse is common. Many of us feel like we are entering a survival camp when we go to work. We do not feel safe. Instead, our amygdala is triggered on a constant basis. Alarm bells ring, indicating life-threatening situations on a continuous basis. Overcontrolled, rejected, or overwhelmed, our ABC becomes depleted. The amygdala hijacks the prefrontal cortex, and survival mode takes over: fight or flight!

An intriguing study by Ryan and his colleagues provides a compelling account of the work-life paradigm and the ABC-depleting nature of workplaces. They followed full-time professionals in various industries (e.g. construction, administration, legal services, health) over a period of 21 consecutive days, assessing their ABC at three random times a day. Participants reported lower ABC during working hours than non-working hours, and ABC levels were also substantially higher on weekends than during the week.

Work Environment Mismatch

It is fair to conclude that there is a mismatch between human nature and workplace conditions. When we are stressed at work, we feel that we cannot have a life at work, that we are not safe beyond mere job security, and that we have to fight for survival or run from danger. The effects on people's health are profound. Psychosomatic symptoms such as burnout, cardiovascular diseases, diabetes, and fatigue have been on the rise. Absenteeism, employee turnover, and disengagement have increased in lockstep. According to Gallup, an American analytics company, over 80% of employees worldwide are disengaged at work.

In addition to the health effects, there are enormous economic costs. According to EU-OSHA, 50% of the 550 million working days lost annually in the United States from absenteeism are stress-related. Productivity losses for U.S. companies due to workers and employees underperforming as a result of switching to survival mode at work are in the hundreds of billions of dollars each year.

It may sound irrational that companies maintain work climates in which employees feel trampled by their bosses, ripped apart by their colleagues, and buried under their workload. However, this is yet another evolutionary mismatch—this time between management theory and economic conditions.

Frederick Winslow Taylor revolutionized the industrial world in 1911 with his book *The Principles of Scientific Management*. It was a time when people were moving from farms into growing cities, taking up work in large industrial plants, and operating heavy machinery and assembly lines. Their jobs were so-called algorithmic tasks that followed a set of established instructions down a single pathway to one conclusion, over and over again! Or, as Taylor described it: "Work consists mainly of simple, not particularly interesting tasks". He outlined how headwork needed to be separated from physical activities. Taylor was also the first to introduce the term *manager*. In his approach, managers were installed to "do the headwork and then systematically and tightly control, observe, measure and optimize workers' performance".

Generations of executives have been trained in Taylorism, which has been passed down by their superiors. All managers are expected to understand and apply Taylor's principles; indeed, such principles have to become part of your DNA if you are to be considered for promotion. Many senior executives today identify people as their company's number-one priority, but when we look beyond the words and examine senior executives' actions, people still rank far behind other company objectives such as shareholder value, earnings per share, customer satisfaction, or infrastructure. I recently concluded a project for a European airline company with several thousand employees. People were a priority for the board, and so they asked me to study their employees' motivation and well-being and to provide suggestions on how to design their organization and train their personnel. The results were shocking: over 90% of employees felt disengaged, and many of them had psychosomatic symptoms. When these results were presented to the management board, the CEO turned to his CFO and asked: "If our employees are so unhappy, don't we have €10,000 somewhere in the budget to cheer them up?" This episode is a great example of how Taylorism still rules modern workplace management.

Western economies no longer run on predictable, large-scale algorithms. An algorithm is a step-by-step procedure for solving problems, but in today's economy, experimenting with options and coming up with novel solutions is the name of the game. Taylor's simple and not particularly interesting tasks have been increasingly substituted by artificial intelligence. In a world where almost anything can be found and replicated in an instant, people's collective intelligence represents the last sustainable source of competitive advantage for companies. In fact, a groundbreaking study by MIT's Human Dynamics Lab identified collective intelligence—or the *c-factor*—as the key performance indicator for organizations. Sandy Pentland and his lab team had the participants in their study wear electronic badges in order to collect data on their daily social interactions at work. When analyzing the information, the c-factor (deduced through a combination of tone of voice, body language, whom they talked to, and how much they talked) was found to be more important for organizational performance than individual intelligence, personality, technical skills, and the substance of discussions *combined*!

The ABC Perspective

This finding may be hardly surprising in the context of our group-based survival mechanism. If companies want to succeed in today's business world, they need to nurture their people's nature, namely, feelings of Autonomy, Belonging, and Competence. When workers and employees feel safe in an organization due to high levels of ABC, they will not be distracted by an amygdala in survival mode. In fact, in light of evolutionary psychology, we can even say that Taylor's methods of management can cause human failure by destroying ABC. The trend since the days of Taylor has been toward valuing the role of the individual for the organization. Whereas workers and employees were a depersonalized resource back then, in today's business world, every head and every heart matters. Organizations need to create ABC-supportive environments for their employees in order to enable them to use their executive functions and in turn create success for themselves and their companies.

Since 2000, the global team of SDT researchers around Deci and Ryan has made it their fundamental mission to investigate and document the impact of people's ABC levels on organizational success. Studies in the manufacturing and service industries, private companies and governments, small to medium-sized local family-owned businesses and large global companies, for-profit and non-profit institutions, business students and alumni all arrived at the same conclusion: ABC levels drive success!

Paul Baard surveyed 200 female and 328 male professionals at a major U.S. investment bank, assessing their ABC levels, perceptions on work climate, and well-being indicators and linking them to their most recent performance evaluations. The results showed that work climate predicted the levels of ABC. In turn, ABC levels drove bankers' well-being and performance evaluations. In another, quite different setting, Juan Carlos Roca and Marylène Gagné studied 480 highly educated employees from four United Nations agencies in an online research project, concluding that their levels of ABC predicted learning-on-the-job outcomes. The higher the ABC, the more useful, enjoyable, and productive the learning experience was and the greater participants' intentions were to continue to pursue further online training.

A team of researchers around Deci and Ryan were curious to find out whether the ABC effect could be identified outside Western cultures. Bulgaria had until 1989 been governed by a socialist totalitarian regime. All industries were state-owned and operated based on central planning principles. Culturally, the country could be described as collectivistic and more or less isolated from the West. In 2001, the SDT scientists collected a large data set from Bulgarian professionals working for ten still state-owned companies. The analysis confirmed the results previously observed in Western samples: employee perceptions of work climates predicted ABC levels, and the higher the ABC, the greater the employees' work engagement was.

ABC Diagnostics

The medical profession teaches us that a cure can only be as good as the diagnostics it is based on. The same can be said of the health of an organization. When I talk to senior executives about their organization, I often ask them "How are your people feeling today?". Some might openly admit that they don't know, but most would pretend and respond that their employees are doing "very well". In the latter case, I always follow up by asking: "Show me!", which tends to cause irritation on behalf of the executive.

If I had asked for the most recent customer satisfaction report or data on the company's financials, the same executive would have immediately been able to locate a file on an electronic device and print out a status report for me. If people were a priority in this company, actual data on how people were doing should be as available to the executive team as the customer data and financial numbers. Given that people are the last remaining source of sustainable competitive advantage, and given that their feelings are critical for their performance, employees' feelings should be monitored on a regular basis. Information on people's feelings are as critical to a company's survival as data on altitude, speed, and navigation are for an aircraft! Imagine you were boarding a plane and at the entrance door you spot a sign saying

ATTENTION
This aircraft only measures altitude, speed, and navigation
every THREE hours

Would you get on that plane? Highly unlikely. But we are expecting hundreds of millions of workers and employees to enter the front doors of their workplaces each day where no one has any idea how those people are feeling. Many companies have never done employee surveys. Some do, but only every one or two years, after which the data are analyzed and immediately shelved.

Sometimes they are shared with the workforce. If steps are taken in response to survey results, there is a lag of about two years on average between the time the survey was conducted and the time the measures were implemented. Two years is a long time given the pace of our twenty-first-century world. In two years, the world, the industry, the company, the employees, and their feelings will have quantum leaped.

Modern information technology allows for more regular, voluntary monitoring of employee well-being. Workers and employees can be invited to share their feelings in a structured format. Julian Troian was named HR manager of the year in Luxembourg in 2016 for installing a unique employee feedback system at the data center company Etix Everywhere in which each employee was asked to confidentially respond to one survey question per day. The questions posed were from different areas such as fairness, reward, or control, and the results were made available to employees in the format of a weather report per workgroup: sun, clouds, rain, thunderstorms. If the sun was out in a specific area and workgroup, no further actions were taken and a question from another area was asked the next day. But if clouds and rain appeared, this was followed up by another question from the same area. Thunderstorms prompted Julian to offer immediate support for resolution.

Etix Everywhere had developed its own HR survey tool due to its in-house IT expertise. Second-generation SDT scholar and entrepreneur Scott Rigby has created motivationworks.com, an open platform based on ABC that uses artificial intelligence to provide detailed action items for individual employees and superiors to boost their ABC. Companies such as Apple, Google, and Johnson & Johnson have been reported using the tool to enable their people to create success for themselves and their company.

Applying and implementing ABC practices requires a new leadership paradigm expressed in company culture, the approach to change, the style of communication, and the structure of compensation.

Leadership

If we were to rank the various fields of research in the organizational sciences in terms of progress over the last 50 years, leadership would be a strong contender for the last spot. Instead of progress, we have seen a lot of sideways movement that has mostly broadened and blurred the area instead of advancing and developing it. Essentially, 50 to 100 leadership models exist in literature today. Four of the most prominent examples include charismatic leadership, authentic leadership, transformational leadership, and servant leadership.[2] Most of the leadership models have one common denominator: leadership is all about how you make people feel! The ABC of work has demonstrated in theory and practice that the more Autonomy, Belonging, and Competence people feel at work, the more successful they are as individuals creating success stories within teams and organizations.

Culture

Company culture is determined by the attitudes and values of individual workers and employees and how the individuals are related to each other. The ABC of work suggests that in successful companies, the success comes not from people collaborating but rather from their inducing feelings of ABC in each other. It is the formal leader's responsibility to lead by example and to create the conditions for instilling the give and take of ABC within the organization.

When I discuss the value of ABC with executives, I am often asked whether this approach has been applied in their specific industry before. My response to them is that as long as their

2   Charismatic leadership energizes people through the charisma of the leader. Authentic leadership generates trust and support through the leader's congruence between who s/he is and what s/he does. Transformational leadership inspires people by the identification of needed change and the creation and implementation of a vision. Servant leadership focuses on people's needs and feelings to help them grow, develop, and perform.

workers and employees are human, the ABC will work. After all, the ABC approach is based on the evolution of the human race and is congruent with our human nature. It may, however, require that the organization go through a process of organizational redesign, training, and personal development—in other words, change!

Change

Change is always a challenge. Our ancestors survived based on stable group relations. Any change represented a potential threat to survival. This is no different today. Many people's daily activities in organizations are on autopilot, so when there is change, this prompts the following kinds of questions in people's minds: How will the change affect the need for my competences? What will be the impact of change on the group that I belong to? How much autonomy will I have after the change? As a result, change always activates people's amygdala and thus generates varying degrees of resistance due to our instinctive fear for survival.

SDT researchers Marylène Gagné, Richard Koestner, and Miron Zuckerman investigated the ABC levels of the employees of a large Canadian telecoms company undergoing a profound change. In addition to ABC levels, they measured the employees' acceptance of change at two times—before the change project kicked off (T1) and 12 months into it (T2). They were not surprised to see that ABC levels had decreased from T1 to T2. Looking deeper, they noticed that the higher the ABC levels were at T1, the greater the acceptance of change was at T2. That means that the ABC of work can facilitate change processes. The trick is to increase ABC levels before and during change by including people in the preparation and implementation of the change process. For instance, if employees are asked for their input on how to implement the change, they are likely to feel Autonomy due to the option they are given. This would also give them a greater sense of Belonging by being included in the preparation and the actual process of change as well as increased feelings of Competence for being asked for their expertise.

Communication

You cannot *not* communicate. Whatever you say and do—or not—you are continuously sending messages to people. Nonetheless, most people are reluctant to provide feedback on the communication they receive and its impact on their feelings. Most of us simply do not like talking about our feelings, especially if it is in the context of work. The ABC framework can help to bridge this gap between feelings and communication.

I teach the ABC framework in an Organizational Psychology course. Each year, I receive emails from students detailing their life stories during as well as after the course. They use the ABC framework to avoid talking about their feelings. For example, one student shared her relocation to another department with me by describing it as "a big Downer for my B". Some students have continued communicating in ABC language with me long after having completed the course and their MBA programs. Recently, an alumnus was asked to present a new innovative solution to the executive committee of his company. He emailed me, saying: "it ticked all the boxes, a big boost for my A, B, and C". I noted the same effect in my work with organizations. Teams that have difficulty communicating are able to open up about difficult issues when they can convey how a certain behavior or rule negatively impacted their ABC instead of talking about their actual feelings of being angry, upset, or hurt. The ABC framework facilitates the constructive resolution of issues that might not be addressed otherwise. One such issue in the workplace is compensation.

Compensation

Many contemporary corporate compensation schemes include some element of reward and punishment. By now, the idea that contingent compensation has a negative effect on employees' performance—otherwise known as the undermining effect—has become an established notion in organizational sciences. Then why is it that companies are still engaging in such unproductive practices? Because it is a tool to fulfill the most basic need of managers who have subscribed to Taylorism—the need for control!

Remember the thought experiment in the previous chapter involving the use of the carrot or the stick to make a person get up from her seat? We saw that over time, the effects of both monetary incentives (the carrot) and fire (the stick) will wear off. I use the phrase "over time" for both scenarios because reward and punishment are both short-term control tools at the expense of long-term productivity. It is hardly surprising that in our business world, which is focused on short-term results such as quarterly company reports, managers engage in Taylor's controlling practices. Yet they are out of line with our human nature, leading to ABC deficiency in workers and employees. What may have worked a century ago will not be sustainable in the digital age. Short-term successes will turn into long-term failures. Such failures will reveal themselves in the underperformance of the company and, less obviously, in workers' and employees' ill-being. Just because your numbers look good today does not mean that your company and your people are healthy and will still be around tomorrow. The sad fact is that, given the amount of time it takes for the failure to materialize, the hired managers are not likely to be around any longer to take responsibility for it.

How a contingent reward-and-punishment program can achieve short-term success and cause long-term failure was examined in a thought-provoking study by Tim Gubler and his colleagues. They used data from an attendance award program introduced at an industrial laundry plant. Attendance awards had an immediate, positive effect on the attendance of employees who had previously had punctuality problems. However, the positive change was not sustainable. Workers started strategically playing the system, leading to deteriorating attendance numbers below pre-program levels. Not only that, employees who had previously had excellent attendance records became less reliable. This spillover effect had even more dramatic implications for the company. Employees who had shown above-average pre-program attendance became less efficient in their daily task performance once the program began. This is a great example of how the undermining effect can cause task underperformance due to ABC deficiency. Company management had no other choice but to suspend the attendance award program entirely, as it had started to threaten the company's economic foundations.

The impact of performance-based pay (PBP) on employee stress levels was the topic of a recent SDT study led by Stacey Parker from the University of Queensland. Previous research data from 1,300 Danish firms had shown a 4-6% increase in anti-depressant and anti-anxiety medication after the introduction of PBP programs. In an experimental lab study followed by a survey-based collection of field data, Parker and her fellow scientists found that PBP predicted higher anxiety, emotional exhaustion, fatigue, and more anti-social behavior.

In 2016, Bard Kuvaas and his colleagues studied the consequences of compensation schemes in a Norwegian insurance company. They had a non-contingent base-pay plan and a pay-for-performance plan paying a bonus based on sales performance. Employees who had chosen the pay-for-performance plan showed lower job performance and greater intentions to leave the company.

We can change the frame of reference from the digital age to the Stone Age to highlight the effects of contingent compensation. The ABC represents our ancestral survival mechanism. By introducing performance-based rewards and punishments, companies send the message to employees that their survival is contingent upon a certain yardstick. It is only if an employee can show a specific Competence (achieving that yardstick) that s/he can receive a reward or avoid punishment, which represents Belonging (or exclusion). The contingency scheme is perceived as controlling by the employee, negatively impacting Autonomy, as survival is perceived as solely based on the yardstick. From an evolutionary perspective, PBP makes employees feel unsafe, causing fight-or-flight behavior and resulting in individual—and eventually corporate—failure.

So What Works?

In a world of increasing speed, uncertainty, and complexity, organizational success depends on employees contributing their heads and hearts and not just their hands. Companies can no longer afford to have managers design work processes and force people into pre-specified boxes. With an increasing number of companies realizing this paradigm shift, a war for talent has unfolded, requiring companies to pursue new approaches to hiring, retaining, and growing employees. Compensation represents a key success factor in the new employee equation. People expect to be rewarded in exchange for their work. However, such schemes need to be consistent with our human nature. In coming up with an appropriate compensation scheme, companies must consider things from the psychological point of view and not just the financial standpoint. What drives ABC and what undermines it?

Marylène Gagné from Curtin University in Western Australia and Jacques Forest from the University of Montréal are the two leading SDT scientists in the area of the link between compensation and levels of ABC. They have collaborated on various research projects to uncover the ABC dynamics around compensation. Their conclusion: unexpected, non-contingent, non-salient rewards (which can be financial) do not drain ABC levels.

There are ways in which compensation schemes can be ABC-supportive. From the perspective of our human nature, this is the case when compensation does not appear to employees as obstacles to survival that would trigger their amygdalas. For example, companies may give employees the choice to have more holiday for less pay, more health coverage for less pay, more pay for fewer pension plan contributions, less pay for more personal development or for the option of working partially from home. Such individualized compensation packages could be adapted by employees in relation to their respective life situations, given that one's needs differ if one is a young, single rookie as opposed to an experienced senior manager who is married with children.

This will give people a sense of control over their work and boost their Autonomy.

Belonging and Competence levels can be supported by avoiding competitive elements in compensation plans. For example, paying a bonus to the top salesperson on your team will destroy the sense of Belonging among the other team members, inhibit their Competence, and impair trust and teamwork. I recently worked with a European telecoms company on designing an ABC-supportive development program for their employees. People could apply to one of three programs. They could become an *Explorer* to acquire new skills and spend time in various departments. They could become a *Manager* by attending an internal mini-MBA program to qualify for more senior responsibilities. Finally, they could become a *Specialist*, deep-diving into a specific area. Even though this was not a formal compensation item that employees subscribed to when signing their contracts, it did represent an unexpected investment by the company in them. Employees perceived it as compensation in recognition of their work. It boosted their Autonomy (as they had a choice in which program to pursue), Belonging (they felt appreciated), and Competence (they acquired new skills).

Designing an appropriate compensation scheme for a company is no longer a standard procedure. It requires agility, flexibility, and an understanding of people—*your* people. You need to include your employees in the discussion of what drives and depletes ABC in your organization and what steps can be taken to increase ABC and to eliminate ABC downers. Equally important, are there financials to back up your decision-making process?

Economics

Financial figures and ratios are the language of business. It would be naïve to propose altruism to business executives. Corporate performance has traditionally been expressed and reported in numbers such as productivity, profitability, or earnings per share. Therefore, it is not enough to make qualitative arguments for corporate investments in people as a source of competitive advantage; one must calculate the quantitative measure of a return on investment (ROI) in order to respond to a C-level executive's question on how the profitability of a specific investment in employees compares to other corporate investments. Only a comprehensive answer to this question will level the playing field between people and other corporate assets and give people the strategic attention they deserve in a knowledge economy. In their joint 2012 report, McKinsey & Company and The Conference Board concede that "worldwide, and in organizations of every type, 'people processes' are failing to keep pace with a changing business landscape," as "the lack of being able to talk the business language of ROI prevents (executive) buy-in".

I spent almost five years of my academic life investigating employee economics and designing an ROI model for people investments. The economic value added (EVA) model is based on the ABC framework. At the core of EVA is an algorithm translating employees' ABC levels into three levels of employee engagement. Engaged employees create more value for a company than they cost. Disengaged employees do as they are told and create value at their level of cost. Actively disengaged employees work against the objectives of the firm, do not create value, and in turn destroy what they cost. By linking the three levels of engagement to the salary statistics of a company, we can calculate the economic value of an increase in employee's ABC levels. An ROI can be calculated by dividing the economic value creation by the cost of an intervention. The cost factor usually consists of employee's time, fees for external facilitators or consultants, and potential overheads. In the original research study published in 2019, the EVA model was validated in a 12-month intervention project with 367 employees of a European pharmaceuticals company. ABC levels were measured before (T1) and after (T2) a series of ABC workshops and coachings. At T2, employees' ABC levels had increased by 10.9%, which translated into an economic value gain of around $817,000. Given the intervention cost of the external consultants ($295,000) and the value of the employees' time ($255,000), the project ROI was calculated at $817,000/($295,000 + $255,000) = 148.5%. The ROI number was stunning, and I had scholars, investment bankers, and practitioners check the model's theoretical foundations as well as its assumptions. The results were particularly surprising given that the economic return was calculated on a 12-month basis only, ignoring any future effects on employee engagement. This essentially assumes that the effects of the ABC intervention would stop after 12 months.

Since its publication, the EVA model has been applied internationally in various settings. Based on the ROI numbers I have been made aware of, no organizational ABC intervention has produced a project ROI below 148%. In fact, most projects scored over 200% and some even over 300% calculated on a conservative 12-month basis. These results were consistent with the work of organizational psychologists Marylène Gagné, Jacques Forest, and their colleagues who used a different economic model but found that every dollar invested in boosting employees' ABC levels generated $3.19 in return.

Both models seem to indicate that a company's people are the most profitable area for corporate investments. People perform the way they feel. The ABC of work provides a structured approach to employees' feelings, enabling them to create sustainable success for themselves and their organizations.

6.   The ABC of Sports

Sport has the power to celebrate our common humanity, regardless of
faith, race, culture, beliefs, gender and ability.
– Sport at the Service of Humanity, 1st Principle of the Declaration
of Principles

January 12, 2016 was a day that Mohamed Masoud will always remember. At only 21 years of age, a lifetime dream had come true. Nicknamed Dola, he and his Egyptian volleyball teammates beat Tunisia 3-2 in the final of the African qualification tournament in Congo's capital Brazzaville. After beating Congo (3-0), Tunisia (3-0), and Cameroon (3-0) in the semifinals, and then Tunisia again in the final, Egypt had qualified for the 2016 Summer Olympics in Rio. Mohamed had the perfect shape and skills for the middle blocker position of a volleyball team. He was quick, strong, and good at reading the opponent's strategies. At 2.11 meters (6 ft 11 in), he also had the necessary height for effectively blocking other teams' hitters. Dola was not only the tallest but also the youngest player of his team and the only player from the Smouha SC club in Alexandria.

Egypt's volleyball team had won the African Cup eight times. The last time was in 2015 in Cairo when they beat their longtime rival Tunisia 3-0. In 2016, it was Egypt's fifth appearance in the Olympic volleyball tournament. The team did not make it to the second round of the tournament in Rio. They lost 0-3 to Poland, Russia, Iran, and Argentina, although they beat Cuba 3-0. What an experience for Mohamed Masoud: between the 7th and 21st of August 2016, he had been a qualified and accepted member of the Olympic family. Despite his Olympic journey, he has remained a modest, down-to-earth individual with his family, friends, and teammates at Al Ahly SC, the club he is playing for today.

Sports display our evolutionary ABC mechanism in a very transparent way. If you can show that you have

	DIRECT	INDIRECT
TEAM	Soccer, Basketball, Volleyball	Bobsleigh, Relay Races, Rowing (2,4,8)
INDIVIDUAL	Tennis Singles, Martial Arts, Chess	Alpine Skiing, Surfing, Athletics

Competence—expressed in points, times, scores, wins, or other competitive outcomes—you will be selected for a team or you will qualify for a tournament, leading to a feeling of Belonging while preserving your degree of Self or Autonomy. This chapter will help you understand the ABC of life from the perspective of sports. But you don't have to be a professional athlete to apply the lessons learned on goal setting, skill application, and persistence to boost your success in life. Overall, competitive sports can be categorized in the above 2x2 matrix.

There is no other area in life where our human nature expresses itself more transparently. The physical, mental, and technical skills developed by foragers in the Stone Age are reflected in the 100-meter dash, soccer, or golfing today. Social and communication skills that helped Stone Age clans to organize themselves as they passed through the savannah plains represent a core ingredient of team-building in sports in our modern world. We are inherently active, playful, social creatures. Practicing and performing natural activities such as running, climbing, or hunting prepared our ancestors for survival. Training and performing sports can serve as a great guide to success in contemporary life. While the link between goal setting, skill application, persistence, and success may be less clear in life domains such as work, sports can show in a very transparent way how our executive functions translate into results.

Goal Setting

There are three types of goals in sports: outcome goals, performance goals, and process goals. Outcome goals focus on qualitative results such as winning, qualifying, or losing weight. Performance goals are specific in terms of times, scores, or points. Process goals include the aspects that a person or team concentrates on while performing a sport. That could be sticking to a specific cadence in cycling, defending against Cristiano Ronaldo in soccer, or paying attention to your breathing in shooting.

Skills Application

Working and progressing toward goals requires the application of certain skills and techniques. For example, a forehand cross in tennis, an effective transition from offense to defense in basketball, and a straight back while lifting weights are specific skills that require individual motoric as well as team co-ordination. A set of mental techniques such as relaxation, visualization, focus, self-talk, and routines have been developed to assist individuals and teams to apply their skills more effectively.

Persistence

Achieving goals through skill application requires persistence in developing such skills. Training in sports is highly repetitive. It takes endless practice to hardwire specific physical and mental patterns into your skill inventory. Over time, individuals and teams can advance their portfolios of abilities. This allows them to create success by achieving better outcomes, performances, and processes.

In Chapter 3, we saw how feelings of Autonomy, Belonging, and Competence provide the energy for performing our executive functions. The ABC also powers the persistent application of skills toward goal achievement in sports. This chapter explores the specific aspects of the ABC of sports, drawing on inspirations from theory and practice.

Professional Sports

Sports has become an industry. Globally, the sports industry market was valued at around $500 billion in revenue per year in 2020, and 20% of that is generated in North America alone through media rights, gate receipts, sponsorships, and merchandise. That has implications for professional athletes and teams. The stakes are high. The rewards come predominantly in the form of money and fame based on outcomes and performances. Scientists Mark White and Ken Sheldon used records from the National Basketball Association and Major League Baseball in a provocative study assessing the impact of such rewards as money on a player's performance. Specifically, they followed players over a period that included a baseline year, a contract year, and a post-contract year. The key question for them was whether the second year's monetary rewards had impacted players' ABC when comparing precontract levels to post-contract levels. What researchers found was that ABC levels were up at the beginning of year two and plummeted below baseline year levels in year three. That had a profound effect on players' executive functions in the post-contract year. Their performances, measured by points scored, batting averages, and defense behavior, suffered substantially, in some cases even falling below the initial baseline levels.

White and Sheldon's findings showcase the undermining effect in professional sports. External rewards—in this case, money—had a negative psychological effect on players' performances. Lower ABC levels led to the decreased activation of players' prefrontal cortex, impairing goal setting, skill application, and persistence. Players underperformed in year three as a consequence. If White and Sheldon's results are correct, why are we still paying professional athletes, knowing as we do the negative impact on performance? Because we have to! Players want to earn a living by practicing and competing, just like plumbers, bakers, and nurses do when performing their jobs. This is still the case even if the stakes and remunerations are so much higher in professional sports due to market conditions. The more practical question is whether the undermining effect can be remedied. This is where sports psychology comes in.

Sports Psychology

The field of sports psychology is diverse and complex. It stretches from optimizing the performance of professional and amateur athletes—often referred to as performance psychology—to the application of exercise and physical activity in order to improve the lives and well-being of non-athletes. Put simply, sports psychology represents a set of tools and techniques such as focus and concentration, imagery and automation, self-talk and positive thinking to boost and maintain high levels of people's ABC in sport. For competitive athletes, professional and amateur, sports psychology teaches them how to use their executive functions to the best of their capabilities and to deliver maximum performance when competing. For non-competitive athletes, non-competitive goals, skill development, and persistent training help improve their quality of life. While success is documented in scores, times, and wins for competitive athletes, non-competitive athletes' success means leisure, recreation, and health.

Psychology research into the ABC of sports started as early as the 1970s. The first studies tried to replicate Deci's 1969 discovery of the undermining effect in the domain of sports. In 1977 and 1980, Ryan examined the impact of scholarships on intercollegiate athletes' desire to play their sport after college. The first study investigated male football players. For them, receiving a scholarship was considered an external incentive, a standard way for teams to "buy" talented players. This external incentive undermined players' interest in continuing with the sport after college. It was substantially lower compared to a control group of non-scholarship athletes. As we now know, the reward overpowered players' ABC and deactivated their prefrontal cortex. In turn, their executive functions were impaired, resulting in a lack of persistence. In contrast, Ryan's second study applied the same research design but involved women receiving scholarships, which at the time was rare. Female athletes interpreted the scholarships as encouragement, which left their prefrontal cortex in active mode. Their desire to move forward with the sport after college was significantly higher in relation to a control group of non-scholarship female athletes. Perceiving the scholarship as encouragement indicates a boost for female athletes' ABC levels.

Since then, the undermining effect has been well documented in sports science. External incentives such as outcome and performance goals are more likely to trigger athletes' amygdala, leading them to slip into survival mode. The translation of a threat to survival into athlete language means fear of failure. When this fear of failure switches off the prefrontal cortex, it prompts the three D's of actual failure: it *distorts* goal setting, makes skill performance *destructive*, and *degrades* persistence. When this happens in a competition, athletes are unable to deliver top performance. There are two ways to overcome this problem: (a) stop the amygdala from being triggered, or (b) boost athletes' ABC to keep a triggered amygdala from shutting off the prefrontal cortex. Two core areas of techniques in sports psychology address these two scenarios for athletes: focus and mental strength. Focusing on the process instead of the outcome or performance maximizes the athlete's attention on the moment and curbs thoughts about the consequences. This mindfulness takes the amygdala out of the equation, thereby allowing the athlete to draw on his/her executive resources. A good example is when a soccer player takes a penalty kick. If s/he focuses on the score after the kick or the consequences of missing, s/he will decrease the likelihood of scoring due to limited execution capabilities. The best way to maximize the chances of scoring is by concentrating on the process of where to shoot. The second technique, mental strength, is based on high levels of ABC. For example, by diversifying the sources of ABC in an athlete's life, the athlete will not feel as though his/her survival depends solely on a particular outcome or performance. As a result, s/he will feel safer. Whenever a critical situation arises in a competition and the amygdala is triggered, an athlete will be more likely to succeed if the ABC of "I will be safe regardless!" is able to overpower the fear of "If I do not win (or score), I am dead!". This facilitates the execution of the sport.

Eliud Kipchoge, the first human to break the two-hour frontier in a marathon, is a great example of both techniques—focus and mental strength. He won the London marathon four times (in 2019, 2018, 2016, and 2015), the Berlin marathon three times (in 2018, 2017, and 2015), and the marathon Olympic gold medal in Rio 2016. One of his early successes was winning the gold medal in the men's 5000m event at the 2003 World Championships in Paris. His well-diversified sources of ABC are his wife Grace and his three children, his extended family, his friends in rural Kenya, his teammates in the Kaptagat training camp, his coach Patrick Sang, and his very strong Catholic faith, the core of Kipchoge's mental strength. When he failed at his first attempt to break the two-hour barrier on the Formula One race course in Monza in 2017, journalists questioned his capabilities. He responded: "We are human. We are going up the tree... I have lifted a branch and I am going onto the next one. This is not the end of the attempt of runners on two hours." After his successful attempt in Vienna 2019, Kipchoge said: "My mind was clear. From the first to the last kilometer, I knew I had it, keeping focus was the key, I just concentrated on myself".

Teams and Competition

Preventing your amygdala from firing up and keeping it in check once it goes off become more complex when we move from individual sports to team sports and from indirect to direct competition.

Teams

In team sports, group dynamics overlay individual goals, skills, and persistence. This adds another dimension to achieving success. There are individual amygdalas and ABC levels, but in a team, they form a kind of group amygdala and group ABC. Individual team members can only succeed by collaborating effectively with the rest of the group. For example, in a rowing eight, you have eight individual team members, eight different physical and mental conditions, eight personalities, eight amygdalas, and eight ABC levels. Success is based on the coordinated maximum performance of individual goals, skills, and persistence over a period of time. How can group focus be maintained and mental strength be sustained in such a complex setting? It becomes even more challenging when we add in the element of competition.

Competition

The more direct the competitive situation, the more salient the potential impact of the undermining effect can be. Let's take boxing, which is essentially two people in a ring, fighting. Modern life can hardly get any closer to a human survival scenario. Preventing the amygdala from signaling danger and maintaining focus seems like an impossible task. And when the amygdala does go off, it may take a superhuman ABC-supported PFC to still behave constructively

But even in a rowing eight, where the competition does not directly impact your performance, the boat's position relative to the other boats influences eight individual amygdalas to varying degrees during a race. Are we in front? Is the competition catching up ? Are we behind? How far? Are we still going to make it? Are we in danger? A case like Australia's 'Lay down Sally' Robbins in Athens 2004 does not happen very often in professional sports. Nonetheless, the effects of teams and the competition on athletes are pervasive. In fact, it takes years of deliberate practice in specific techniques to avoid failures.

A Gameplan

A key technique for shifting focus from outcomes and performance to the process of execution is a game plan. The more complex the competitive situation—the larger the team and the more direct the competition—the simpler such a game plan has to be. If it is too complicated, focus will be lost. Rowing is a good example. When Germany won the gold medal at the 2012 London Olympics, they kept focus with a clear and simple game plan: lead from the start with 10 maximum hard strokes, control the race after the start phase with a cadence of 38 strokes per minute, stay in the lead until the 1,500m mark, then finish strong with all you have. In more direct competitive sports such as tennis or boxing, athletes may even focus on only one element or sequence of elements as their game plan. Identifying Novak Djokovic's key element, Craig O'Shannessy, the strategy analyst for Wimbledon, the Australian Open, and the ATP and WTA Tours notes: "It's particularly his backhand return... It's the best backhand return in the world. That's where it all starts." Floyd Mayweather Jr. has often been referred to as the best defensive and most accurate boxer in history. His combination of shoulder roll and subsequent counterattack became the signature feature of his successes in boxing. Obviously, there is much more that goes into rowing for gold in the Olympics, winning a Grand Slam, or becoming a world boxing champion. However, each success had its focus that the team or athlete could hold on to.

Feeling Safe

Athletes can lose that focus in competitive situations. That is when high levels of ABC are needed to overwrite amygdala signals. We saw how the marathon runner Eliud Kipchoge had built a portfolio of close relationships as sources of ABC in support of his career that helped him deal with failures such as Monza. This approach can be translated into any individual sport, regardless of whether that sport is a direct[3] or indirect competition sport. The higher the ABC level, the better the athlete is able to focus on goal setting, skill application, and persistence.

With regard to team sports, ABC levels depend not only on individual team members' relationships outside the team but to an even larger extent on how team members boost each other's ABC levels. How teammates look out for each other's feelings, rely on each other's talents and skills, and care for each other's needs determine how safe each of them feels as part of the team. It is a tribute to our human nature of leveraging groups as our survival mechanism. In today's practice, this feeling of safety has often been referred to as trust.

As we have seen in the case of Sally Robbins, one athlete cannot make a team but s/he can break a team. Therefore, they say that only soccer teams of 11 friends can win championships. The cycling team Ineos, which won the Tour de France seven out of eight times between 2012 and 2019, credits a big chunk of its success to its riders having spent time with each other in on- and off-season bonding programs. As Phil Jackson, who won two NBA titles as a player and 11 titles as coach of the Chicago Bulls and Los Angeles Lakers, once said: "Good teams become great ones when all members trust each other enough to surrender the 'me' for the 'we'." His philosophy for team success is shared by other legendary professional sports coaches such as NFL legend Bill

---

3　Direct competition means that an athlete is able to interfere with and influence the performance of the opponent(s); Indirect competition means that an athlete cannot interfere with and influence the performance of the opponent(s)

Walsh, who won three Super Bowls as coach of the San Francisco 49ers, was named NFL Coach of the Year in 1981 and 1984, and was inducted into the Pro Football Hall of Fame in 1993. Walsh believed strongly that individual team members could wreck a team through their feelings of insecurity. Therefore, according to Walsh, the key factor for team success was being "sensitive to feelings, loyalties, and emotions that teammates have toward one another"—in essence, enhancing each other's ABC levels.

Meaning

Eliud Kipchoge is not only a good example of the application of sports psychology techniques such as focus and mental strength; he also stands for the power of meaning in sports. Subjecting oneself to endless rounds of detailed goal setting and planning, persistent and repetitive skills training, and countless sequences of trial and error requires substantial energy. The secret of the successes of Kipchoge as well as other great athletes such as Michael Jordan, Wayne Gretzki, or Michael Schumacher was that they saw meaning in what they were doing. They may not have been the most talented people from the start. Michael Jordan, for example, was cut from his high school basketball team for lack of potential. It takes deliberate practice in the key elements of a discipline to achieve success. The senior editor of *Fortune Magazine*, Geoff Colvin, examined history's sports geniuses such as Jerry Rice of the San Francisco 49ers and golf champion Tiger Woods and concluded that "Hard work always beats talent, especially when talent does not work hard." Or as Vince Lombardi, the man for whom the NFL Super Bowl Trophy is named, put it: "The only place that success comes before work is in the dictionary." Ten thousand hours of deliberate practice has been touted as the magic number for a person to arrive at a world-class level in any given discipline, in and out of sports. Rice was not particularly gifted as a wide receiver in football. Due to his lack of speed, 15 teams passed him by before Rice was drafted by the 49ers in 1985. In San Francisco, he practiced sprinting on the steepest slopes of his home area under a self-developed, excruciating, repetitive training regime, in particular during the off season. He became one of the fastest wide receivers of the NFL. However, it was his extra training of specific muscle groups as well as the endurance components of his program that turned him into the most successful wide receiver in NFL history. Rice was not only fast; he had the endurance to deliver top performances and to decide games in the fourth quarter of a game. He also had the physical condition that enabled him to sustain his performance level to age 35.

At the age of 7 months, Tiger Woods' father, a self-proclaimed golf addict, put Tiger in a highchair in their garage where his father practiced golf shots for several hours a day. At the age of 2, Tiger practiced his first putting shots on the golf course. At 4, his father and various golf professionals trained Tiger in the specific elements of golf on a daily basis. When in primary school, everyone in the area knew him. At college, he was known nationwide. At 19, he was selected to represent the US team at the Walker Cup. By then, he had already had 17 years of deliberate practice. And since then, he has won the most titles ever on the PGA tour—82—and 15 major championships. He wore the green jacket five times as winner of the Masters Tournament in Augusta, where he was also the youngest winner ever at age 21.

Rice, Woods, Jordan, Gretzki, and Schumacher all achieved scores, times, wins, or world-class excellence that elevated them to the very top of their respective sports. They were able to succeed and became legends only because they enjoyed what they were doing all along the way. This meaning is what created more ABC-based energy for them than they put in, which helped them sustain incredibly hard levels of deliberate practice.

At the same time, we have all seen countless one-hit wonders that had a single successful moment in their sports lives. Leon Spinks beat Muhammad Ali in 1978, Buster Douglas defeated Mike Tyson in 1990, Mario Götze scored the winning goal for Germany in the 2014 World Cup, Timmy Smith set a Super Bowl record of

204 yards and two touchdowns for the Washington Redskins during Super Bowl XXII, Michael Chang won the French Open in 1989 at age 17, and Rich Beem beat out Tiger Woods at the 2002 PGA Championship. There may be multiple salient reasons for the lack of sustainability of success in each case. The ABC of sports suggests that these athletes did not derive enough meaning from their sport to sustain the amount of ABC needed for them to overcome external factors such as rewards, fame, and money or the pressure of adversities, expectations, or competition.

One could say quite the opposite about Eliud Kipchoge. After his run in Vienna, he commented on the meaning of his long career in running: "I'm sending a message to every individual in this world, that when you work hard, when you actually concentrate, when you set your priorities high, when you actually set your goals, and put them in your heart and in your mind, you will accomplish, without any question."

Beyond Undermining and Meaning

The ABC framework not only sheds light on the mechanisms underlying sustainable success in sports. Research also suggests that it could have prevented what many commentators have described as the biggest and longest scandal in sports history. Lance Armstrong won the Tour de France seven times between 1999 and 2005. Since his first win in 1999, there had been allegations of doping, a claim he consistently denied. In 2012, the U.S. Anti-Doping Agency (USADA) concluded that Armstrong had used performance-enhancing drugs during his career, calling him the instigator of "the most sophisticated, professionalized and successful doping program that sport has ever seen". Following the USADA report, Armstrong was stripped of his seven Tour de France titles and has been facing several lawsuits since then. In January 2013, after years of denial, he publicly admitted to doping in a TV interview with Oprah Winfrey. In an effort to achieve eternal glory as a winner, Armstrong's scandal had produced only losers: Armstrong himself, his family, his community, his teammates, his sponsors, his fans, and the sport of cycling.

Several scientific studies have shown that athletes' ABC levels are related to their susceptibility to performance-enhancing drugs. In 2006, Eric Donahue and his colleagues surveyed 1,290 elite Canadian athletes in baseball, gymnastics, swimming, basketball, hockey, skiing, athletics, soccer, and speed skating. The researchers asked athletes about their goals in the sport, their sportspersonship, and their use of performance-enhancing substances over the last 12 months. Those athletes who were focused more on outcome and performance goals displayed less sportspersonship behavior and were more likely to engage in doping practices. The findings were confirmed by a 2011 study in which a team around Vassilis Barkoukis examined 1,075 Olympic-level participants from nine different sports. They also found that goal orientation predicted sportspersonship and, in turn, doping behavior. In essence, focusing on outcome and performance goals triggers the undermining effect. The lower the athletes' ABC levels are, the more likely their prefrontal cortex will be overpowered by their amygdala, prompting them to engage in anti-social and self-defeating behavior such as doping. More generally, Nikos Ntoumanis and Martyn Standage have found that higher ABC levels had a positive impact on fair play and respect for other athletes.

Burnout and Dropout

Together with his colleague Alison Smith, Ntoumanis has identified athletes' lower ABC levels as an indicator for giving up earlier when faced with challenges. Burnout and dropout are two aspects of giving up. A number of studies have identified ABC deficiency as a driver of burnout. Thomas Raedeke (1997) as well as Chris Lonsdale et al. (2009) and Patrick Holmberg and Dennis Sheridan (2013) have demonstrated that low ABC levels drive athlete burnout, using North American samples of 236 adolescent swimmers, 201 elite athletes, and 598 college athletes. A study of more than 7,000 youth players from five European soccer leagues showed that a lack of feelings of Autonomy, Belonging, or Competence fueled dropouts.

Over the past decade, the ABC of sports and its ability to boost competitive performance has increasingly gained attention across disciplines, cultures, and gender. A particularly noteworthy study was completed by Ken Sheldon, Ruixue Zhaoyang, and Michael Williams in 2013. They studied undergraduate basketball players in a pre/post-game design. Data on ABC levels were collected before and after games and correlated with game performance, including shots taken and shooting percentages. The study found that pre-game ABC levels predicted game performance and, in turn, post-game ABC levels. In other words, maintaining high levels of ABC not only supports athletes' executive functions during a game but also helps them to sustain demanding training regimes and peak performances in the long run. Coaching plays a decisive role in managing the ABC levels of individuals and teams.

Coaching

Many factors can influence outcomes and performances in sports. The coach-athlete relationship has turned out to be one of the most critical ones. Coaches may have exquisite knowledge of the game and may be great strategists and game planners. But if they do not understand people, they do not understand coaching. Coaches need to be sensitive to athletes' ABC levels. Coaching behavior needs to support athletes' feelings of Autonomy, Belonging, and Competence to enable the three E's of success: *evident* goal setting, *effective* skill application, and *enhanced* persistence. Coaches who neglect their athletes' ABC levels may achieve short-term successes but will fail in the medium to long run. Felix Magath is a good example. Even though he won titles, he never completed more than three seasons with the same club, indicating that his coaching style ran out of steam. Over time,

Magath's methods caused increasing ABC deficiencies in his players. At each of his assignments, his relationships with the players fell to pieces, along with their trust and feelings of safety. As a result, success was not sustainable.

Scientific evidence points in the direction of Autonomy, Belonging and Competence as the sources of coaching success and failure. Anthony Amorose and Thelma Horn studied 386 college athletes, aged 17 to 23, from a variety of sports in Division I, the highest division of college sports in the U.S. They found that autocratic and controlling coaching behavior depleted athletes' ABC levels. In a subsequent investigation, Doris Matosic and Anne Cox were able to show how coaches using rewards to control the behavior of 165 college swimmers triggered the undermining effect. Luc Pelletier et al. followed 369 elite Canadian swimmers over a 22-month period. Those athletes who perceived their coaches as being ABC-supportive showed more persistence. Studies have also demonstrated that ABC-depleting coaching behavior leads to higher levels of dropout. When Laura Healy et al. collected data from competitive athletes from a wide variety of sports, they found that participants who perceived their coaches as being ABC-draining reported more burnout, ill-being, and physical symptoms such as pain or fatigue. Ken Hodge and Chris Lonsdale studied 229 university athletes to show that lower ABC levels led to more morally disengaged and anti-social behavior toward the athletes' own teammates as well as their opponents.

The former American football player and coach Bill McCartney pointed out that "coaching is about taking a player where he cannot take himself". Feedback plays an important role in this process. Conventional wisdom suggests that criticism does not make people feel good, ultimately leading to ABC deficiency. That is why Joelle Carpentier and Geneviève Mageau designed a study to examine if and how negative feedback could be given to athletes in a way that increased their feelings of Autonomy, Belonging, and Competence. The researchers surveyed 340 athletes and 58 coaches after training sessions to investigate the delivery and impact of different styles of change-oriented (i.e. negative) feedback to athletes. Results showed that negative feedback and ABC levels were not necessarily at odds. In fact, when negative feedback is "empathic, constructive, accompanied by choices of solutions, based on clear and attainable objectives known to athletes, paired with tips," and "given in a considerate tone of voice avoiding person-related statements", it increases ABC levels. Spectacular manifestations of an ABC-based coaching style are the consecutive world championship titles of the All Blacks New Zealand rugby team in 2011 and 2015. Together with All Blacks head coach Graham Henry and assistant coach Wayne Smith, Ken Hodge from the University of Otago summarized and published the success story as a case study in the journal *The Sports Psychologist*. Multiple sources of data from in-depth interviews, books, and videos obtained from coaches, players, and journalists were drawn on to paint a comprehensive picture of the coaching climate during the 2011 campaign. What they outline as the foundation of their success is a so-called dual management model based on ABC principles. First, coaches came up with a theme for selecting players for the team—"Better people make better All Blacks"—which focused much more on character and personality than on technical rugby skills. Selection was no longer all about rugby. In that sense, players *behaved* themselves into or out of the team. As a result, coaches selected a team of players who obtained meaning from the sport and created a team atmosphere in which the players boosted each other's ABC levels. In a second step, the coaching team delegated responsibility to the players. A leadership group of players was formed that gave them a say and ownership in decision-making. A subset of the leadership group was the on-field leadership team. The integration of the two ensured that off-field decisions were effectively translated into on-field performance. It also diversified on-field responsibility. The team had one captain but there were a number of further on-field leaders, each of whom knew his role within the team structure. Choice gave players Autonomy; the method of selection and the team atmosphere gave them a sense of Belonging; and ownership and responsibility gave them

Competence, meaning, and the power to persist. The results were sustainable peak performance and two consecutive world titles.

If there is one coach who seems to represent the ABC of coaching more than any other at this point in time, it is Jürgen Klopp. A mediocre soccer player in Germany's second division who "stuck around like a bad smell" (as he himself says) for 11 years at the FSV Mainz 05 soccer club, he was appointed head coach in 2001 and led the team to its first promotion to Germany's first division, the Bundesliga, in the 2003/2004 season. After moving to Dortmund in 2008, he led the team there to two Bundesliga trophies in 2011 and 2012, the German Cup in 2012, and the UEFA Champions League finals in 2013. In October 2015, Klopp replaced Brendan Rodgers as head coach at Liverpool FC, which became the winners of the 2019 UEFA Champions League. Following this success, Klopp was named Best FIFA Men's Coach in 2019.

Spanish player and coaching legend Pep Guardiola once described Klopp as the best team-building coach on the planet. Based on his round face and round glasses, the British press even bestowed him the esteemed nickname of Harry Potter. The secret of Klopp's coaching style, however, is based much less on magic than on the ABC approach. In his first press conference as the new head coach in Liverpool, a journalist asked Klopp: "When José Mourinho came to England for the first time to coach Chelsea, he described himself as *The Special One*. How would you describe yourself?" After some hesitation, Klopp responded: "Maybe I am *The Normal One*". This statement sums up his coaching philosophy. From his perspective, he is not doing anything special. He simply treats human beings in a human way.

Where Klopp coaches, people feel safe. In a recent British documentary, he remarked: "Life is a gift. So you should enjoy it and help the people around you enjoy it". His nurturing, caring coaching style gives players and staff the feeling that each one of them is important and has a role to play. He gives people Autonomy in interpreting their roles, a sense of Belonging by appreciating and supporting their contributions, and Competence by providing encouraging feedback for change and ensuring them of their qualities. When no-name Oliver Kirch made a surprise appearance in Dortmund's starting lineup in the 2014 UEFA Champions League quarter finals, he became the man of the match against Real Madrid. In a post-game interview, Kirch commented that Klopp had given him unconditional support regardless of any mistakes he might make. As a result, Kirch felt that he could invest all his energy in performing his role and give 100% or more. Neven Subotic, who played under Klopp in Mainz and Dortmund, once said: "Klopp sometimes shouts at me. However, I always know that he respects me as a person and appreciates my qualities as a player." Klopp's teams succeed because high levels of ABC prevent individual amygdalas from signaling danger. When players and staff feel safe, their prefrontal cortexes can operate at maximum capacity in terms of goal setting, skill application, and persistence. When individual amygdalas are triggered during critical situations, teammates will be there to lift each other's ABC levels, preventing the amygdala from overpowering the prefrontal cortex and impairing performance.

Liverpool's stunning 4-0 win over Barcelona at Anfield Stadium in 2019 is the perfect example of what ABC-based teams are capable of. After losing 0-3 in Barcelona in the first leg, Klopp's team made it into the history books with one of the greatest comebacks in the history of the competition. Despite the absence of their star forwards Mohamed Salah and Roberto Firmino, Liverpool scored four goals to advance to the finals, where the team beat Tottenham to win the UEFA Champions League. Leading up to the final, Klopp had boosted players' ABC levels. He assured them they had the qualities to score four or more goals (Competence). They were given the freedom to try and make mistakes (Autonomy). And regardless of what happened out there that night, the players knew they would be appreciated for giving their all and would still be part of the Liverpool family (Belonging). When players got on the pitch that night, there was no fear of failure on their mind. Instead, the combination of A, B, and C gave players trust, confidence, and a "We can do it" attitude that allowed them to focus all their energy on the process. And what could better represent Klopp's coaching philosophy than Liverpool, the club whose fans developed the tradition of singing *You'll Never Walk Alone* during matches? The team players know that the coach is always on their side. Klopp once said: "When signing players, they are often surprised. When I first meet them, we don't talk about soccer at all. Success is about people and making sure that they are fine."

This style of coaching is a skill that can be trained. A team of scientists led by Sung Hyeon Cheon worked with coaches involved in the London 2012 Paralympic Games. The coaches and their athletes were assigned to either a control group or an ABC group. The ABC group coaches received ABC-based training in coaching practices that supported the athletes' Autonomy, Belonging, and Competence. This included providing rationales when making requests, acknowledging athletes' feelings, and using non-pressuring language and being patient with their athletes. As a result, athletes coached by ABC-trained coaches were more motivated and engaged and won significantly more Olympic medals than the control-group athletes.

Non-Competitive Sport

Coaching also plays a role in sports where people do not compete. Non-competitive activities such as yoga, aerobics, Tae Bo, jogging, walking, or weight training are usually referred to simply as exercise. They can be performed individually or in groups. When instructors or trainers are involved in non-competitive sports, they are there to help people maintain or regain their quality of life through health, fitness, and recreation. The ABC also plays a crucial role in this context.

Autonomy

Exercise programs boost participants' Autonomy when they include elements of choice such as flexible timetables, varying activity modules, or individual versus group sessions. A long list of scientific work in the area shows that feelings of Autonomy enhance people's enjoyment and engagement in the sport and also lead to sustained involvement in exercise. An example from my personal experience is the so-called boxercise program I followed at a fitness club in Australia. Boxercise is a combination of sandbag boxing and fitness that involves both technical elements and cardio work. Each Monday, Wednesday, and Friday night they ran three classes in parallel, each with a different level of intensity. I started with the easy level and worked my way up to level three. When I felt really tired from work, I had the option of picking the easy level that night. I could even move over from one level to another between modules. As a result, I always felt in control in all ways, giving me a feeling of Autonomy.

Belonging

People feel a sense of Belonging and are more likely to be engaged in something when they are looking forward to social interactions related to that activity. In a clinical trial in 2011, Matthew Buman et al. tested the effectiveness of a peer-volunteer program for promoting physical activity among sedentary older adults over an 18-month period. Participants in the intervention group who had a peer were found to be much more active and persistent over the 18 months than those exercising alone. My colleague Geoff Lovell invited me to be part of a study investigating the effects of Belonging on exercising mothers. Data showed that mothers performing their activities in groups (e.g. participating in an aerobics class) were more motivated and engaged and derived more enjoyment from exercise than mothers exercising alone (e.g. going for a run).

Competence

People feel a greater sense of Competence from an activity when they perceive it as being optimally challenging—that is, it should be neither too hard nor too easy. Exercise programs offering various levels of difficulty support participants' feelings of Competence. In reference to my Australian boxercise program, I never felt overwhelmed or underwhelmed, given that I could move between levels one, two, and three whenever I felt like it.

The ABC framework is key for the success of exercise programs. Our executive functions of goal setting, skills application, and persistence drive people's participation and, in turn, their quality of life. The design and implementation of exercise programs need to account for Autonomy, Belonging and Competence. Frederiki Moustaka, Symeon Vlachopoulos, Chris Kabitsis, and Yannis Theodorakis compared two groups of middle-aged women, one participating in an ABC-based exercise program, the other in a similar program but not including ABC elements. The women in the ABC program were more motivated, engaged, and alive. A review of published ABC studies in the field by Pedro Teixeira et al. revealed a substantially higher persistence in ABC-based exercise programs.

Undermining Exercising

If people do not compete to win, what are their goals in exercising? Essentially, there are two types of goals people tend to have in exercising: one is external (improving one's appearance, showing off, boosting one's ego) and the other is internal (improving one's health and fitness level, enhancing well-being). In exercise, the undermining effect also plays a role. A focus on external rewards (and punishments) distorts goals, makes skills destructive, and degrades persistence. Exercising to lose weight or build muscles may be aimed at enhancing one's appearance, showing off, and ego boosting. Alternatively, an individual may aim to lose kilos to prevent overweight-related illnesses such as diabetes or coronary heart disease. And building muscles can help to prevent such things as osteoarthritis. A focus on external factors and related outcomes rather than the process of achieving health and fitness for oneself has been shown to be detrimental to exercise activities. A study by David Markland from Bangor University demonstrated that women who had greater discrepancies between their actual weight and an ideal external benchmark experienced lower ABC levels and thus exercised less. In another study, Markland teamed up with David Ingledew to investigate the exercise regimen of 252 office workers. Participants with health/fitness goals were much more effective in maintaining their exercise programs than those focused on weight/appearance goals. Speaking of health, this will be the topic of the next chapter.

7. The ABC of Health

The foundation of success in life is health.
— P.T. Barnum

Everything would be nothing without health. Jan Frodeno is the only professional triathlete to have won both Olympic gold and the Ironman World Championship. He is also the world record holder for the Ironman distance triathlon: 7:35:39 hours for a 3.8 km swim, 180 km bike ride, and a 42 km marathon run. When you ask experts, they describe Frodeno as the best swimmer, the best cyclist, and the best runner in the Ironman triathlon. In their opinion, all he had to do was bring it all together. His debut appearance at the Ironman World Championship in Hawaii in 2014 was his greatest learning experience. Frodeno finished in third place after a flat tire and a four-minute time penalty, just six minutes behind the winner, Sebastian Kienle. In 2015 and 2016, Frodeno, praised as the best athlete across disciplines, dominated the race. Many commentators saw Frodeno as the legitimate twenty-first-century successor to triathlon legends Mark Allen and Dave Scott who had won the race six times each in the 1980s and 1990s. They predicted a winning streak for Frodeno for years to come. However, this is not what happened.

In 2017, Frodeno led the race on the bike, but excruciating pain in his lower back and hamstring forced him to walk large parts of the marathon. Despite the pain, he did not give up but kept walking, finishing the race in 35th place. The following year, he failed to even make it to the starting line after suffering from a sacral fracture in his lower back. But Frodeno came back in 2019. Free from injury, he won his third Ironman world title with a new course record and a whopping margin of over six minutes on runner-up Tim O'Donnell. The story of Jan Frodeno showcases the enabling role that health plays in life: health drives success, while health deficits cause failure. Looking at the mental health issues and related suicide of Avicii, health can play an even more fundamental role for us beyond success and failure: it can be a question of life and death!

Health for Survival

When our evolutionary ancestors suffered physical or mental impairments, their chances of survival were severely limited. This was not because their illness in itself was fatal; it was because they could no longer pull their weight by contributing their physical, mental, or social skills to the group. They could no longer travel large distances, go on hunting missions, build camp, navigate, communicate, or carry loads. As a result, debilitated foragers represented a burden to their group and had to be carried by others, both figuratively and even literally. Instead of contributing to the survival of their group, they only consumed group resources such as time, food, and emotional and physical energy. As a result, unhealthy group members could only be carried up to a point. Limited care or abandonment by the group was essentially a death penalty. Evolution has coded individual health as an "if-then" trigger into our survival program: 'IF you are healthy, THEN you are part of a group and will survive'. Alternatively, 'IF you are not healthy, THEN your group will no longer support you and you will die'. Let's take a look at the implications of this algorithm in modern life.

Modern Health

In today's world, most health issues have far less fatal consequences. They are more a question of lifestyle than of life and death. In the majority of cases, health problems prevent us from doing what we love or dampen our enjoyment of what we do. Examples include the hobby athlete who can no longer do his running sessions due to cartilage damage in his knee, the employee nearing burnout and suffering from emotional exhaustion, the patient with cardiovascular problems causing restrictions in physical activity, or the depressed parent who has no energy to care for their children.

I have met quite a few people whose most important values in life were power, money, and reputation. The moment they suffered substantial blows to their physical or mental health, all of the above did not matter to them anymore. This was true of the young, high-potential investment banker after a heart attack, the Olympian gold medalist in cycling rendered paraplegic after an accident, the adored singer songwriter after losing a child, or the aging billionaire facing the first signs of dementia.

For all of the above, the health issue they were suffering from had no immediate life-or-death implications. Instead, a knee injury, cardiovascular problems, a burnout, depression, and dementia represent limitations to people's lifestyles. But our instincts are pervasive. Disease and its "associate" pain prompt our amygdala to signal danger, thus overpowering our prefrontal cortex and sending us into fight-or-flight mode. We can see how health issues decrease our feelings of Autonomy, Belonging, and Competence. When we are limited in the activities we do and how we were used to perform them, both our Autonomy and Competence suffer. Not being able to socialize with people, for example due to exhaustion or physical symptoms, negatively impacts our Belonging. The longer the disease and/or pain persists, the more often the amygdala alerts the prefrontal cortex for danger, causing continuous stress to the body and the mind. This means that health issues can make you much sicker than you actually are due to the prefrontal cortex receiving signals of survival threats that do not exist in reality.

Health gives us another perspective on the mismatch between our ancestral instincts and modern life circumstances. Foragers did not have access to emergency telephone numbers, hospitals with intensive care, technologies such as ultrasound or life support machines, and medication including morphine-based painkillers. Today, even substantial health issues such as losing a limb can be treated. Neither physical nor mental problems will result in the kind of individual death penalties (due to social exclusion from a group) that our ancestors experienced. Nonetheless, in our modern world, we often react to even minor health challenges as if our life was under threat, causing stress and triggering the three D's of failure. This behavior can be attributed to the modern way of defining health.

A Dangerous Definition

According to the World Health Organization (WHO), health is "a state of complete physical, mental and social well-being and not merely the absence of disease or infirmity". In fact, the WHO considers physical, mental, and social well-being a human right, enabling a life without limitations or restrictions. This definition has two implications. First of all, health is psychosomatic. Both physical and mental dimensions and their interplay matter for our health. No informed person will take issue with that statement, given that the psychosomatic field has made it into mainstream scientific and popular literature over the last decades. The second part of the definition deserves more scrutiny. If health is not the mere absence of disease or infirmity, what exactly is it? When the WHO talks about health as a human right enabling a life without limitations or restrictions, it is referring to the restrictions we face based on our race, religion, political belief, and economic or social conditions. But defining health as a human right also provides a fertile breeding ground for the modern movement of self-optimization. Living in an accelerating society where everyone can be anything without limitations and restrictions can make healthy people sick when trying to keep up with societal ideals. But let's take a look at psychosomatics first.

Vitality as a Measure of Health

As outlined in Chapter 3, Richard Ryan and Christina Frederick developed the foundational theory and practical applications of vitality as a tool for capturing psychosomatic health. Vitality supplies the energy for powering the three E's of success: evident goal setting, effective skill application, and enhanced persistence. A stream of scientific studies since then has underlined the role that people's ABC levels play as a vitality booster across life domains. For example, the social scientists Symeon Vlachopoulos and Eleni Karavani studied close to 400 Greek exercise participants with ages varying between 18 and 61. Competence levels were the main predictor of participants' vitality over a six-week intervention research project. Various studies by Richard Ryan, Edward Deci and Netta Weinstein have shown how helping and supporting others boosted the sense of Belonging in both the givers and the receivers of support and in turn their vitality. In the organizational context, Richard Ryan, Jessy Bernstein and Kirk Warren-Brown uncovered how Autonomy, Belonging, and Competence drove employees' vitality in a sample of adult U.S. workers.

Parallel to investigations on how the ABC levels impact vitality, SDT research teams started examining objective outcomes associated with vitality. The results have demonstrated how vitality was associated with better physical and mental health and performance, higher creativity, more stress-resilience, and better social skills. A series of neuroscientific studies by Lisa Feldman Barrett et al. in 2004, Alan Rozanski et al. in 2005, and Eva Selhub and Alan Logan in 2012 has provided explanations for previous psychological research findings. Higher levels of vitality were associated with increased levels of brain activity, enabling people's executive functions responsible for the three E's of success. In summary, the higher your ABC is, the higher your vitality and the better your psychosomatic health is as an energy provider for the executive functions of a successful life.

Jan Frodeno had the ABC levels, the vitality, the energy, and the mental health to bounce back from his injuries in 2017 and 2018 in order to regain his physical health for an even stronger comeback in 2019. Instead, Avicii's ABC levels were not sufficient to cope with his psychosomatic health problems, resulting in fatal consequences due to a lack of vitality and a shortfall in the energy to cope with adversity.

There are two ways in which ABC levels impact people's health: before health issues occur (the ABC of Prevention) and after they have occurred (the ABC of Cure).

The ABC of Prevention

The higher your ABC levels are, the more resilient you are against health problems. Why is this? People high on Autonomy, Belonging, and Competence are less likely to engage in the three D's of health failures: distorted goal-setting such as overambitious sports performances causing orthopedic or cardiovascular problems; destructive skill application leading to work accidents; and degraded persistence in maintaining a healthy lifestyle. In addition to these obvious conditions, higher levels of ABC energize the prefrontal cortex and prevent it from being constantly overpowered by the amygdala. Bolstering the prefrontal cortex means we are also more resilient against stress. Less stress translates into lower heart rates, lower glucose levels, and lower cortisol levels. As a result, we are less receptive to societal epidemics such as obesity, diabetes, or coronary heart disease. In essence, the ABC of Prevention makes it less likely for the hobby athlete to have a knee injury, the patient to have cardiovascular problems, the employee to suffer a burnout, parents to be depressed, the investment banker to have a heart attack, and the billionaire to develop dementia.

The ABC of Cure

Once you experience a physical or mental condition, the ABC represents a powerful tool for treatment. Change in patient behavior is a key determining factor in the success or failure of a medical treatment. Geoffrey Williams received his Ph.D. in health psychology from the University of Rochester Medical Center (URMC) in 1986. He led the first ABC-related study into how patients change and maintain healthy behavior in the treatment of diseases. In 1996, his team of scientists followed 128 morbidly obese patients over a 24-month period. For the first six months, study participants underwent a medically supervised, very-low-calorie diet program for losing weight that included weekly group meetings. Patients provided ABC-related survey data four times over the two-year period. Results showed that higher levels of ABC predicted greater attendance at the six-month weekly program, better compliance with dietary guidelines, sustained exercise, and the maintenance of weight loss after 24 months.

Encouraged by the findings, Williams went on to apply the ABC framework to patients with diabetes in the fall of 1997. Would differences in patients' ABC levels correlate with their management of diabetes? Over a 12-month period, Williams, together with Zachary Freedman and Edward Deci, assessed patient behavior and hemoglobin levels as a biomarker for health-related outcomes after 4 and 12 months respectively. Participants were 128 outpatients between the ages of 18 and 80 who took medication for diabetes, had no other major medical illnesses, and were responsible for monitoring their glucose and taking their medications. What the researchers found was consistent with the previous obesity study. Diabetes patients who felt more Autonomy, Belonging, and Competence exhibited healthier behavior. At both assessment points, after 4 and 12 months, higher ABC levels correlated with better adherence to program guidelines and, in turn, lower and healthier hemoglobin levels.

Since the completion of the two initial studies in the late 1990s, investigating the ABC framework in the context of treating health conditions has branched out into various streams of research. For example, the field of addiction has received particular attention. In fact, Williams' team of researchers developed an ABC-based intervention framework for addicts, hypothesizing that increasing patients' levels of ABC through a clinical intervention would increase their energy levels to resist their temptations, leading to successful cessation and sustained abstinence. In early 2001, the research team started testing its hypothesis on an adult sample of 1,000 smokers. Participants were people who smoked at least five cigarettes a day and were willing to visit the clinic on four occasions over a six-month period to discuss their health and tobacco use with health professionals and to complete questionnaires. Notably, wanting to quit smoking was not a requirement. In fact, in the initial intake questionnaire at the beginning of the study, more than 50% of study participants said that they had no intention to quit. The intervention involved health professionals who were trained to apply the ABC framework during the four counselling sessions. The participants' Autonomy was boosted by giving them a personal choice in deciding whether to quit or not, by not pressurizing or criticizing them, and by accepting their decisions both verbally and nonverbally. Competence levels were enhanced by discussing smokers' potential anxieties and perceived difficulties with quitting. If they tried and failed, the attempt was acknowledged, and their feelings about it were analyzed. Such attempts were not framed as failure but as learning experiences in discovering what worked and did not work. Finally, the participants' sense of Belonging was bolstered by showing concern and empathy. The message to smokers was that their acceptance as a human being was not contingent upon their smoking habits.

When Williams and his colleagues analyzed the results of the study, they found that participants were three times more likely to quit smoking compared to community care program statistics. This effect was still evident 18 and 24 months after the treatment. Thus, the ABC approach had increased the chances of cessation and abstinence from smoking by 3:1. The results are equally compelling from an economic perspective. The cost of the ABC intervention for tobacco cessation was calculated at $1,258 per quality-adjusted life year saved (QALY), an impact-related measure to benchmark the cost of medical treatments. By comparison, the cost per QALY for smoking-related diagnostics such as hypertension screening for men between the ages of 45 and 54 is around $5,200. The QALY cost for most surgeries and treatments such as lung cancer are in the tens of thousands of dollars.

Eric is a prominent singer songwriter. He was no typical addict, if there ever was one. The wealth he had amassed throughout his career allowed him to indulge in alcohol and drugs. According to his own account, in his worst condition, he spent around $16,000 a month on heroin. After three years of being addicted to heroin, he finally managed to quit, only to fall in love with cocaine and alcohol as compensation. All in all, Eric spent about 20 years addicted to alcohol and drugs. "In the lowest moments of my life, the only reason I didn't commit suicide was that I knew I wouldn't be able to drink and get high any more if I was dead. It was the only thing I thought was worth living for." When his son was born in 1986, Eric claims that it was only through the love of his son that he was convinced to give sobriety a chance. He held on to his newfound sobriety even after his son's tragic death when falling from the 49th floor of a building.

Addiction does not differentiate between poor and wealthy, weak or strong, man or woman. There are only three potential outcomes for all addicts: being treated for substance abuse, being held hostage by the substance, or escaping captivity through death. In retrospect, Eric Clapton considers his peers and loved ones as the source of energy that enabled him to overcome his long-term addiction. His strong message to the addict community is that having people who love you and who you can be honest with are the most valuable and powerful support in this fight (Belonging). They show you that you have other options in life than consuming alcohol or drugs (Autonomy) and encourage you on your path of becoming and staying clean (Competence). This is how the ABC approach saved Clapton's health and life, allowing us to further enjoy his unique rock and blues music.

Since Williams' initial studies in the late 1990s, there has been an exponential growth in ABC-related health studies. This has been due to the practical and economic effectiveness of the ABC framework. A 2006 publication by a team of scientists around

Williams reported that patients with elevated cholesterol levels showed twice the reduction in the harmful low-density lipoprotein cholesterol (LDL-C) as part of an ABC intervention compared to common community care programs. Similar positive effects have been revealed by studies in the context of healthy eating, physical activity, and adherence to medication.

Healthy Eating

You are having lunch with your partner and children at home when your son hands you his plate, asking for some more broccoli and a couple carrots. Would that not be any parent's dream? Well, the ABC can help this dream come true. There is sufficient evidence showing that higher ABC levels predict more fruit and vegetable intake in both adults and children. For example, when children were offered a choice of vegetables in a study led by Ligia Dominguez et al., they ate significantly more vegetables than those who were offered no choice. In another study, Nida Shaikh and his team monitored the diets of 1,021 African American adults. Those who received ABC-based counselling substantially increased their intake of fruits and vegetables over a six-month period.

Physical Activity

Improving our eating habits is one aspect of personal health management. Another important factor is getting enough physical exercise. More and more people in our modern societies are failing to engage in enough vigorous physical activity to maintain their health. Michelle Fortier, a researcher at the School of Psychology and Kinesiology at the University of Ottawa, wanted to test how the ABC could help improve people's activity levels. A randomized clinical trial was conducted with 120 comparatively sedentary patients between the ages of 18 and

70. Half the participants received a general physician's advice to increase their physical activity, while the other half underwent ABC-based counselling. After three months, the results of actual activity patterns showed that the level of physical exercise for the ABC intervention group had increased substantially more than that of the control group.

Medication Compliance

Statistics suggest that around half of all medication prescriptions are not followed properly, which impedes the positive effects of the medication. A 2013 publication by the National Community Pharmacists Association estimated the economic cost of nonadherence to medication prescription at close to $300 billion for the U.S. health care system. Multiple SDT studies have demonstrated that the ABC approach helps improve compliance and health outcomes and therefore makes economic sense.

In one such study, over 200 HIV-positive patients were surveyed by Sarah Kennedy, Kathy Goggin, and Nikki Nollen. Patients who felt they received more feelings of Autonomy, Belonging, and Competence from their practitioners and families exhibited better medication compliance. A Rochester team led by Williams examined this adherence effect in over 2,000 diabetes patients and arrived at the same conclusion. In short, when ABC levels are high, prescriptions are more likely to be filled and used at the given dose and over the prescribed time horizon, leading to better health while saving billions of dollars for the public health system.

Caring for the Elderly

Aging represents a challenge for many of us. We are faced with reductions in mobility, for example when we are no longer able to drive a car. Our physical condition may prevent us from doing our favorite activities. Both can impose significant lifestyle changes. Meanwhile, our brains show a dwindling capacity to process information. Socially isolated and marginalized, one can see how older people might lose purpose and meaning and slide into depression. Financial concerns often further impair their well-being.

The two most compelling research studies illustrating the positive impact of high ABC levels on elderly patients were conducted by Virginia Kasser and, more recently, by Annette Custers. Kasser followed 50 nursing home residents in a full-care facility over a one-year period. She interviewed and surveyed them on several occasions. Patients indicated how much ABC they received from their families, friends, and nursing home staff as well as from their daily lives and activities in the facility. These data were correlated with outcome variables for determining patients' health. Not only did higher ABC levels predict more vitality and life satisfaction, better well-being, and fewer physical symptoms and cases of depression in nursing home residents, Kasser was surprised to find that the recorded data established the ABC as a marker for patients' life expectancy. The higher the patients' ABC levels, the lower their mortality rate was.

The results of the above study were replicated by a research team led by Annette Custers who interviewed 88 elderly people living in facilities for older adults. Custers' work confirmed the impact of patients' ABC levels on their quality of life and resulting longevity. This means that the ABC of health, which predicts success and failure in life, can—with increasing age—be a determining factor for life and death.

Caregivers and the Medical Profession

There is now a wealth of evidence, supported by a recent review of 184 SDT research studies, on how ABC levels are related to a wide range of psychological as well as physical health outcomes. One aspect that has repeatedly surfaced in ABC investigations into healthcare was the salient role that caregivers and medical professionals play in influencing patients' ABC levels. What researchers discovered was that physiotherapists, paramedics, nurses, and medical doctors have a very powerful instrument to contribute to patients' health beyond their respective disciplinary tools. Through the ABC approach, caregivers and medical professionals can touch patients' lives and contribute to their health—all without using their hands. Research data confirm that when healthcare practitioners support patients' ABC levels, such patients experience better health outcomes. Communication turns out to be key in this. For example, giving patients options for treatment or medication drives their feelings of Autonomy. Taking time and showing empathy supports how much Belonging they perceive. Finally, patients' Competence increases when their questions and concerns are taken seriously and addressed appropriately. A good case of how not to do that is Dr. Richard Hoffmann's communication with Sarah after her horse-riding accident. Dr Hoffmann neither took the time nor took Sarah's concerns seriously. Instead, he talked down to her. With ABC levels depleted, Sarah left the hospital hurting both physically and psychologically.

ABC-supportive communication can be learned. It is like training a muscle. In 2015, Aileen Murray and her team trained physiotherapists in communication skills intended to enhance patients' ABC levels. In order to assess the effectiveness of the training, the verbal communication between physiotherapists and patients was recorded before and after the training sessions. The findings revealed that after receiving training, the physiotherapists became far more effective in increasing patients' ABC levels through their style of communication. Given the impact of ABC levels on health outcomes and its essence as a communication skill that can be trained, the concept and practice of ABC should be part of any education and training for caregivers and medical professionals.

The ABC effect on patients also comes with a kicker for healthcare practitioners. Helping also helps the helper. SDT research has uncovered how giving ABC also increases the ABC levels of givers, also referred to as the "helpers' high". This is an important finding. Healthcare professions are among the most susceptible to burnout. According to a 2017 Medscape Lifestyle Report based on over 20,000 surveyed physicians in the U.S., more than half of them experienced symptoms of burnout, and that number has been increasing. This is twice the rate of U.S. workers in other professions after controlling for hours worked, age, gender, and other factors. But burnout is not limited to physicians. A survey on nurses in the U.S. yielded a 33% rate of burnout in hospital nurses and a 37% rate in nurses providing direct patient care in nursing homes. In conclusion, the ABC approach makes a substantial difference to the health of both sides of the practitioner–patient relationship.

Burnout

Burnout was long considered a pseudoscientific phenomenon, the product of "pop psychology". Originally introduced into the psychological discourse by the American practicing psychologist Herbert Freudenberger in the 1970s, he had borrowed the term from the drug scene, which describes the devastating effects of drug abuse. Given that our modern world only recognizes what can be measured, Christina Maslach's development of a measurement tool for burnout in 1981, known as the Maslach Burnout Inventory (MBI), marked the start of an almost 40-year journey to recognition of the phenomenon. In May 2019, the WHO finally included burnout in its eleventh revision of the International Classification of Diseases (ICD-11), but not as a medical condition, only as an "occupational phenomenon". This means that, according to the WHO, burnout only exists in the workplace.

According to Maslach, burnout can be defined as psychological and physical—that is, psychosomatic—exhaustion. The exhaustion can be attributed to a "fundamental mismatch between the nature of a person and the nature of the circumstances" says Maslach. Unlike depression, a condition that occurs within a person, burnout occurs in the context of an environment. It remains unclear why the WHO believes that only workplaces qualify as burnout-related environments and family or social life contexts do not. Humans are social animals. Any group—be it work, family, or social life—can stress us by triggering our amygdala and its associated survival mechanism. As soon as a gap is detected between the levels of Autonomy, Belonging, and Competence we need to feel safe and the actual levels of ABC we perceive as provided by the context, the danger scanner sends an alert signal. If and when that happens, it takes psychosomatic energy for us to stop the amygdala from overpowering the prefrontal cortex and to respond in constructive, prosocial ways instead of sliding into the fight-or-flight mode. The more often that energy is required to weather the storm, the more people's psychosomatic energy reservoirs are being depleted. Stressful situations that arose for our ancestors every once in a while now disrupt us multiple times a day, every day! It is no wonder our energy reservoirs run dry over time. Due to the increasing numbers and extent of stress triggers in modern life, we see substantial increases in rates of people who continuously burn more psychosomatic energy than they generate, ultimately leading to a burnout.

There are two strategies that can be used to combat this problem: the energy outflow can be limited somehow or the inflow of energy can be increased. As shown earlier, SDT research identified vitality as a tool for assessing people's psychosomatic energy levels, and Autonomy, Belonging, and Competence were found to predict vitality. Claude Fernet at the University of Québéc à Trois Rivières is one of the leading next-generation SDT scholars. As part of his scientific work, he has studied burnout from numerous perspectives. In one study, Fernet and his team investigated the ABC levels and burnout rates of 356 school board employees. What they found was that higher levels of ABC helped limit the energy outflow related to energy-depleting job demands. At the same time, feelings of Autonomy, Belonging, and Competence boosted energy inflow as a resource for coping and performing. In summary, Fernet's research project revealed the role of ABC as a tool for the prevention and treatment of burnout.

COVID-19

Much has been said and written about the corona pandemic. It has become increasingly difficult to have honorable discussions on the measures being enforced by governments. Anxiety and fear have taken over in large parts of the global population, with hysteria overpowering rational thinking and behavior. The world has been going digital on the topic, but not from a technological point of view. The discourse has become paradigmatically black and white. On the one hand, if you acknowledge the positive aspects of governmental measures, this immediately throws you into the authoritarian camp. On the other hand, if you signal the slightest doubts over some of the steps being taken, you are considered a grandma murderer. In this chapter on health, let me contribute a few words on the pandemic from an ABC perspective to lay out some common ground.

The coronavirus attacks the most vulnerable feature of human existence: it leverages our nature as social beings to spread, grow, and kill. We have been repeatedly reminded by political leaders to follow the science in overcoming this corona crisis. The scientist in me applauds this approach. However, the question needs to be asked: which science are we talking about? Science is about creating knowledge in pursuit of truth. A substantial amount of knowledge about COVID-19, in many cases contradictory, has been uncovered. Nobel Prize winners, chief epidemiologists, and other highly reputable specialists disagree on pretty much every aspect of the scientific studies conducted on the virus—the research design, the data collection, the data interpretation, and the conclusions. As a result, even the science surrounding the coronavirus has gone black and white. For one side, lockdowns, face masks, and apps are useful measures to flatten the curve and limit the reproduction number (R) to prevent the spreading of infections. For the other side, this is all nonsense and all efforts should be made to serve and protect seniors without restricting the rest of the population. At this point in time, we can conclude that we do not have a sufficient understanding of the COVID-19 algorithm. Instead, conspiracy theorists, politicians, scientists, and the media have all picked that part of the COVID-19 science that fits their purpose—sowing paranoia, boosting approval ratings, gaining attention and recognition, and increasing readership or TV ratings. Due to their executive power and media presence, governments around the world have gained the upper hand in the quest for truth. What is needed are more open and balanced and less hysterical societal discussions without accusing each other of dictatorship or murder. The solid science behind the ABC can facilitate such discourse.

Fear drives failure. When the amygdala overpowers the prefrontal cortex, people suffer from distorted goals, destructive skill application, and degraded persistence. This applies to all human beings, political decision-makers and citizens alike. King's College in London recently criticized the "irrational diversion" of resources to COVID-19 as failing preventable cancer patients, resulting in more additional cancer-related deaths than COVID-19 deaths. According to U.S medical statistics, cardiac arrests have been down by 38% since the start of the pandemic. Unless COVID-19 is found to be a magic cure for cardiac arrest, the only other explanation is that patients who need treatment fail to go to the doctor for fear of infection. The United Nations Children's Fund (UNICEF) reckon that around 1 million children will die globally due to the effects of economic devastation caused by governments' corona-related measures and subsequent decisions taken by industry. What can stop the amygdala from overwhelming the prefrontal cortex, ensuring rational responses as opposed to irrational reactions? Feelings of Autonomy, Belonging, and Competence!

We have seen how an individual's feelings are based on the information the person receives and how s/he interprets it. Social distancing is a great example of an ABC depletion process. By being imposed on people (information), it decreases people's levels of Autonomy (interpretation). Being separated from one's family, friends, and co-workers (information) negatively impacts one's Belonging (interpretation). Being restricted in terms of activities (information)—be it work or leisure—shrinks their Competence (interpretation). Even when we are not locked up in our homes, our ABC levels are depleted by social distancing measures. Wearing non-transparent face masks disrupts an important channel of communication—facial expressions. And what about shaking hands or hugging? When feelings are taken out of the equation of human interaction, we can no longer be social beings and instead are reduced to being a vegetable. There is much more to human nature than biological existence. How long do we think we can limit, restrict, and withhold the one key ingredient of our evolutionary human survival mechanism—social interaction?

To be clear, I am not suggesting that we abandon all social distancing measures immediately. But such measures can only be short-term solutions. They have already started to negatively impact people's health. Feelings drive behavior and outcomes. The lack of feelings of ABC as a result of social distancing has already resulted in fight-or-flight behaviors that have taken many shapes and forms. For example, the increased consumption of alcohol, drugs, cigarettes, and videogaming reflects the behavior of those who are compensating their ABC deficiencies by fleeing the real world. Other examples of flight responses include the considerable rise in cases of depression and suicides since the start of the measures. In terms of the fight response, there have been reports of greater levels of aggression reflected in the material increases in domestic violence or enraged public protests. Retrospectively, statistics will show previously unseen numbers in negative health outcomes. Commentators will look back on this period and say: "Remember that was the start of the COVID-19 pandemic?". Are these living conditions what we are willing to accept as the new normal?

There is no point in offsetting actual or projected COVID-19 death numbers against the collateral deaths related to social distancing. Both camps have a point. As a society, we need to have a pragmatic instead of a paradigmatic dialogue on how we want to live long-term. Over the last half century, SDT researchers have demonstrated in tens of thousands of studies that feelings of Autonomy, Belonging, and Competence are as essential to the human species as oxygen, food, and water. COVID-19 seems to be deadly for some parts of the population. The ABC is a question of life and death for all of us. Therefore, it's time we shifted the focus from the dictatorship-versus-grandma-murderer blame game to finding ABC-based solutions. How do we make sure that people get the ABC levels they need to survive and thrive under different pandemic scenarios, consistent with the WHO's definition of health—a human right enabling life without limitations or restrictions?

Self-Optimization

As helpful as the WHO's definition of health may be for surviving COVID-19, it can also kill people. This is because it champions an ideal state that countless people strive to attain in the course of their lifetime, some of them even dying in the attempt. From an early age, we are being taught to accept no limits or restrictions, to achieve anything we want, and to become the best version of ourselves, which will be reflected in a perfect body and a perfect mind. Countless apps like MyFitnessPal, Fitbit Coach, Fitocracy, Samsung Health, or Apple Health now exist to help our prefrontal cortex set SMART (Specific, Measurable, Achievable, Relevant, Timebound) goals and to support our persistence in pursuing them. Along this journey, apps further assist us in training, improving, and optimizing our portfolio of skills. Embedded success algorithms based on goals, skills, and persistence promise us upgrades of all the physical and mental parts of our lives, which in turn will guarantee us success. This includes the parts we did not even know about or the ones we did not feel needed improvement. Gamification features benchmark your activities, help you to find virtual friends supporting Belonging, and give awards for higher performance levels, boosting Competence. They also assist you in designing your individual, optional exercise regime, increasing Autonomy. Feeling healthy is not good enough anymore. Innovative technological solutions deliver on-the-spot, objective proof of our health condition. They measure steps, distances, speed, repetitions, calories, biomarkers, and even thoughts and compare data to other subscribed users. How are we doing in the daily races? Are we set up and ready to go for success or are we still a not-good-enough failure?

The part of the WHO's definition of health suggesting a life without limitations and restrictions can kill people. By pushing the limits in our pursuit of perfect bodies and minds, we are running the risk of improving ourselves to death. "We are living in an age of perfectionism, and perfection is the idea that kills ... People are suffering and dying under the torture of the fantasy Self they are failing to become" writes UK journalist Will Storr in his book on self-optimization. The need for self-optimization addresses our fears and perceived inadequacies, which trigger our amygdala. Marketing primes us to believe that we can only ensure our survival with a body-mass index (BMI) in the low 20s, a sixpack like Chris Hemsworth, lips like Angelina Jolie, the body shape of Gigi Hadid, the ability to run a marathon in under three hours, or the stamina to climb Mount Everest. However, what this message actually does for us is lead us into disaster. Our external incentives become Autonomy downers by controlling our behavior, Belonging downers by fueling competition and individualistic actions, and Competence downers by overwhelming our physical and mental resources. There is a wealth of SDT research underpinning how so-called "external aspirations" decrease our ABC levels, leading to negative health outcomes. What about the ABC supply in apps? The ABC provided by apps is nothing but a mirage—virtual and not sustainable. It reminds me of Mary Chase's Pulitzer Prize-winning Broadway comedy

Harvey in which the main character Elwood Dowd lives with a white, human-sized, invisible rabbit. Ultimately, not only Elwood but also his mentally healthy sister end up in a psychiatric clinic due to his delusion.

Self-optimization deprives us of ABC and instills stress in us and in the people around us, in addition to all the other stress factors in our lives. As we have seen in previous chapters, continuous stress kills!

If self-optimization is dangerous and harmful, why are so many of us subscribing to the perfectionist ideal of our time? The answer is much bigger than health. A life without limits or restrictions promises perfect, never-ending happiness, the subject of the next chapter.

8. The ABC of Happiness

Happiness is the highest form of health.
– His Holiness the 14th Dalai Lama

If you received a dollar for every "How are you?" uttered on this planet each day, you would be far ahead of Jeff Bezos, Elon Musk and Bill Gates on the list of the world's richest people. The responses you might get can vary widely, however, from something like "Not so good", "I have had better days", and "Not bad" to "Pretty good" and "I'm doing fine, thank you!". But do you remember the last time someone responded by saying "I am really, really happy!"? If you do, it must have been unusual and related to exceptional circumstances such as just being married—or perhaps divorced!

Happiness is not part of our everyday lives. We may love schmaltzy, tear-jerking films, but when the main characters live happily ever after and the movie ends, so does most viewers' happiness experience. They have had their 90 minutes of rollercoaster emotions with a monster dose of happy feelings at the climax. When the movie ends, it is back to the harsh and unforgiving reality of daily struggles.

Happiness is the last class I teach in my elective course called *Organizational Psychology.* After 11 three-hour sessions of highly interactive class discussions, this final class always starts like a funeral service. It is so silent that you can hear a needle drop amidst frozen faces, many of them looking down at the floor. I throw some provocative statements into the classroom, statements like "You seem to me to be the unhappiest cohort of students I have ever had!", in order to agitate students into breaking the ice with some initial comments. And after a slow start, students finally get going. They venture such comments as "Happiness is a very personal thing", "There is no standard", "It's different for everyone", "My happiness is not anyone else's business", and "We were not born to be happy". I wait for the one key comment that is my cue to switch from a moderating role into intervention mode, and that is: "Why is happiness part of a business school course anyway?"

When you survey people to choose their number-one aspiration in life from a list of say 30 items including beauty, love, wealth, personal growth, reputation, fame, helpfulness, power, success, and health, a large majority will pick happiness over all the other items. If you then conduct follow-up interviews with survey participants who did not choose happiness in order to dig deeper into why they picked the particular item they did, almost all of them eventually arrive at the same destination—to achieve happiness in life! Not only do people want some happiness in some parts of our lives. If we could have it our way, most of us would go for perfect, never-ending happiness! This is not surprising. There is now an abundance of scientific evidence showing that happier people have more friends, live healthier and longer lives, and are more successful in business. These are the exact reasons why happiness is a relevant module in my organizational psychology course.

A Short History of Happiness

The term "happiness" can be found in some governmental constitutions around the world. But for generations it has never been a topic high on the agenda of societal life. Over the centuries, people were more concerned with survival, which had to do with avoiding diseases, plagues, and death. As a result, there are no long-term studies on the evolution of happiness throughout humankind. The sciences discovered the topic in the last decades of the twentieth century. Ed Diener's seminal 1984 article in the *Psychological Bulletin*, "Subjective Well-Being", paved the way for a paradigm shift beyond pathologies and healing. It took another 15 years before Daniel Kahneman opened up a new field of psychology called "positive psychology", starting a new era of scientific inquiry in the social sciences. This was around the same time that Richard Davidson received permission from the

Dalai Lama to study the brains of Tibetan and Nepalese Buddhist monks using EEG and MfRI scans.

Davidson, born in Brooklyn, made his first steps in the medical arena as a summer intern in the sleep laboratory of Maimonides Medical Center during his high school years. After receiving his B.A. in psychology from New York University, he obtained his Ph.D. in personality, psychopathology, and psychophysiology in 1976 from Harvard University. Davidson joined the University of Wisconsin at Madison in 1984 (the year that Diener published his article), where he has been a professor of psychology and psychiatry ever since. As you would have expected at the time, his initial work focused on psychopathologies. Then something happened that Davidson describes as a "pivotal moment" and a "total wake-up call" in his life. He met the Dalai Lama in 1992.

When challenged by His Holiness on why he was only investigating negative states and feelings and not positive qualities such as kindness, compassion, and happiness, Davidson did not have an answer. Since then, his work has shifted, applying state-of-the-art technologies to study the neural bases of positive emotions. What he found in the brains of monks after years of meditating on love and compassion has since been extended to the rest of us. Happiness is a skill that can be trained like a muscle. Due to the plasticity of the brain, mental training such as meditation can change the wiring of our brains to have more frequent and more intense experiences of happiness. This is good news for all of us. Perfect, never-ending happiness is within our reach, and Davidson's research uncovered a path to achieve it—Buddhist monks' meditation practice.

The same technological tools that Davidson used in his research were applied by Kahneman, who won the Nobel Prize in Behavioral Economics in 2002 for studying happiness. For example, in one research study, he and his colleagues examined the brain activity of participants undergoing the following procedure. Participants were promised a financial reward for their participation—say, $20—and were given certain tasks to perform under the scanner. At some point, participants were told that they were doing so well that they would be rewarded

$50 instead of $20. What the research team detected was a spike in activity in participants' "happiness center" within the brain the very moment they were informed of the increase in reward. In conclusion, happiness spikes can be prompted in untrained people. Also, happiness can be trained by understanding the cause and effect relationship in terms of what drives happiness spikes in my own brain and those of other people. They are two types of happiness: short-term and longer-term happiness. Despite the conventional belief that everyone differs in their happiness, there are common features applicable to all of us.

One Human Nature, Two Types of Happiness

Despite its low historical profile in the sciences, happiness has been subject to a longstanding debate from a philosophical perspective. Two opposing concepts have been clashing since the fourth century B.C. I will refer to them as episodic happiness and sustainable happiness.

Episodic Happiness

The Greek philosopher Aristippus taught in the fourth century B.C. that happiness was about maximizing the amount of pleasure as aggregated by a person's so-called "hedonic" moments or episodes. One of the most influential protagonists of this philosophy in terms of today's happiness discussion, the eighteenth-century utilitarian philosopher Jeremy Bentham, argued that a good society is built on people pursuing the maximization of their individual pleasures and self-interests. Over the past 25 centuries, hedonism has developed throughout the various human epochs from a historical philosophy into a modern life religion, the religion of consumption!

We can buy happiness. Takeaway coffee with caramel flavor, a chocolate doughnut, a bagel with raisins for breakfast, a Thai dish and a good chat with colleagues at lunch, a new pair of running shoes from the shopping mall, another coffee and a muffin in the afternoon, booking the next holiday online, a plate of delicious pasta and a treasured glass of red wine for dinner, a good book or a blockbuster movie before bedtime. This is the very mechanism that Kahneman discovered in his research. Each of these pleasures causes an emotional spike in the happiness center of your brain. It is an episode that subsides in the short run, only to be replaced by another pleasure spike to experience another happy moment. When psychological studies measure episodic happiness, participants are asked to respond to statements such as "Life gives me pleasure" or "Life excites me" on a scale of 1(strongly disagree) to 5 (strongly agree).

From the day we are born, we are being trained as happiness junkies, always on the lookout for the next shot in happy feelings. Massages, fitness, food, alcohol, drugs, sex, video games, or information—there are endless bodily and mental pleasures that can be consumed. However, their happiness effects are only short-lived. The moment the feeling of happiness drawn from one episode starts fading, we develop withdrawal symptoms, a black hole of emptiness slowly opening up that needs to be filled with another pleasurable experience. That is what the scientists Philip Brickman and Donald Campbell describe as the "hedonic treadmill". Each of us has a relatively stable happiness component with emotional episodes of positive and negative life events oscillating around our base-level happiness. Regardless of how much effort we put into creating positive episodes for ourselves, the effects evaporate pretty quickly and we return to our base-level happiness. What is even worse, happiness shots can turn against us. Experiences such as scratches in a new sportscar, the end of our holidays, or a headache from too much red wine transform originally happy episodes into miserable feelings detrimental to our episodic happiness level. We can conclude that hedonic, episodic happiness comes and goes. The provocative question that Brickman and Campbell's work then raises is: what determines base-level happiness?

Sustainable Happiness

Around the same time that Aristippus postulated the foundations of hedonic happiness, opposing views were formulated. One of Aristippus' most reputable adversaries was Aristotle. According to his philosophy, episodic happiness was a misconception, reducing humans to slavish followers of their desires. The twentieth-century social psychologist and philosopher Erich Fromm picked up on the Aristotelian view on happiness. He proposed that there were two dimensions to happiness: purely subjectively felt needs satisfied by episodic, hedonic pleasures like shopping, and objectively valid, sustainable needs that were requirements of human nature. Such needs pertain to contributing to the community and the greater good instead of one's individual pleasure. The Greek term often used to refer to this dimension of happiness is "eudaimonia". The combination of "eu", which means "good", and "daimon", which stands for "spirit", translates into having purpose and meaning in life and living in congruence with one's true nature. Scientists measure sustainable happiness by asking people to indicate on a scale of 1 (strongly disagree) to 7 (strongly agree) to what extent the following statements apply to them: "I lead a purposeful and meaningful life", "I actively contribute to the happiness and well-being of others", or "My life serves a higher purpose". The helpers' high is a perfect example of eudaimonic happiness. Helping others provides your life with the meaning that boosts your own sustainable happiness level. Scientists and philosophers from the eudaimonic camp can explain why success without meaning is not sustainable. If people do not have a meaning in life, they lack base-level happiness. In their pursuit of happiness, they need to engage in continuous, episodic experiences to lift their happiness levels. As soon as the effect fades, another event will be required to boost their happy feelings. On aggregate, without base-line happiness, we are trapped. As soon as a single life event pushes happiness into the negative zone, we feel increasing pressure to make up for the shortfall. We invest additional energy into further episodes of happiness to compensate. If and when that fails, we find ourselves in a downward spiral of energy depletion. Over time, we run out of fuel, ultimately leading to burnout.

Happiness has two overlapping parts. Sustainable happiness is wired into our brains during the first eight to ten years of our lives. It represents a stable base-level happiness driven by meaning and purpose, that is, focusing on contributing to the lives of others. Mother Teresa, for example, is the embodiment of eudaimonic happiness. It also shows that happy feelings can be achieved without hedonism. As discovered by Davidson's research, the wiring of your brain can be changed through training. The same can be said of your sustainable happiness level. It is stable unless you decide to upgrade it through specific mental practices such as dedicated meditation.

Episodic happiness has only short-term effects. It is self-focused and emphasizes the pursuit of maximum mental and physical pleasures. Positive emotional episodes subside and can even turn negative. Both developments can trigger addiction-like behavior, a continuous hunt for happiness shots, for example through consumption. There is no need to train for that. We are all experts in hedonic treadmill behavior. Instead, a bit of untraining may help us limit the negative consequences for our lifestyle and happiness.

What about Life Satisfaction?

Let's conduct a little experiment. Please answer the following two questions using a scale of 0 (not at all) to 10 (absolutely):

Question 1 – How happy are you with your present life?
Question 2 – How satisfied are you with your present life?

Are both of your scores the same? If not, you are in good company. This simple exercise demonstrates that happiness and life satisfaction are not one and the same thing, neither in theory nor in practice. There has been long-standing confusion and controversy about the terminology surrounding happiness in the social sciences. While there is a common understanding among scholars on the two dimensions of episodic and sustainable happiness, there has been contentious debate over whether life satisfaction is part of hedonism, part of eudaimonia, part of both, or a separate concept.

Let's take a look at the definition of life satisfaction. Diener and two of his colleagues defined it back in 1985 as "a cognitive judgmental process dependent upon a comparison of one's circumstances with what is thought to be an appropriate standard". In laymen's terms, this means that people compare the circumstances of their lives—housing, work, education, disposable income, partnership—to a self-chosen benchmark. For example, a family owning a Toyota Prius in a neighborhood where most people drive Bentleys or Aston Martins is likely to experience lower life satisfaction. Thus, life satisfaction represents a process of cognitive assessment of your situation, quite different from the emotional moments of hedonic happiness. When surveying life satisfaction, we can ask people how satisfied they are with their life in general or, more domain-specific, how satisfied they are with their respective work, housing, education, or financial situation.

Unlike eudaimonia, life satisfaction is not focused on what you can contribute to others. Instead, it is about the essential building blocks of your own life, i.e. your situation, your abilities, and your personal growth—in essence, what you consider the important components of a good life. Others only serve as a benchmark for social comparison.

How stable is our life satisfaction over time? Is it full of ups and down just like hedonism, or is it as stable as eudaimonia? Richard Lucas and Brent Donellan from Michigan State University studied two data sets from Germany and the UK to shed light on this question. One included over 8,600 participants who had taken part in the German Socio-Economic Panel Study (GSOEP) for an average of 12 years. The other data set involved close to 9,500 respondents to the British Household Panel Study

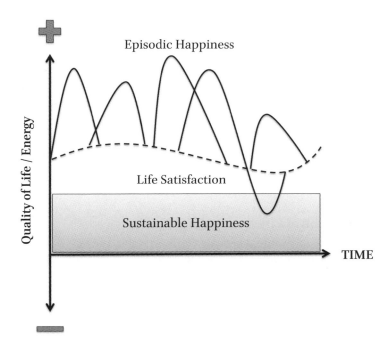

Episodic Happiness

Quality of Life / Energy

Life Satisfaction

Sustainable Happiness

TIME

(BHPS) who had participated for an average of seven years. In both surveys, participants were asked a single question to indicate on a scale of 1 to 10 how satisfied they were with their lives in general. In their data analysis, Lucas and Donellan identified how stable the responses were over time, and for both the GSOEP and BHPS samples, the responses were very similar and pretty stable! The conclusion was that around 40% of an average person's life satisfaction is perfectly stable over time. Another 35% is moderately stable in the medium term. This is the case for lasting but adaptable life circumstances. For example, widows and widowers experience strong reactions to the loss of a spouse. When moving to a new country, people may respond very vividly to the new environment. Both can lead to short-term instability in life satisfaction. But the effect subsides over time through adaptation. The remaining 25% of life satisfaction overlaps with hedonic happiness and is influenced by daily life events.

In a nutshell, a small proportion of life satisfaction overlaps with episodic happiness. There are no commonalities with sustainable happiness. The scientific evidence suggests treating life satisfaction as a separate construct, one that is distinct from happiness. In fact, recent literature integrating philosophical and psychological directions conveys the view that sustainable happiness, episodic happiness, and life satisfaction each contribute specific aspects to a person's "quality of life": a stable basis, moderate medium-term stability, and short-term spikes.

A Question of Lifestyle

Even though happiness components and life satisfaction complement each other, individuals differ in the expression of each aspect in their daily lives. For most of us, our lifestyles will consist of a combination of some sustainable happiness, life satisfaction, and happy episodes as icing on the cake. But there are three extreme scenarios that people can engage in: the episodic life, the satisfied life, and the meaningful life.

The Episodic Life

One can see how a person can indulge in all the pleasures of a hedonic happiness junkie and be a pain or parasite to society due to a lack of eudaimonia. An episodic life also disregards developing the building blocks of your life. The fragile setup of a lifestyle focused solely on happy episodes lacks foundation. Life satisfaction and meaning are insurance policies against negative episodes in your life. When misfortunes strike, as they sometimes do, episodic lives are at an extremely high risk of failure.

When Eric Clapton decided to fight his addiction to alcohol and drugs, a circle of close friends and his love for music were the sources of power he drew upon in order to prevail. This was quite different for episodic happiness junkie Brian. His lifestyle

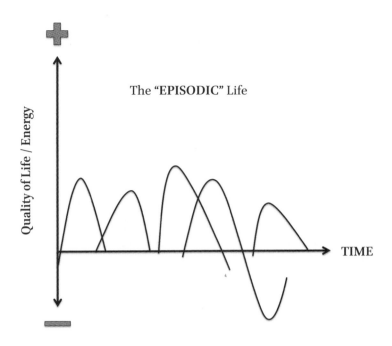

The "EPISODIC" Life

had left him no friends. The only person he loved was himself. The London investment banker enjoyed life to its fullest. His happiness shots involved bullying clients and colleagues, earning million-dollar bonuses, buying sportscars, seducing women, frequenting gentlemen clubs and nightclubs, and enjoying Cohiba cigars, champagne, and cocaine. Brian could not sit still. If he was not part of another happy episode, he felt he was missing out on life. While sitting in his general practitioner's waiting room, he would doodle on his smart phone to create informational spikes related to stock market data or yellow press revelations. When his doctor revealed Brian's recent medical results, they promised everything but another happy episode in his life. Diagnostic data indicated testicular cancer. "Live fast, die young" is the title of a biography of James Dean, one of Brian's idols. Brian was 31, seven years older than James Dean when the latter died in a car crash in California. Brian had certainly lived fast in recent years. The "dying young" part of Dean's story had given Brian an episodic thrill. But now, facing potential death did not feel thrilling at all. In his mind, he started plowing through his life in alphabetical order. 'A' for assistance. Who could he call on to collect some necessities from his apartment so he could spend the next couple of weeks in hospital? No one came to mind. 'C' for colleagues. His job was very competitive, and Brian had a reputation for taking advantage of his colleagues. His bosses did not care as long as he made money for the bank. Why would they care about his disease? 'F' for family. Brian had no brothers or sisters, and he had been suing his parents in court over an early share of his heritage. Another 'F' for friends. Brian had plenty of friends when he was partying with women and drugs. But none of his so-called friends would be interested in the sad story of a cancer patient. 'M' for meaning. There was nothing that Brain really felt proud of except for his ability to create a constant stream of happy episodes. His entire life centered around himself. What would he leave behind in case he died from cancer? Meaning? No way! 'S' for support. Was there anyone close enough that Brian could rely on for some emotional support? His love life had been nothing but a collection of meaningless episodes. There was no partner he could turn to. When he arrived at the end of his mental exercise, Brian was faced with the emptiness of an episodic life. He spent a couple of weeks at the hospital for further testing. Fortunately, his cancer had been detected early and could be treated and ultimately cured. Six months later, Brian was back in business living his episodic life. The experience just proved to him that you had to indulge in as many happy episodes as possible, as life could end all of a sudden. But what if his cancer had been terminal? The last months, maybe years, of his existence would have been determined by emptiness.

The Satisfied Life

When you are going through life, the building block of high levels of life satisfaction will support you. You will be able to draw on your internal and external resources such as self-confidence,

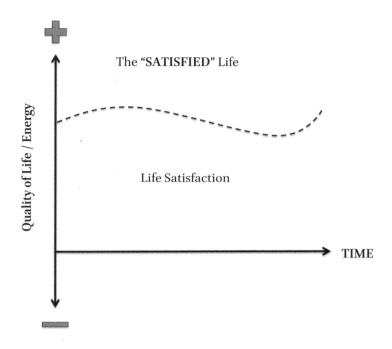

The "SATISFIED" Life

Life Satisfaction

Quality of Life / Energy

TIME

knowledge, competences, your network of contacts, and financial means.

I have met so many people who lead good lives. They all feel comfortable and are sometimes even bored by their comfort. At some point, many of them develop this nagging feeling that there is something missing in their life. Is this it? Is this what life is all about? When that happens, some people turn to charity work for more meaning or higher purpose in their lives. Others try to spice up their lives by engaging in hedonic episodes such as buying sportscars or running city marathons. While the buildup of sustainable happiness through benefiting others is an applaudable effort, over-engaging in happy episodes can go awfully wrong. We all know about rich entrepreneurs who are killed climbing Mount Everest, swimming with sharks, or feeding crocodiles. Take Richard Branson, who crossed the Atlantic in a hot-air balloon and almost died when the balloon crashed. It was also Branson who barely escaped an avalanche while climbing the Mont Blanc mountain. Cheating on your partner is also a great way of falling into the hedonism trap.

I had known Bob and his wife Belinda for over 20 years. He worked as head of sales and marketing in a large multinational company. The family had three kids and lived a pretty stable, satisfied life. But stable increasingly meant boring for Bob. Even though he was very successful in business, Bob had long felt the nagging need to engage in new episodic adventures: sports, investments, exclusive gentlemen clubs, extravagant holiday locations. It was pretty obvious from our conversations that he did not have much meaning in his life. His competitive mantra was faster, further, higher. Bob's hedonic episodes required increasing emotional impact to create moments of happiness for him. Whenever the end of an episode was near and the excitement of happiness was receding to the zero line again, Bob set his sights on planning his next adventure. That was no different when Bob met Amy. She was an attractive 31-year-old finance professional in Bob's company. After some initial conversations, lunches, and dinners, Bob started an intimate relationship with Amy. The more time they spent together, the less time Bob spent with his family. After three months, short afternoon episodes were no longer enough. Bob invited Amy to join him for a conference where they spent a full week together. Finally, after six months, Bob revealed his affair to his wife and kids, rented an apartment, and had Amy move in with him. How was Bob able to increase happiness levels from here, you might ask. Bob bought expensive gifts, helped Amy advance her career in his company, and contemplated marriage and having kids. This was around the time that Amy hooked up with the company's finance director and got Bob fired due to all the intimate details he knew about her. The source of his moments of happiness had turned into a nightmare. Bob lost everything, the foundation of his life satisfaction based on his family and his job. He also lost his energy to engage in any episodic happiness activities for compensation. The happiness spikes he previously experienced with Amy were too high for them to be matched by alternatives. His actual happiness level was too far in the red to provide any energy for new hedonic episodes. And due to the lack of meaning in his life, his sustainable happiness was too low to bolster his happiness levels against such an episodic blow. Bob suffered a burnout that took him more than two years to recover from. He spent six months in a psychosomatic clinic. Today, he runs a yoga center in Australia.

The Meaningful Life

Buddhist philosophy advocates love and compassion for others as a source of happiness on people's path to enlightenment. Needless to say, this extreme scenario of a meaningful life is unlikely to catch on in the modern Western world. As trained episodic happiness junkies, many of us may have some meaning in our lives. But what would life be without the happy episodes of chocolate or wine? And what happens when we run out of chocolate or

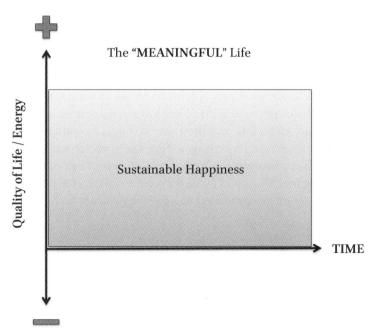

wine? What we find is that the more meaning people develop in their lives, the less craving they have for episodic happiness. Let me share Andrea's story with you.

Andrea was an important person. She was part of the political establishment in Washington D.C. Well-educated with a network of innumerable political and industrial contacts, Andrea was on her way to glory. Maybe she would be working in the White House one day, maybe even in the Oval Office. She also had a boyfriend, and together they indulged in all the episodic pleasures you can think of. But wherever she was and whatever she did, Andrea never felt fulfilled. She felt a kind of vacuum in her soul. One day in May, she attended a talk by the Dalai Lama when he was travelling through North America. It changed her life. She went on to spend time at Kopan Monastery in Kathmandu to meditate and study Buddhism. She became ordained as a Buddhist nun and later ran one of the Dalai Lama's Buddhist centers in the U.S.

This is the story of someone who converted full circle from an episodic, satisfied life to a meaningful life by giving up all worldly pleasures and concerns. Andrea's story is an extraordinary example of untraining our episodic mind. I am not suggesting that we should all follow Andrea's path. In Western societies, it is hard to persevere in leading a life of sustainable happiness. That is why people like Andrea become ordained and live in monasteries. As the Dalai Lama once put it, give Buddhist monks or nuns a family, a mortgage, and a job, and they may struggle as well. As part of a non-monastic community, we engage in social interaction that involves consumption, and we pursue happy episodes. But developing meaning and a focus on benefiting others in our lives can help to reduce our slavery to episodic pleasure and desires.

Cultural Shift

When there is a topic as popular and important for society as happiness, there are also countless individuals and institutions trying to benefit from it. Happiness is no exception. Capitalism is the economic system that Western democracies have been built on. Private ownership in pursuit of the maximization of profits has become a key feature of capitalist economies. Another idea—liberalism—promoted free markets with only limited government interference as catalysts for profit maximization, economic development, and societal prosperity. The eighteenth-century economist and philosopher Adam Smith, author of *The Wealth of Nations* and often referred to as the father of capitalism and liberalism, would have been proud of the various ways that Western societies have implemented his vision. Societies, communities, and families have prospered. Infant mortality has plummeted, families can now buy fridges instead of digging holes in their gardens to cool groceries, and people have expanded their lives by covering larger distances due to railroads and automobiles. But then something happened around the middle of the twentieth century.

David Brooks is a Canadian-born American political and cultural commentator for *The New York Times*. In a speech to college students in Davidson, North Carolina in January 2018, he revealed his perspectives on the cultural shifts taking place in American and Western societies in recent history. Since the beginning of the twentieth century up until the end of the 1960s, people have faced two world wars and the Great Depression. To overcome adversities, there was a feeling that "we are all in this together". People formed groups, worked in big organizations, and were very skilled in building tight communities. Your identity was by and large determined by the family, ethnic group, and neighborhood you belonged to. An individual's mission was to contribute to the lives of others. According to Brooks, the key values at the time were loyalty, modesty, and humility. But at the same time, this era had its downsides, which included racism, sexism, anti-Semitism, emotional coldness, and conformity. As a result, the younger generation rebelled, and there was a transition to a new culture that found its expression in the 1968 student revolts around the globe. The old culture was not working for them anymore, so they created a new ethos that Brooks called

"I am free to be myself". From this point onwards, an increasing number of people subscribed to the goal of human independence, pursuing one's self-interest, doing with one's life whatever one wants, and breaking all the rules of conformity. This cultural shift found its expression in various movements such as feminism, civil rights, peace, and rock and roll. It also triggered a shift in economics.

Margaret Thatcher and Ronald Reagan are two of the most quoted protagonists of the so-called "neo-liberalist" camp. Minimal government regulation and maximum freedom for market participants became the name of the game in the late 1970s and 1980s. No more rules; life is what you make of it! It was the time when books such as *Liar's Poker*, *The Bonfire of the Vanities*, and *Barbarians at the Gate* sold millions of copies, showcasing how finance professionals were making money by deceiving, exploiting, and intimidating others. In the movie *Wall Street*, the ruthless corporate raider Gordon Gecko embodied the "greed is good" mantra to become an idol for a generation of young, ambitious investment bankers. It may not come as a surprise that Ed Diener's first inquiries into happiness took place in that era. Due to a lack of historical scientific data on happiness, we cannot comment on the impact on happiness of that cultural and economic shift. What we can say, however, is that there have been enormous efforts since the 1980s to explore the link between economic self-interest and individual profit maximization on the one hand and happiness on the other in support of a neo-liberal, "money buys happiness" paradigm.

The Devil is in the Detail

In November 2013, the German TV station ARD ran a week-long special on happiness. They interviewed people on the streets of Germany, in big cities and the countryside, prominent people, ordinary people, successful entrepreneurs, people who had lost it all, students in schools, employees at work. A month before

Christmas, the year's peak shopping period, the question on everyone's mind was: "Does money buy happiness?". In order to explore this question from a scientific point of view, ARD had teamed up with Infratest dimap, a German institute with strong credibility and an excellent reputation. Most German citizens know and trust the company due to its TV presence related to political research as well as polls and projections on regional and federal elections in Germany. Infratest dimap decided to run a representative survey called "Happiness Trend 2013" with over 50,000 German citizens from all over Germany. On a scale of 0 (not at all) to 10 (absolutely), participants were asked to respond to the following question: "How satisfied are you with your present life?". A key finding of the statistical data analysis was that all participants with a monthly net disposable income of €3,000 and higher had an average happiness score of 7.9. The same score for all participants with a monthly net disposable income of €1,500 and lower was 6.8. Once the results of the happiness study were released in November, media headlines all arrived at the same conclusion: money buys happiness. The implication was clear: spending more money for Christmas shopping will make everyone happier!

It is okay when people use happiness and life satisfaction interchangeably in everyday life. What is not okay is to label something a happiness survey, measure life satisfaction, and prompt the media to promote money as a happiness candle for Christmas. A disclaimer in the subtext of the ARD/Infratest dimap publication reads: "money may not make you happier but more satisfied". Such a disclaimer may not be good enough to make up for the specious claim of the survey's happiness headline and the subsequent media frenzy and change in people's behavior. What about all the Germans who went out and spent all their savings on buying happiness for Christmas 2013, and all they got was life satisfaction instead?

Anyone investigating the psychological effects of economic indicators such as disposable income on the quality of life has a responsibility to clearly advertise what perspective they are examining—episodic happiness or sustainable happiness, or perhaps not happiness at all but life satisfaction. One of the field's burning research questions since the turn of the century has been as follows. If there was a relationship between income and one of the dimensions of quality of life, would the link be infinite? Would the person making $100,000 be two times as happy as the person making $50,000, and billionaires a thousand times happier than millionaires?

Can Money Buy Happiness?

From Diener's first contribution to the literature on happiness, it took 25 years to come up with an initial response to that question. In 2010, Nobel Laureate Kahneman published the results of the first large-scale investigation on the topic. His findings would spark further research activity, leading to a startling observation on the relationships between money and quality of life. Let's start with Kahneman's original study.

In 2008 and 2009, the Gallup Organization collected data from US residents through their Gallup-Healthways Well-Being Index (GHWBI). Kahneman and his team studied 450,000 participants' data records from the GHWBI to examine a potential relationship between episodic hedonic happiness and annual disposable income. Would money buy episodic happiness? The answer to that was: it depends. Statistical analysis revealed a satiation point. Up to an annual income of $75,000, there is a clear link between hedonic happiness and income. Beyond this threshold, the relationship collapses. Increases in income are no longer reflected in happiness levels. Kahneman argued that below the $75,000 threshold, the lack of income produced low hedonic happiness due to challenges such as social isolation or health issues. This effect was offset by increasing income, leading to a correlation between episodic happiness and income up to the $75,000 threshold. Beyond that point, additional income did not buy people more frequent and more positive moments of mental and physical pleasures. Instead, they were satiated with social contacts, health, or leisure. Kahneman concluded his data analysis with a visionary hypothesis for future research: "It also is likely that when income rises beyond this value, the increased ability to purchase positive experiences is balanced, on average, by some negative effects."

Ed Diener himself, surrounded by a team of scientists from Purdue University and the University of Virginia, picked up on Kahneman's work. What would the satiation effect look like in other countries around the world? Diener's team studied a dataset of 1.7 million individuals worldwide, provided by Gallup Poll, to answer this question. In 2018, eight years after Kahneman, the threshold levels of this more granular study are shown in the table below:

REGION	LIFE SATISFACTION	EPISODIC HAPPINESS
Global	$95,000	$70,000
Western Europe	$100,000	$50,000
Eastern Europe	$45,000	$35,000
Australia/New Zealand	$125,000	$50,000
East Asia	$110,000	$60,000
Latin America	$35,000	$30,000
Middle East	$115,000	$115,000
North America	$105,000	$80,000
Africa	$40,000	$40,000

In essence, the satiation effect of income on episodic happiness could be reproduced in any region studied by the research team. A new revealing finding was that life satisfaction also plateaued. In some areas such as Africa, the Middle East, and Latin America, life satisfaction and episodic happiness flattened at around the same annual disposable income. In Africa and Latin America, both measures may be related to the bare necessities of survival such as food and shelter. Any improvement in life circumstances and resulting satisfaction adds to people's chances of survival. Survival may not be an issue in the Middle East, but people there seem to value and appreciate any positive changes in their respective situations as happy moments unrelated to survival.

For all the other regions, the satiation points for life satisfaction were considerably higher than for episodic happiness. One way to interpret this is that when episodic happiness stops, there is still a lot of room for upgrading your life domains and increasing your life satisfaction, but this does not add to episodic happiness. But there was another, unexpected finding hidden in the Gallup Poll data: life satisfaction did not remain stable after the satiation point but dropped! Before, some scientists had speculated that very high incomes may lead to reductions in happiness. However, this was the first, preliminary evidence that an effect actually existed—but on life satisfaction and not on happiness. The scientists hypothesized that higher incomes may be related to increased pressure and stress. For example, higher job demands such as time, workload, and responsibility could limit opportunities for life satisfaction. Increased materialistic values, unfulfilled desires, social comparison pressures, moving to more expensive neighborhoods, having more children, taking on mortgages, buying expensive cars, and going on exquisite vacations could also be seen as contributing to the detected decline in life satisfaction related to higher incomes.

So having sifted through the academic baggage, can money buy happiness? Yes, it can...up to a point. Money helps us attain episodes of bare human necessities such as health, social exchange, and leisure. Beyond a certain threshold point, more money does not add to episodic happiness anymore, but it can further increase your life satisfaction. But be careful: your life satisfaction only increases to a certain turning point. The more incomes increase beyond that threshold—which differs by culture and level of economic development—the more life satisfaction decreases. What about sustainable happiness? Due to its nature of being inward-focused rather than driven by external desires, it is unaffected by economic factors such as income. However, you can create meaning and purpose in your life by leveraging a high income position. The best way to do this is to identify ways you can contribute to communities and society. In doing so, it is best to leave your ego at the door and to focus on how you can benefit others. This is a smart strategy for everyone, not only those with high incomes. Meaning and purpose represent the foundation of any sustainable success.

The ABC Perspective

Happiness could be described as the supreme misunderstanding of modern life. Through the lens of an evolutionary microscope, we can uncover it as another mismatch between our ancestral human nature and contemporary culture. On the surface, consuming a bottle of red wine in compensation for a hard day at work may give us a happy episode in the evening. Buying a sportscar to match living standards in our neighborhood may give you life satisfaction. Supporting the local soccer club by volunteering to chauffeur youngsters to games on weekends may add meaning and sustainable happiness to your life. Yet from an evolutionary perspective, all three are nothing but expressions of our embedded survival mechanism.

For our ancestors, recovering from a hunting trip, upgrading one's arsenal of tools to compete with rivalling bands, and contributing to one's community were a question of life and death. In modern society, associating a hard day at work, the lifestyle demands of your neighborhood, or the needs of the local soccer club with actual survival would be an exaggeration. And yet we are prompted to react to such situations with red wine, a sportscar, and a taxi service. This modern life behavior can be explained by taking our human nature into account.

Work, our neighbors' lifestyle, and the soccer club needing our help all trigger our amygdala, which is constantly scanning the environment for dangers to ourselves and our community. Stress is all around us. What keeps the amygdala from persistently overpowering the prefrontal cortex are feelings of Autonomy, Belonging, and Competence that make us feel safe. We are intuitively looking for ABC as sources of survival. When we find ABC in our present world, it gives us happy moments, life satisfaction, or sustainable happiness. In short, happiness is the modern life equivalent of ancestral survival.

There is sweeping, scientific evidence supporting the ABC as a driver for all three elements of quality of life: episodic happiness, life satisfaction, and sustainable happiness. Tim Kasser has been widely recognized as a scholar for his work in the field of consumerism and materialism. He was part of Rochester University's Human Motivation Research Group when he and Richard Ryan teamed up to develop the so-called aspiration index questionnaire. It allows for a detailed investigation on which sources of ABC were contributing to which quality of life element. The index broadly distinguishes between two dimensions—external and internal aspirations. For example, external aspirations could be "to have many expensive possessions", "to be famous", or "to look attractive". "To help others improve their lives", "to help people in need", or "to work to make the world a better place" represent internal aspirations.

Scientists first started addressing the research question in the late 1990s. Since then, a body of knowledge has accumulated on the relationship between ABC sources and quality-of-life dimensions.

External aspirations as sources of ABC correlate with episodic happiness and life satisfaction. Consumption and materialistic values drive external aspirations, making people slaves of their desires. They become dependent upon external factors such as material things and other people. A life determined by external aspirations means you are surrendering control and putting yourself at the mercy of external events and circumstances. This engenders an endless cycle of a need for ABC, followed by a period of temporary relief, followed in turn by a new need for ABC, followed by another period of relief, and so on. The only difference between episodic happiness and life satisfaction in this context is the time horizon. For episodic happiness, the relief is only short term, such as a piece of chocolate, alcohol, or drugs. Buying houses, cars, and videogames or posting something on Instagram add to a person's life satisfaction through medium-term ABC effects. However, the rollercoaster pattern remains the same. People are constantly under pressure to engage in activities that boost ABC from external sources.

This is different for internal aspirations. Values, attitudes, and beliefs focused on supporting others without the involvement of one's ego create behaviors that produce ABC independent of aspects in your environments. You are in control of your own happiness destiny. With a mindset of helpfulness and meaning, you generate ABC, which in turn drives sustainable happiness. There will be no yo-yo effects as in the case of episodic happiness and life satisfaction. The supply of ABC will be stable based on your inner approach. Internal aspirations therefore represent a foundation for sustainable happiness.

Happiness for Sale

Happiness has become an industry. This is not the case for sustainable happiness, however, for how could you make money from a self-sufficient ABC producer? But those without much meaning in their lives whose ABC levels go through daily turbulences become easy prey for advertisers exploiting the people's pursuit of happiness. I will share two illustrations of that scenario with you, consumer products and pharmaceuticals.

Both the consumer product industry and the pharmaceutical industry have become experts in selling short- and medium-term happiness to customers. If you buy Marlboro cigarettes, you get Marlboro Country with its endless wilderness and horseback riding, which promises Autonomy—which will last for as long as the smoke of a cigarette. Your friend Johnny Walker gives you a warm sense of Belonging—as long as there is some left in the glass. Apple computers push your Competence by making you 'think different' every time you use them. Instead of switching to another program tonight, deliberately watch a couple of TV commercials. What specific feelings are they addressing in you? A, B, C, or maybe all of them in one clip? Buying happy episodes and life satisfaction indirectly by feeling ABC is one option, but from some companies, you can even buy happiness directly. Febreze will make you "Breathe Happy", Kinder provides "Happy Moments", and McDonald's offers you a "Happy Meal".

Whenever low ABC levels come knocking on people's doors, pharmaceutical companies are there to offer help. If you feel depressed, deflated, down, or overwhelmed, there is always a pill to instantly brighten your day. For as long as it lasts, the pill will give you spikes of Autonomy, Belonging, and Competence. According to MEDCO Health Solutions, at least one in five adults in the U.S. is already taking at least one psychiatric drug today. At the same time, competitive pressure has contributed to a substantial increase in self-optimizing, performance-enhancing drugs, often referred to as "brain boosters". Ritalin, amphetamines, and Modafinil have become very popular among students and employees—not to cure any disease but to boost short-term mental performance through biochemical ABC triggers (but only for the duration of the trip).

Short and medium-term happiness are great business models. As soon as the effects subside, happiness junkies rush to replenish their ABC levels with new shots, generating repeated revenues for consumer products and pharmaceutical companies.

How Money Can Undermine Happiness

Since its groundbreaking publication in the scientific journal *Nature Human Behavior* in 2018, much has been written about the turning points in the study conducted by Diener and his colleagues. It also prompted a stream of future research activity that is currently underway. But the key to unlocking the turning point puzzle may be found in ABC-related research from the past.

In 2005, three scholars from the disciplines of marketing and psychology set out to explore the impact of money on human behavior. Kathleen Vohs, Nicole Mead, and Miranda Goode designed nine experiments in which they compared the behavior of two groups: money-primed participants (the test group) and non-money-primed participants (the control group). Priming is a manipulation technique that researchers use to activate specific ideas in the minds of participants. In this study, test group participants were asked to read a text out loud in front of a video camera. The text included money-related terminology such as capital, investment, rich, profit, dollar, millionaire, and so on. In some of the nine experiments, researchers also used word puzzles for priming. For example, test group participants were asked to form sentences from several four-word puzzles, each containing a money-related term. After the completion of such an exercise, test group participants had the 'thought of money' in their heads. All the researchers had to do now was compare test group behavior to a control group of participants who had been manipulated with neutral, non-money texts or puzzles. In their 2006 article in *Science* magazine, Vohs, Mead, and Goode outlined their profound findings. In one of the experiments, when participants were asked whether they preferred to work in a team or alone on a forthcoming task, 83% of money-primed people opted to work alone compared to only 25% of the control group. Another experiment asked participants to move two chairs together for a get-acquainted conversation. Researchers measured the distance between the two chairs. For the money-primed group, the distance was an average of 118 centimeters, while the neutral control group put only 80 centimeters on average in between the chairs. When all participants were rewarded with $2 in quarters for participating in the experiments at the end, they were all asked for a small donation to the University Student Fund. Money-primed participants donated an average of 77 cents, whereas the non-money-primed control group gave $1.34 on average. Further tests saw control group participants asking help from researchers and peers earlier and more often when confronted with an impossible task, volunteering for more work, spending more time helping peers, and helping collect more pencils from a box that had been dropped to the floor. Overall, the research team concluded that "money brings about a self-sufficient orientation in which people prefer to be free of dependency and dependents ... money-primed people prefer to play alone, work alone and put more distance between themselves and others".

Money undermines our human nature. By conveying a feeling of independence, it negates the 'survival in groups' mechanism, prompting us to invest less Competence in the group. We also rely less on Belonging from the group. Instead, we think we increase our Autonomy by feeling more independent from others. Money often artificially substitutes for our feelings of Belonging and Competence. Beyond a certain turning point, money becomes a burden. We no longer control money, it controls us. Relationships with people are different from a relationship with money. Money does not smile, hug, or listen. It is a non-responsive, fragile, disloyal partner. Due to its unreliable nature, it triggers our amygdala for fear of losing it. Money can spark a vicious circle. In order to accumulate lots of it, people may sacrifice relationships for it. Once they feel independent with exclusively money to rely on, the fear of losing it creeps up on them due to the lack of alternative safety nets such as colleagues, families, or friends.

When I interviewed senior executives around the world for an ABC research project, 82% of participants said the equivalent of "I do not need anybody" at some point during the interview. And when asked to cluster their relationships into categories of close family and friends, acquaintances, and shallow contacts, over 55% of them admitted that they did not feel close to anybody. The bottom line is that money is the equivalent of artificial ABC that allows for happy episodes. In the medium term, it increases life satisfaction to the point where it becomes a burden, causing fears of losing it due to one's dependence on it. Because money induces people to be self-focused, it also sabotages sustainable happiness, which is about meaning and helping others.

Were We Happier in the Stone Age?

There was no money in ancestral times, so perhaps people were happier without money during the good old Stone Age. We have no way of knowing. There were no researchers back then asking people to rate their happiness level on a scale of 1 to 10. The scientific knowledge we have accumulated over the short history of happiness studies suggests that the mechanism and level of happiness may not have changed much. Our embedded human survival mechanism is still the same. What has changed, however, is our environment. Quality of life is a relative concept embedded in respective life circumstances. It may be much more relative in episodic happiness and life satisfaction due to their focus on external factors. Sustainable happiness has its sources in internal factors, which may not have changed much throughout human evolution.

Without scientific evidence, however, we are left to guess. But drawing on what we know by now, quality of life seems to be related to life circumstances at the time. If you are born in a dark house, you may lead a happy life in darkness. The first glimpse of light you see—through a gap under a door or through a window—you will enjoy a happy moment. But you will instantly adapt to the brighter environment. From that moment on, mere light will no longer trigger happy moments for you.

In the same way, it is fair to assume that our quality of life has adapted throughout humankind to our changing environments. The categories of happy episodes, life satisfaction, and sustainable happiness are likely to be still the same. And our best bet is that happiness levels are no different from our ancestors. The only difference is that what makes us happy—what satisfies and nurtures our ABC today—has made quantum leaps since the Stone Age.

Where from Here?

Just to be clear: I am not a radical leftist. All the discoveries presented in this chapter have been revealed using so-called 'gold-standard' research methods. The research articles mentioned in this book were published in top academic journals such as *Nature* or *Science*. The takeaways from this chapter are much more common sense than radical. They are not suggesting that we should refrain from having a good glass of wine, buying a new car, or going on holiday. More importantly, they educate us not to expect lasting effects from such experiences. There is no perfect, never-ending happiness to be found in consumption. Instead, the key messages can be summarized as follows.

Do not become a slave to your momentary desires. Do not let marketing trick you into spending money on artificial ABC through impulse purchases. Take a step back for a few seconds and ask yourself: do I really, really need that? If you understand that it will only lead to a short happiness trip, and if you still decide to engage in it, you should go for it and enjoy the experience. You will not expect any long-term effects and will therefore not be disappointed, which in turn makes it unlikely that you will degenerate into junkie-type behavior.

Do not blindly chase after money, possessions, or approval from others as sources of ABC. While they are core ingredients of our modern lifestyle, they also wear off, just like happy moments. The only difference is that wear and tear usually happen in a more medium-term timeframe. Nonetheless, you become dependent upon external factors. Entering into a spiral of faster cars, bigger houses, and more fame will not yield long-term effects. Being aware of that will help you better manage your ABC levels. You will control your urge instead of being controlled by your environment.

Design your life in a way that combines a sustainable, self-reliant foundation of meaning with deliberate aspects of life satisfaction and occasional, intentional happy episodes. Attitudes, values, and beliefs are sources of ABC that are unaffected by circumstances. Developing these sources will enable you to experience a happier, more stable life in the long term. Happiness is not a destination but a journey. Do not benchmark your feelings against a perfect, never-ending happiness ideal. Rather, benchmark yourself against yourself from yesterday and try to become a little happier each day.

Designing a happy life can be seen as a core human capability that each of us can learn. And learning and education is what we now turn to in the next chapter.

9. The ABC of Education

Education is the passport to the future;
tomorrow belongs to those who prepare for it today.

– Malcolm X

Learning is key to human survival. When we are born, we are totally unprepared for life, defenseless and dependable. At birth, each of us is equipped with a genetic, in-built construction manual and a toolbox. One set of tools enabling our learning are our senses. Information collected through experiences of play and exploration provide the building blocks in the construction of a functioning human being fit for survival. This amazing process of creation can take up to 20 years. That is roughly how long our brain grows naturally, learning by wiring experience-based information into our brain cell connections. After age 20, more brain cells die than grow naturally. But natural brain cell generation, also known as neurogenesis, never stops. It tunes down. To give you an idea of magnitude, in our mother's womb, we grow an average of 250,000 new cells per minute. In old age, neurogenesis is still at around 700 per day. The secret to maintaining our mental fitness even at old age is the effective use of newly generated cells. Use them or lose them. Through life-long learning activities, more available brain cells can be kept alive and productive by wiring them into our existing network of brain connections. In essence, learning is a core element in our survival and well-being from the cradle to the grave.

However fascinating the human learning mechanism may be, no other species on our planet takes longer to become self-sufficient: 20 years, compared to six and five years respectively for orangutans and elephants. But how is it that humans came to run such a risky reproduction scheme? The answer is that that is the way evolution solved an existential human problem.

From about six to three million years ago, our ancestors started combining apelike and humanlike movements, gradually transitioning to walking upright. The function of our pelvis changed. It increasingly adopted the role of a hinge between a heavy upper body and two legs carrying it. As a consequence, our hip shape changed for more stability, and that made childbirth more difficult. To make things worse, the human brain—for example, the prefrontal cortexes, grew in size at the same time. If the earliest humans had brains the sizes of oranges, today's human brains are more akin to cantaloupe melons. In other words, they almost tripled their dimensions. Together, the changes in hip shape and the growth of the brain intensified the difficulty and risk for mothers to give birth. The evolutionary compromise to combining upright movement and bigger brains was for humans to give birth prematurely and deal with the fit-for-life question later. From that perspective, learning is a key tool in bridging humans' twenty-year gap in achieving and sustaining self-sufficiency.

From Learning to Education

In recognition of the importance of effective learning for our survival, our ancestors developed approaches to learning, conventionally referred to as education. Combining the Latin "e" (out of, from) and "ducere" (to lead or take someone with you), education can be seen as the *leading* of offspring *out of* the womb through the acquisition of fundamental survival instruments.

Our genetic code holds an in-built construction manual preparing children for this process of learning. It is an instinct that intrinsically motivates us to figure out how things work, to solve problems, and to discover capabilities and limitations. In other words, an interest in learning is part of our human nature. A successful education system needs to nurture this intrinsic mechanism.

The Archives of Education

There are informal educational settings such as play and trial and error as well as institutionalized settings for education such as preschool, primary school, secondary school, high school, college, or university, which represent the dimensions of formal education. Some 100,000 years ago, learning was about imitation and basic oral communication. Imagine our ancestral children sitting around a campfire with adults and older children as their teachers. They were watching, imitating, playing, and pretending to be the teachers around them. The teachers were sharing observations or correcting behavior with head nods, gestures, or vocal signals. This is how ancestral children learned the physical, technical, and mental skills to ensure their own survival and, in turn, contribute to the survival of the group.

About 70,000 to 30,000 BCE, the human body underwent a genetic mutation enabling humans to communicate more effectively. By connecting a limited number of sounds to words and sentences, learning became more efficient and precise, for example through storytelling.

Literacy propelled learning. Starting in India and Egypt around 3,000 BCE, literacy soon spread to China, Greece, and Rome, with the first books written during the Roman Empire around 30 BCE. Since then, reading and writing have represented the core ingredients of any formal education system. In 1880, 90% of the world population—some 900 million people—was illiterate. Today, only 10% of people living on our planet are still illiterate. As the world population is now close to 8 billion, this equates to 800 million people. This means that despite all the innovation and economic development, the mere number of illiterate people has hardly changed over the last 150 years. It may be difficult to grasp in the developed parts of the world, but 800 million illiterate people means that there are still substantial inequalities globally with regards to literacy today. Notably, in sub-Saharan African countries such as Burkina Faso, Niger, and South Sudan, less than 30% of their population has access to humankind's most fundamental learning tool—literacy.

Education Impact

The World Bank, the WHO, and the United Nations (UN) all agree that education is key to economic development, health, and well-being. Their stance is reflected in such axioms as "Knowledge is power", "The more you know, the further you go", and "Give a person a fish and you feed the person for a day; educate to fish and you feed the person for a lifetime". The UN's sustainable development goal #4 of "quality education" states that:

> Education enables upward socioeconomic mobility and is a key to escaping poverty. Over the past decade, major progress was made towards increasing access to education and school enrollment rates at all levels, particularly for girls. Nevertheless, about 260 million children were still out of school in 2018 — nearly one-fifth of the global population in that age group. And more than half of all children and adolescents worldwide are not meeting minimum proficiency standards in reading and mathematics.

Education is an investment. Statistically, another year in school raises earnings by 10% a year—a better return on investment than most other investment opportunities today. Better education also leads to better health and well-being. People with more education live longer and healthier lives because they understand their healthcare needs better. More income means more resources to cope with health issues due to access to medical advice and medication. Higher incomes further reduce the stress that comes from social and economic hardships. Overall, education leads to higher incomes and better health and well-being for the individual. In turn, the individual is enabled to contribute more to the community. As such, education represents the backbone of any society. It is a determining factor in the survival of nations.

Much More than Maths

The way we educate our children today determines how we will live tomorrow. A student today could be your caregiver in a nursing home tomorrow. How would you like to be treated by that caregiver? Would you only be interested in the person's technical, medical, or maybe scientific skills? Or would being treated with respect, compassion, openness, warmth, and encouragement be vital for your health and well-being? Most people I have met would answer 'yes' to that last question. But if we want future adults to live by and apply these values and attitudes, they need to learn them as children in educational environments governed by the same values and attitudes.

Education is much more than acquiring competences in science, technology, engineering and maths (STEM). Skills are neither good nor bad. The person applying them turns them into one or the other. For example, let's take a scientific researcher. The person could use STEM expert knowledge to either research a new vaccine for a virus or, alternatively, develop weapons of mass destruction. This choice depends on the values and attitudes of the person.

So how can education make a difference in a person's life? At its core, it is how we make children feel. By supporting children's ABC levels, we make them feel safe, as a result of which they flourish and show their natural curiosity about everything and everyone. By creating environments that foster feelings of Autonomy, Belonging, and Competence, we boost their learning. Giving them choice, being open and warm and compassionate with them, making them feel respected, and acknowledging their individual development will energize their prefrontal cortexes. Learning thrives by providing inherent satisfaction. As a result, the three E's of success will be wired into children's brains. Learning will enhance their persistence in applying effective skills in the identification and pursuit of evident goals. Children will grow up to make meaningful contributions to their own lives as well as their communities.

But education can also do substantial developmental harm in children. When they feel overcontrolled, pressured, cornered, excluded, alienated, discouraged, degraded, and insecure, their brains will build highways of stress to their amygdalas. This would make these children much more likely to display fight-or-flight behavior in the future, leading to anti-social and self-defeating outcomes. Let's face it, the impact of education on the wiring of a child's brain represents a major factor in the behavioral pattern of the later adult. Unfortunately, the overwhelming evidence points in the direction of modern, formal education being increasingly ineffective and out of touch with our human nature—in one word, species-inappropriate.

According to recent data from the *Democratic Schools for All* study of the Council of Europe, 60% of school students report feeling stressed and pressured, and 60% of girls and 40% of boys say that they feel anxious and stressed about school testing even when they are well prepared. Back in 2008, a European Commission consensus paper called *Mental Health in Youth and Education* had already suggested that about 10-20% of school children were suffering from at least one mental health issue. A 2017 study by Germany's largest health insurer DAK analyzed data from 370,000 children between the ages of 10 and 17. They found that over 25% of these schoolchildren experienced forms of depression, anxiety, and an array of psychosomatic symptoms such as eating or sleeping disorders.

"It was higher than we expected. We know from talking to students that they are feeling tired, stressed, and bored (by school), but we were surprised by how overwhelming it was," remarked the scientist Zorana Ivcevic of the Yale School of Medicine. She and her co-author published their findings in the academic journal *Learning and Instruction* in 2020. The study surveyed over 20,000 high school students in the U.S. Across all 50 states and demographic groups, they found the same pattern. Over three-quarters of students reported negative feelings toward school.

By stressing and pressuring students and instilling negative feelings in them today, we prepare the ground for stress, pressure, negativity, and ill-being in tomorrow's communities. The problem with modern education seems to be twofold. First of all, it is rooted in *what* we teach our youngsters in combination with an equally important second problem, which is *how* we do it. Organizations such as the Council of Europe, the OECD, and UNICEF are calling for non-coercive learning environments to protect children. They know that feeling safe is crucial for the natural development of children. It is only in such environments that children will learn to habitually use their prefrontal cortexes rather than their amygdalas as drivers of their behavior. This will enable them to engage in the three E's of success and help create the conditions for societies' future economic development, health, and well-being. The field of pedagogy will help us gain some insights into how to keep children's in-built curiosity, make them feel safe, and avoid coercion in education.

From Education to Pedagogy

Education and pedagogy are often used interchangeably, but they are not the same thing. The difference between the two is like the difference between science and logic. Education is the 'where', and pedagogy the 'what' and 'how'. Education is the destination, pedagogy the path to get there. In essence, pedagogy is the act, art, practice, or method of teaching. As such, it accounts for how we make children feel in educational settings. Who is "we"? Usually, the two main pedagogic caregivers in human upbringing are parents and teachers. In this chapter I will focus on formal, institutionalized education.

When you ask students about their formal education, they will tell you how they like or dislike certain subjects. They will also tell you how they feel about their teachers supporting or scolding them and how they perceive assignments, tests, grades, competition, and facilities. This indicates that there are three pedagogical lenses through which students analyze their educational environments. The first is the content being taught; the second the configuration provided by classrooms, assignment

Pedagogical Dimension	Today	50,000 BCE
Content	Institutionally prescribed; reading, writing at elementary level; science, technology, engineering, maths at secondary level; specialization at tertiary level: **Individual, specific qualification for disciplinary task(s)**	By interest and natural circumstances; climbing trees, developing tools, carrying loads, group communication and collaboration, dealing with changing territories and dangers: **General training targeted at survival of community**
Configuration	Structured classroom, with one student per seat and desk; no eating, no drinking, no speaking; teacher-directed problems that have one solution and the instructor knows it; high-stakes testing; reward and punishment e.g. through grades, promotion, detention; conditional regard: **Individual control, selection and gatekeeping**	Campfire and nature as classrooms; open-ended, often self-selected experiments and problems including trial and error; each student a valuable member of the pack; logically rewarded and punished by life through risks, failures, and mastery of experiments; creating space for natural development: **Individual flourishing in support of sustaining community**
Climate	Hierarchical, controlled, orderly, formal, high pressure, little space for individual interest, clear separation of teachers and parents, one formal teacher: **Individual success oriented**	Open, informal, communal; teachers are mothers, fathers, older children, students themselves; following natural interests: **Community survival oriented**

types, grading, and promotion; and the third is the climate or class atmosphere created by the teacher's behavior. Allow me to take you on a tour of what modern education is offering along the three pedagogical dimensions of content, configuration, and climate.

Modern Education

Children's default setting at birth is to learn. The core ingredient of our in-built construction manual is curiosity in discovering the magic of the world around us. Healthy three-year-olds cannot wait to help their parents hoover the lounge, bake in the oven, or understand how cars work and how to drive them. They love to imitate, experiment, play, and explore. Children have an innate urge to figure out how things work, discover their own capabilities and limitations, as well as master challenges in their respective environment. Our human nature of learning to survive has not changed over the last 50,000 years. The construction manual built into our genetic code is still the same. But the way we teach has undergone a dramatic mutation.

The above table shows another great example of the mismatch between evolution and innovation. How could our nature and our education drift apart so spectacularly? And what are the implications for our children's learning, health, and well-being today?

Education 1.9

Compared to the last 50,000 years, modern education is a relatively new experiment. Its origins go back about 200 years to the beginning of the nineteenth century. It was at that time that governments in Western and Central European countries such as Prussia, France, and England introduced elementary education. The political agenda was to instill values, beliefs, and civil order in their populations by early teachings including reading, writing, and arithmetic. Russia created a state boarding school system for its children. Ivan Betskoy, the educational advisor to the Russian Tsarina Catherine II, described education's mission as a way to "create a new form of citizen, a new race of man". Over the following decades, secondary and tertiary layers were built onto the initial elementary part. Education now covered all children's developmental stages, from

5 years to over 20. I will refer to the origins of formal education at the beginning of the nineteenth century as Education 1.9.

The mindset of Education 1.9 saw schools and colleges as learning factories. Education became an institutional matter. Of course, children were able to learn to read, write, and multiply, which was a good thing. But that kind of learning is not what boys and girls are naturally interested in. And it also does not help them thrive as human beings. Instead, the political agenda of civil control determined the pedagogical dimensions of content, configuration, and climate. The curriculum dictated basic, narrow content of the three Rs of Reading, wRiting, and aRithmetic. Hierarchy, control, and highly structured environments were key features of the learning climate and configuration of Education 1.9. In a way, education was seen as a way of domesticating the unpredictable human factor in society. Pedagogy was not about children's flourishing, health, and well-being but was instead determined by the political storms surrounding education driven by ideologies, institutional interests, and conflicts.

Education 2.0

The application of Education 1.9 continued into the twentieth century. During the first half of the 1900s, politicians were busy leading their nations through two World Wars and rebuilding countries afterwards. The crowd control features of Education 1.9 served as a useful tool along the way. In parallel, the second industrialization revolution started to heavily influence the mindset of Education 1.9. Assembly lines and large industrial plants required workers to perform simple, very specific tasks all day, as per managers' instructions. The intention of nineteenth-century policymakers had been to educate children to become obedient citizens in a stable civil order. Similarly, Taylor's dehumanized view of workers in 1911 portrayed them as noiseless machine parts in efficient assembly lines. This common paradigm added an economic, industrial layer to the original political agenda of civil order under Education 1.9. Children became a human resource.

Education 2.0 turned into a training camp preparing boys and increasing numbers of girls for their lives as industrial workers. Education 1.9 provided the perfect setting for the second industrial revolution. It was only a small step for Education 2.0 to "manufacture" the human resources needed for the nation's economic and industrial development. Children were able to transition seamlessly from the learning factories to industrial factories The educational content in both settings was narrow and specific. Both climates were hierarchical and highly controlled. The configuration of structured classrooms, instructional teachers, and rewards and punishments were mirrored by highly organized assembly lines, supervising managers, and carrots and sticks. Then, midway through the century, a development in economic theory added another feature to Education 2.0: an overemphasis on individual assessment through grades and high-stakes testing.

Milton Friedman's principle of shareholder value, postulated in a *New York Times* essay in 1970, identified a company's sole responsibility as increasing its profits in order to create value for its shareholders. In his 1962 book *Capitalism and Freedom*, Friedman had already concluded that "there is one and only one social responsibility of business—to use its resources and engage in activities designed to increase its profits so long as it stays within the rules of the game, which is to say, engages in open and free competition without deception or fraud". In 1976, Friedman won the Nobel Prize in economic sciences. The so-called Friedman doctrine was widely adopted by companies over the following decades. In fact, it spurred another economic development in the 1980s and 1990s—neo-liberalism, often referred to as turbo capitalism.

A wave of privatization, deregulation, and free trade instilled a paradigm of unleashed institutional as well as individual freedom in societies. In reference to Friedman, neo-liberalism proposed that the sole social responsibility of every company and every person was to maximize its self-interest. In turn, deregulated markets freely organized the supply and demand of goods and services, and skills promised welfare for all. This development did not go unnoticed by educational policymakers and administrators.

Grades and Tests

Education 2.0 became heavily influenced by neo-liberalism at the end of the twentieth century. The educational agenda was to create a free and transparent market for educational achievements. The way to introduce neo-liberal ideas into education was by expanding the role of grading to boost competition between children. You are the architect of your own fortune. Your grade will determine your future. Your fellow-student today will be your competitor for a job tomorrow. Those were the kinds of messages that the spotlight on grading intended to convey to children. They were further emphasized by high-stakes testing (HST), in which a single or small number of exams had major consequences for students. Examples include the gaokao in China, the concours in France, and the high school or baccalaureate exit examinations in the U.S and elsewhere. The implied logic was that if you do not perform well on the test, it will negatively affect the rest of your life.

Since the beginning of the twenty-first century, the turbo capitalism saga has suffered substantial cracks. For example, a best-selling book by the French economist Thomas Piketty, *Capital in the 21st Century*, demonstrated the way capitalism drives inequality. He argues that capitalism needs state intervention for a redistribution of wealth. Unless capitalism is reformed, Piketty sees its current form leading to social unrest and a threat to Western democratic orders. If he is right, the adult products of Education 2.0 children may well destroy the very pillar that modern education was originally designed for—civil order!

This kind of scientific evidence of the downsides of capitalism has been echoed by business practice. In 2019, a group of nearly 200 CEOs of major U.S. corporations issued a statement revoking the shareholder principle. Instead, they outlined their companies' responsibilities as "investing in employees, delivering value to customers, dealing ethically with suppliers and supporting outside communities". It seems that a wind of change has been blowing through scientific labs and executive suites.

Unfortunately, it does not seem to have reached modern education yet. Two decades into the twenty-first century, Education 2.0 with its traditional content, configuration, and climate still prevails.

Education in the Twenty-First Century—The Story so Far

Democracy is the form of government in most Western countries today. At its core, it gives citizens the right to choose. For example, one way of choosing is the right to vote. Another one is the right of free speech. But democracy does not seem to have found its way into modern education yet. Why would the Education Department of the European Union Directorate General of Democracy (DGII) otherwise run a campaign on Democratic Schools for All? Under the tagline "Free to Speak —Safe to Learn", the department outlines an educational framework for all European Union member states. It reads that the DGII "sets out, for the first time, the core values, skills, attitudes and critical knowledge and understanding that every citizen needs in order to be active in a democratic society".

Germany is a great example of a lack of democratic principles in Education 2.0. Parents are legally obliged to send their children to school. If they don't, they can go to prison (and some have indeed been imprisoned). In a 2014 ruling by the German Federal Constitutional Court (Bundesverfassungericht), it was confirmed that homeschooling was illegal in Germany and a prison sentence was within the scope of possible verdicts. By the way, even under the COVID-19 lockdowns, German legislation did not change; it was only suspended until further notice. But Germany is not alone. Most democratic countries display a lack of democracy when it comes to their educational systems—maybe not as drastically as Germany, where parents can be imprisoned for failing to send their children to school, but their pedagogical paradigms certainly are far from democratic. Why is this the case? The short answer is the need for control.

There are two major factors influencing the governmental need for control in education. There is a lack of trust in children's in-built construction manual. Most policymakers and administrators do not believe in natural development. Even if they did, they would be loath to allow children to explore, experiment, play, and pursue their innate curiosity in an undirected manner. For how could natural learning ensure the two main missions of Education 2.0—civil order and the supply of skills for the nation's economic and industrial development?

If they were searching for answers to the above questions, modern education does not seem to have found any. Its foundations are still built on the three big C's: control, control, and control!

Control and Content

Content is prescribed in very detailed curricula. Narrow intellectual goals focus on what governments determine as important educational ingredients and outcomes. Teachers are under pressure to translate overloaded curricula into daily classroom activities in increasingly shorter timeframes. For example, many countries have cut school times over the last decade to provide younger talent to job markets and tertiary education. Although the curricula were revised, the quantity of the content remained the same. Teachers are being held responsible for finding ways to implement these new educational policies. A common strategy for dealing with control is passing it on to the next level. Consequently, teachers have engaged in increasing control over schoolchildren to deliver on the policies imposed upon them. Increasing control in teaching comes with many costs. Two of them are conflict and disengagement.

When children are bored by content that is outside of their scope and interest, they can express their displeasure by disturbing their environments. When bored, negative attention can be better than none at all. The continuous disruptions and interferences cause mounting conflicts between students and their teachers. Alternatively, students who see little rationale in the content being taught can become disengaged.

Between 2012 and 2015, the federal states in Germany one by one shortened their secondary education from nine to eight years. All of them kept the quantity of the content untouched. When my family and I moved from Australia to Germany in 2013, our federal state had already adopted the new policy. My daughter sat her first math exam shortly after our arrival. To solve one of the problems, she could draw on the knowledge and techniques she had learned in her math class back in Australia. She arrived at the correct answer but scored zero points for her solution. Even though she had solved the problem correctly, she had not followed the prescribed path taught by her German math teacher. In a 2012 publication, the Leibniz Institute for Educational Science in Frankfurt outlined activation, arousal, curiosity, openness, independence, and mental space as prerequisites for inspiring engaged learning in children. All of that was missing in my daughter's case. My daughter was frustrated and became disengaged and disinterested in math.

This is what happens when modern education's controlled, narrow focus on content meets children's natural, broad, creative spirit. Teachers' and children's ABC levels are adversely affected. Both feel restricted in their Autonomy. Both feel left alone, leading to a drop in their sense of Belonging. Both feel helpless, negatively impacting Competence. Low ABC levels pull the plug on teachers' and children's prefrontal cortexes, allowing their amygdalas to drive their actions. Fight-or-flight behavior on either side leads to increasing conflict or, as in my daughter's case, disengagement. Our modern education system addresses undesired behavior by tightening up control even further through pedagogical configuration.

Control and Configuration

Teachers' control extends far beyond content and prescribed problem-solving techniques. There are classroom rules for almost everything: one person per seat; no speaking; no food; no drinks; special permissions required to go to the bathroom; and sitting still for hours. While this regiment may help teachers control their classroom and related content teaching, it certainly is not species-appropriate for their students.

While teacher control over configuration may increase their Autonomy and Competence, it increases the distance between them and their students. Belonging suffers. In turn, students' ABC levels sink further. In addition to content control, schoolchildren have to cope with additional controls on when and how to sit, speak, eat, and drink.

Our nature is still determined by thousands of years of having led a nomad lifestyle—wandering through the savannah, covering large distances, and overcoming new challenges on a continuous basis. A bit more than two centuries of modern education have perverted this identity of the Homo Sapiens child. And it is having dire consequences.

Attention Deficit and Hyperactivity Disorder (ADHD) is a serious mental illness in children, adolescents, and to a lesser extent adults. The neuroscientist Lukasz Konopka explains ADHD as a brain disorder related to children's prefrontal cortexes. As two of the prefrontal cortex's core functions are controlling our attention and our movements, one can see PFC malfunction leading to a lack of executive control over one's behavior in both areas. ADHD is associated with a lack of attention, hyperactivity, and impulsivity. Children suffering from the condition have problems concentrating and cannot sit still, sustain effort, or follow instructions. They are fidgety and forgetful. They further display high levels of impulsivity by running around, climbing, talking excessively, answering without thinking, interrupting, and not waiting for one's turn. In the past, there were doubts over whether ADHD was a real affliction. But today, scientific evidence confirms ADHD as one of the most common psychiatric disorders.

There is no cure for ADHD. Treatments range from behavioral therapies to prescribed medication and often a combination of both. The prescribed medicine makes children calmer and less impulsive. Their interactions become more socially acceptable, and they can concentrate more on learning. Its side effects include decreased appetite, headaches, sleep problems, stomach aches, dizziness, and fatigue. Nora Volkow, director of the U.S. National Institute on Drug Abuse, conducted a number of neuroscientific imaging studies to better understand how ADHD medication affected the brain. When they compared the brains of kids treated for ADHD before and after a year of medication, they found that brain structures facilitating the functioning of the prefrontal cortex had changed substantially. Since the findings were revealed in 2013, researchers and clinicians have disagreed over the extent to which the detected neural changes had long-term effects on children's personalities, health, and well-being.

While scientists agree about the existence of ADHD today, there is now another area of considerable disagreement: the assessment method to be used as a basis for treatment. The scientific world still lacks a generally accepted way to diagnose the condition, which means that there is much confusion over its actual prevalence in children. Statistics show significant differences in ADHD numbers by countries as well as among socio-demographic groups. A 2010 study led by Michel Lecendreux found an ADHD rate of between 3.5% and 5.6% in close to 5,000 participants aged 6 to 12 in France. In comparison, CHADD, an organization for Children and Adults with ADHD in the U.S., estimated in 2010 that 7% of American 4- to 11-year-olds had ADHD. Six years later, the 2016 National Survey of Children's Health (NSCH) in the U.S. showed that the overall percentage of children with ADHD had substantially increased over time—rising from 6.1% in 1998 to 10.2% in 2016. Moreover, its prevalence was increasing with age: in 2016, 7.7% of those between the ages of 4 and 11, and 13.5% of those between the ages of 12 and 17 had ADHD. The incidence of the condition also differed by ethnic group: in 2016, 6.1% of Hispanics, 12.0% of Non-Hispanic White, and 12.8% of Non-Hispanic Black were diagnosed with the condition.

The discussion on what drives such significant deviations has been heated and messy. Research has indicated that two elements appear to be responsible for much of the discrepancies: the method of assessment and children's access to healthcare diagnostics. Despite the significant gaps in our knowledge of ADHD, there is one area that has remained uncontested—the difference in ADHD prevalence by gender!

According to OECD data, the ratio of boys to girls diagnosed with ADHD has been 9 to 1 in clinical studies and 4 to 1 in the general population. Disregarding the discrepancies between laboratory and field research, we can conclude that boys are much more likely to be diagnosed with ADHD than girls. According to Mark Mahone, director of the department of neuropsychology at the Kennedy Krieger Institute in Baltimore, ADHD seems to express itself differently in boys and girls. Caryn Carlson's scientific work on gender differences in ADHD at the University of Texas supports Mahone's observation. ADHD boys show much higher levels of hyperactivity and impulsivity than ADHD girls. Given the fuzzy assessment methods surrounding the condition, it is not surprising that boys are more likely to be diagnosed with ADHD than girls due to the more apparent symptomatic behavior. There is a rationale for the hypothesis that far too many boys are being treated for ADHD without actually suffering from the condition. In scientific terms, these cases are called "false positives".

Evolutionary Psychology and ADHD

Imagine the "big cat" area in a zoo somewhere. You can see lions, jaguars, leopards, or cheetahs in captivity. Some zoos will also have a black panther on show. There is a magnificent, telling poem by the German poet Rainer Maria Rilke describing a panther's caged life:

His vision, from the constantly passing bars,
has grown so weary that it cannot hold

anything else. It seems to him there are
a thousand bars; and behind the bars, no world.

As he paces in cramped circles, over and over,
the movement of his powerful soft strides
is like a ritual dance around a center
in which a mighty will stands paralyzed.

Only at times, the curtain of the pupils
lifts, quietly--. An image enters in,
rushes down through the tensed, arrested muscles,
plunges into the heart and is gone.[4]

The panther's behavior is natural. It is wandering up and down its cage due to its in-built drive to move. To my knowledge, no veterinarian at any zoo ever considered medicating a panther to prevent it from wandering about in its cage. Now let's take a look at the Homo Sapiens' classrooms, our modern education zoos.

For tens of thousands of years, ancestral females gathered berries and herbs or nursed children and the elderly. Their male counterparts carried heavy loads, built camps, and hunted dear, bear, or mammoth in groups. As a result, forager men were constantly active and alert. They ran around, climbed, and communicated with each other. If this list of behavior sounds familiar to you, then take a look at the checklist of ADHD symptoms. It is natural for boys to be active. From an evolutionary perspective, it is also natural for boys to be more active than girls. ADHD is another great example of an evolutionary mismatch. Sitting still and concentrating on hypothetical tasks for many hours a day is unnatural for children/humans. The demands of 200 years of modern education do not fit with what tens of thousands of years of evolution have prepared us for.

Evolutionary psychology contributes new perspectives on ADHD and education. It raises significant issues on diagnostics

---

4   English translation by Stephen Mitchell.

and treatment in general. There are particularly uncomfortable questions around false positives in boys—questions about health, well-being, and ethics. These issues become even more striking when we take the brain-changing impact of medication into consideration. Interest groups like the World Wildlife Fund (WWF) fight to free the wild animals being caged in zoos. Who fights for our children being caged in classrooms? Who determines the difference between active and hyperactive?

If learning is so important to the survival and future of our societies, we may want to pay more attention to a natural design of modern education rather than one based on institutional interests. The current system of control via configurations of sitting, speaking, eating, and drinking substantially constrains students' ABC levels. In turn, it pulls the plug on their prefrontal cortexes, which are crucial for persistently applying their skills to achieve meaningful learning goals.

Given the confusion around ADHD assessment standards, it is all too easy for schools to use ADHD as a control tool for classrooms. I have personally witnessed several cases in which schools pressured parents to have their children diagnosed and treated for ADHD. Some schools even blackmail parents with the threat of referring their children to special education.

I am not suggesting that this is common practice. ADHD is just one example of how modern education is trying to control self-inflicted problems. Such configuration tools are harming the natural development of children. Grading and high stakes testing is another one.

Grading

Grading has played an increasingly important role in recent years. It is so pervasive today that is has become an unquestioned feature. It is hard for us to imagine school without grades, pressure, successes, and competition. Modern education uses grading for two main reasons: feedback and selection.

On the one hand, tests should provide feedback to students on how they are doing, what to improve on, and how. It is meant to be part of a personal development plan. Unfortunately, this informational character of feedback is not how children perceive it. Instead, exam topics feel arbitrarily imposed instead of driven by natural interest. Marking is mostly mistake-oriented instead of encouraging and forward-looking. It merely lets students know how their individual development compares relative to others. The purpose of grading is skewed toward its second purpose— institutional control over selection, or gatekeeping.

Gatekeeping is an important educational function. It is a selection tool. As such, it is useful at the end of a process. Tests make sense for the licensing of physicians, plumbers, or bakers, for example, but they are less useful when it comes to continuous assessment. While they are not detrimental by definition, the way in which they are designed compromises people's interest and cognitive performance because they are socially comparative, judgmental, and stressful. From Deci's famous SOMA puzzle study and Murayama's neuroscientific inquiries, we know that the controlling features of external rewards decrease ABC levels and, in turn, activity in the prefrontal cortex. Testing may be a necessary tool for institutional control. However, the undermining effect of modern education designs corrupts its fundamental mission—learning!

To make things worse, testing not only happens at the student level. In 2000, the OECD first introduced PISA, the Programme for International Student Assessment, to evaluate educational systems worldwide by measuring 15-year-old schoolchildren's academic performance on mathematics, science, and reading. Benchmarking, another economic tool rooted in neo-liberalism, may be helpful in comparing, say, the cost structures of automotive manufacturing. But the informational benefit of PISA seems questionable. It reduces different socio-economic levels and cultures to numbers. According to the American psychologist Abraham Maslow, people have a cognitive bias that involves an over-reliance on a familiar tool. He once wrote: "If the only tool you have is a hammer, you treat everything as a nail". Applying this to PISA reduces children and modern education to statistics about maths, science, and reading. As those numbers are the only global information we have on school systems, they are being used as performance indicators for schools and teachers. PISA numbers have turned into carrot-and-stick-type control tools. Various governmental and administrative levels are using them to reward or punish schools and teachers. In turn, schools and teachers pass on the pressure they feel to students by controlling content and configuration. This mechanism has consequences for the third pedagogical C—climate.

Control and Climate

When students are forced to engage in unnatural activities that they see little meaning in, they become stressed. On top of that, teachers under pressure bring their own stresses to the classroom. It should by now be obvious to you what that mix will produce: the hijacking of the amygdala and a fight-or-flight response!

Fight

In such an explosive atmosphere, teachers exert their power to downgrade, detain, or degrade. This usually applies to younger colleagues who are still "fighting" to get it right. Or they give up, become disengaged, and wait for retirement, like many older-generation teachers. When I worked on a local school project, one of the teachers told me in an interview: "It is my birthday today. I have only 14 years to my retirement!".

A recent report from the American Federation of Teachers revealed that over half of the nation's teachers were suffering from stress-related mental health concerns. Patricia Jennings, a University of Virginia professor and founder of the *Care for Teachers* initiative, observes that teachers are emotionally exhausted from being held responsible by administrators for their students' performance. In addition, teachers felt increasingly exposed to school violence. The Sixth European Work Conditions Survey 2019 mirrored the situation of teachers in the U.S. They suffered much more often from stress, anxiety, fatigue, and sleeping disorders than any other profession.

Both the European Council data and the Yale study show that students are as stressed, anxious, fatigued, and sleep-deprived as their teachers. Some fight back through the mediums of disobedience, disorder, and disrespect. This includes physical threats and violence against teachers. In fact, The American Psychological Association (APA) reckons that almost 80% of American teachers have been a victim of physical threats or violence by students.

Flight

Alternatively, children distance themselves from school and from their teachers by disengaging, being disinterested, or deflecting. One way that students deflect are drugs, which offer them temporary escapes from toxic educational environments. According to a recent European School Survey Project on Alcohol and Other Drugs (ESPAD), on average 17% of school children between the ages of 15 and 16 had used illicit drugs such as cannabis, amphetamines, cocaine, crack, ecstasy, LSD, or other hallucinogens. And they had also used heroin at least once in their lifetime (referred to in the scientific world as lifetime prevalence). The number varies wildly between EU countries from around 2% for countries like Norway, Sweden, Greece, or Romania to 29% in the Czech Republic. By comparison, U.S. statistics suggest a lifetime prevalence of illicit drugs as high as 35% in 2019.

In a nutshell, modern education serves as a pressure cooker for school climates. Teachers and students wear each other out under the tight controls exerted by policymakers and administrators through the content and configuration they prescribe.

Too Much Control

Modern education is still stuck in the second industrial revolution. It has not advanced sufficiently to fulfill its mandate of educating children for the modern world we live in. The prevailing feature of our times is no longer algorithmic, that is, we no longer follow a set of prescribed instructions down a single pathway to one predicted conclusion. On the contrary, life has become volatile, uncertain, complex, and ambiguous (VUCA). Such a fast-changing world demands that we be free to experiment with new ideas, explore new avenues, and come up with novel solutions. These features need to be reflected in modern education systems, enabling today's children to solve the world's complex problems tomorrow.

Learning factories put rigid fences around children. Too much control is incompatible with our human nature. Throughout evolution, we have survived due to our creativity in adapting to our environment. The last 200 years of tightening control through educational reforms have increasingly distorted and degraded our creativity as humans. When putting inhumane fences around humans, they adapt by turning into other species. They either become will-less sheep or elephants trampling everything and everyone as they escape. Both are undesirable educational outcomes for human behavior in a world of mounting VUCA challenges.

Wildlife organizations fight for the conservation of our nature. That includes creating species-appropriate, natural living conditions for animals in zoos. We should be fighting for the development, health, and well-being of our children in our overstructured, unnatural educational zoos that suppress instinctive learning. After all, learning secures the conservation of the human species.

The Sciences of ABC in Education

For over 40 years now, ABC researchers have been studying the psychology of learning. They have interviewed, surveyed, and designed experiments for children, adolescents, and teachers. Data collected from elementary schools all the way through to post-graduate settings and across age groups, cultures, and socio-economic status have provided a solid foundation for empirical analysis. After four decades of scientific groundwork, the results send a clear message: ABC levels drive interest, curiosity, resilience, engagement, social development, and, in turn, academic performance. In other words, feelings of Autonomy, Belonging, and Competence are vital to learning—from the classroom to the lecture hall. And there is another conclusion: too much external control over the content, configuration, and climate of educational institutions is detrimental to learning, as it harms ABC levels in students and educators.

ABC Studies

When Ed Deci and Richard Ryan were joined by Allan Schwartz and Louise Sheinman in 1980, they did not foresee that their research would pave the way for a wave of ABC-based investigations that would refute the principal component of modern education: control! Their initial investigation into the impact of controlling versus supportive teacher behavior on ABC levels sparked substantial doubts about the efficacy of control.

At the beginning of a new school year, teachers in grades 4, 5, and 6 were contacted by the researchers to assess their teaching styles. The teachers were given scenarios of classroom challenges and asked to propose solutions. Some exhibited controlling behavior (the controlling teachers group), endorsing tools such as rewards and punishments as well as controlling language (e.g., "should", "have to", "must") or giving very specific directions and guidelines. Other teachers were more focused on supporting students (the supportive teachers group). They were oriented toward findings ways to support students by trying to understand their perspective, providing choice, and offering constructive, encouraging feedback.

The self-reported styles were collected from the teachers before they met their students for the first time. In a second step, the researchers measured students' ABC levels in the first week of school, again after two months, and finally at the end of the school year. The results revealed that the ABC levels of the students under the supportive teachers had increased after two months and the effect had lasted throughout the school year. In contrast, the behavior of controlling teachers was a downer for their students' ABC levels, both after two months and at the end of the year.

A further study by Yi-Miau Tsai and a group of researchers in 2008 revealed that much of this effect is teacher-related. They measured students' ABC levels in several subjects over a three-week period. What they found was that students' ABC levels showed extremely high variability even within a single school day. A more detailed analysis uncovered the reason. ABC levels fluctuated wildly lesson by lesson depending on the teachers' controlling or supportive behavior.

Fluffy Outcomes

There is plenty of scientific evidence based on the ABC mechanism pointing to how pedagogical support rather than control translates into interest, engagement, and effort in education. Johnmarshall Reeve is a professor with the Institute of Positive Psychology and Education at the Australian Catholic University in Sydney. He completed his postdoctoral work at the University of Rochester, where he met Deci and Ryan. Reeve's research has a particular focus on how teaching styles drive student engagement. For example, in an experiment with college students studying conversational Chinese, the students were either given a supportive rationale and choice or received controlling, directive instructions. Those students who were given rationale and choice put in considerably more effort into learning. Together with Hyungshim Jang and Ed Deci,

Reeve examined engagement in a group of 1,584 9-11 graders from 133 public high schools in the Midwest. Students who felt supported rather than controlled in their classrooms were much more engaged.

Now you may be thinking that engagement, effort, curiosity, resilience, or social development are fluffy nice-to-haves in the classroom. But do teaching styles affect academic performance?

Academic Performance

ABC levels can predict academic achievement in education. Geneviève Taylor and several research colleagues reviewed the literature in the field in 2014. Subsequently, they designed and conducted three studies of their own with high school and college students in Canada and Sweden over a one-year period. Both their review findings and their own research confirmed that ABC levels predicted academic performance. Taylor's work was extended by Purdue University's John Mark Froiland and Frank Worrell from the University of California in 2016. Their investigation into the link between ABC levels and academic achievement included 1,575 students from an ethnically and racially diverse high school. They found that ABC levels were driving GPA scores even when accounting for performance prior to their research. In other words, ABC-supportive teaching environments can boost any student's academic performance, independent of prior achievements.

This finding also applies to graduate education. Ken Sheldon is an SDT researcher at the University of Missouri. He and his fellow researcher Lawrence Krieger followed an initial group of 216 law school students over a three-year period. The final 79 participants reported a decline in ABC levels over the course of their three-year study program. Those students who had supportive instructors displayed less of a decline in their ABC levels. They also received higher grades and performed better on the bar exam.

Dropping Out, Ill-Being, and Stress

When a pedagogy based on control leads to depleting ABC reservoirs, students suffer from ABC deficiency. This can have harmful effects for them beyond decreased engagement and academic underperformance while in school. Patricia Hardré and Reeve surveyed close to 500 high school students to explore the effects of teacher behavior on students' intention to stay in school. Supportive teaching styles were associated with higher ABC levels and lower dropout intentions. Those who thought that school dropouts were mainly linked to low grades were in for a surprise. The best predictor of dropouts was not low academic performance but teaching style. Even students with high academic scores considered leaving school due to their frustration with what they saw as an over-controlled environment.

From the outset of ABC research into the educational sciences, student well-being has been studied and found to be closely related to teaching style. Reeve was joined by Ching-Mei Tseng for a clever study in 2010. By collecting salivary cortisol data from 78 undergraduate students, they wanted to uncover the biological underpinnings of student well-being under three conditions: supportive, neutral, and controlling teaching style scenarios. Given cortisol's role as an indicator of stress, the team's hypothesis was that higher levels of control would trigger students' amygdala, leading to increased stress and thus the release of cortisol.

The participants were engaged in a 20-minute puzzle-solving activity while exposed to a teacher who enacted a controlling, neutral, or supportive teaching style. Salivary cortisol was assessed before, during, and after the learning activity, and a post-experimental questionnaire assessed participants' perceptions of the teacher's style. The results confirmed the researchers' hypothesis. Students exposed to a controlling teacher had higher cortisol levels than those in the neutral scenario. The supportive teaching style was related to the lowest cortisol levels in students. So biological indicators reinforce previous psychological findings in terms of teaching style impacting student well-being.

ABC-supportive features	ABC-depleting features
– Providing rationale for topics and processes	– Monopolizing learning material and processes
– Listening to students	– Issuing directives and narrow instructions
– Making time for students' independent work	– Rewarding compliance with instructions and punishing deviations
– Giving students an opportunity to contribute	
– Acknowledging signs of improvement	– Putting students under time pressure for their work
– Encouraging students' effort	– Using controlling language such as "should" and "have to"
– Offering hints when stuck	
– Being open and responsive to students' feedback, comments and questions	– Focusing on students' mistakes and shortcomings
– Acknowledging students' experiences and perspectives	– Using directive questions to control the flow of conversations

* ABC features of content, configuration, and climate; based on Reeve and Jang (2006)

Grading

The control feature of grading has distinct negative effects on learning. A rare field study from Sweden provides some staggering insights. Alli Klapp is an associate professor of educational sciences at the University of Gothenburg. Her 2008 PhD dissertation, *Grades and grade assignment: effects of student and school characteristics,* was the start of her research journey into the world of school grading. A nagging question that her dissertation had prompted was whether grading per se had any longer-term effects on learning. In the years following her PhD, Klapp designed and implemented a study that specifically looked at how grading or not grading students in primary school affected their course grades in the middle school years 7, 8, and 9 as well as their final grade in year 12. Data collection was based on over 8,000 Swedish students. Some of them were not graded in primary school, while others attended schools using traditional grading schemes. The results were astounding. Grading in primary school had a substantial negative impact on academic achievement in grades 7-9. Students who had not been graded in their primary school years showed much better academic performance in years 7-9. Also, weaker students were less likely to graduate from secondary school if graded in primary school.

Klapp's study highlights modern education's naïve view on human functioning. The belief that grades are like money and that all you need to do is work harder to get more could not be more wrong for learning. There is no reason to subscribe to the traditional educational mantra of lower grades prompting harder work and, in turn, more learning. It is quite the opposite. There is an inherent psychological problem with the foundation of grading: testing!

As early as 1987, Richard Ryan and fellow researcher Wendy Grolnick discovered the detrimental effects of testing on learning. In a public elementary school, they randomly separated 91 fifth graders into three groups. All of them were asked to read the same textbook passage. However, each group was given a different condition. In the non-directed (ND) group, students were asked to read the passage and simply rate it for how interesting they found it. ND students were not expecting a test and therefore were under no pressure to learn or perform. The second, non-controlling-directed (NCD) group was told that it would read the text and be tested on it. But NCD students were also told that the purpose of the test was not to be graded but to help researchers understand how and what children learned from the text. The controlling-directed (CD) group received the typical instruction students get in modern education: read the text, take a test, and you will be graded on your performance! All three groups were tested, even ND group students. Here are the findings:

1. Both of the non-controlled groups (ND and NCD) reported more interest in the text than CD students.
2. Both ND and NCD students scored better on questions that assessed deep, conceptual learning.

3. Even though CD students who expected to be tested and graded did worse on deep, conceptual learning, they were quite good at memorizing material.

4. A follow-up test one week later revealed that the CD group had forgotten substantially more of the facts they had memorized than students in groups ND and NCD.

In summary, testing for grading negatively impacts deeper, conceptual learning and retention of knowledge.

The role of ABC levels in that context has been studied from multiple perspectives. Caroline Pulfrey conducted several experiments at professional schools in which she studied what happened to students when they expected to be graded. Her conclusion was that it impaired their ABC levels. We have seen how ABC deficiency leads to the amygdala hijacking the prefrontal cortex. So the fear of failure in the expected test expresses itself by amygdala-driven distorted goal setting, destructive skill application, and decreased persistence, the three D's of failure! Put simply, testing and grading compromise deeper, conceptual learning and knowledge retention through ABC deficiency.

There has been an increase in continuous testing and grading in an effort to create a quantifiable, transparent benchmarking system in education, which is a dangerous trend. A single test to certify plumbers or to issue driver's licenses fulfills a gatekeeping role that is necessary, which justifies the negative psychological consequences of testing. But there is a wealth of scientific knowledge showing that control through continuous testing impairs learning. For example, it promotes what is described as "bulimic learning", in which students get caught in an ongoing cycle of memorization and regurgitation. Permanent testing creates an environment in which students do not learn out of interest but due to perceived pressure. The challenge for them is to memorize vast amounts of information in the short term to be immediately reproduced in tests on a weekly and sometimes daily basis. Attention and understanding as a basis for knowledge retention suffer. This sounds more like the consumption of entertainment than a thoughtful process of learning. But continuous testing and grading not only sabotage learning; it also fosters other undesired outcomes.

The Belgian scientist Maarten Vansteenkiste and his research team arrived at conclusions similar to Pulfrey when they examined a participant group of 10-12th graders. Controlling goals such as expected tests and grading were associated with less interest, less initiative, and less engagement in learning as well as lower academic achievement. In addition, they found that such control features nurtured cheating.

The highlighted effects of testing are amplified when the stakes involved are high. This is true for students sitting potentially life-changing exams as well as teachers and institutions being assessed and benchmarked by programs such as the Programme for International Student Assessment (PISA) or Trends in Mathematics and Science Study (TIMMS). In all cases, policymakers believe that increased control through what they advocate as "increased accountability" for students, teachers, and institutions will lead to better education. Instead, as ABC research would predict, tightening control has resulted in a variety of detrimental outcomes at all three levels. The final report issued by a U.S. National Academies task force concluded that high stakes testing (HST) did not provide an adequate assessment of student learning, encouraged teachers to focus narrowly on the material expected to be tested, and had essentially no positive effects on academic achievement. The task force moreover detected additional undesired outcomes of HST such as higher student dropout rates and increased cheating, this time at the levels of districts and schools. Some students were even excluded from test taking, as they were expected to lower the school scores. Student answers were changed and false performance data reported. School administrators tightened their control over teachers, holding them accountable for student results. Increased control of teachers translated into teachers being more controlling with their students, a domino effect with negative consequences for all.

Teachers

When you ask policymakers or school principals, they will both tell you that their key focus is students' development and well-being. If that were true, they would care much more about the development and well-being of their teachers. As the successful British entrepreneur Richard Branson once said: "Clients do not come first. Employees come first. If you take care of the employees, they will take care of the clients." There is ample scientific evidence that the same applies to the field of education.

In a groundbreaking study, a research team led by Guy Roth and Avi Assor looked into the interplay between teachers' ABC levels and students' ABC levels. The participants were 132 teachers from elementary schools and 62 classes with 1,255 students from grades 3-6. Questionnaires were used to assess teachers' and students' levels of ABC, well-being, and engagement. What researchers found provided scientific validation of Branson's business philosophy for the educational sciences. Higher levels of teacher ABC were associated with higher well-being in teachers and less controlling teaching styles. On the flipside, students of teachers with high ABC levels and lower control behavior displayed higher ABC levels, higher well-being, and engagement in learning. The resounding message of Roth and Assor's work to modern education's control culture was that students do not come first; *teachers* come first. If you take care of the teachers, they will take care of the students!

When education turns up the heat on teachers, administrators are responsible for causing two negative effects. First, teachers become more instructive, use more directive language, talk more, give students less time to solve problems independently, and provide solutions instead. In turn, students show less interest and engagement, causing their learning and performance to suffer. These effects were shown in an experiment led by Deci, Nancy Spiegel, Ryan, Richard Koestner, and Manette Kauffman in 1982. Second, teachers' well-being suffers. The increasing accountability pressure sparks a vicious downward spiral, running teachers' health into the ground. Pressure from above leads to teachers behaving in a more controlling way. Students respond with disruption, disengagement, and underperformance. This creates pressure from below. Suddenly, teachers find themselves in a pressure sandwich, further depleting their levels of ABC. A number of recent research studies by such scientists as Claude Fernet and Kimberly Bartholomew have looked into this sandwich effect. Across the board, data showed that the combination of pressure from above and below squeezes teachers into burnout.

Burnout statistics around the world show that teacher burnout has been among the highest across all industries and continues to rise. Eight percent of teachers in the U.S., 7% in Australia, 5% in Canada, and 5% Germany have been diagnosed with the condition in recent years. Experts believe the actual numbers could be more than double the official rates when accounting for undetected cases. Prevalence is substantially lower in countries such as Finland and Singapore, however, where the rate is about 3%.

Beyond low burnout rates, Finland and Singapore have consistently been at the top of academic performance league tables. Even though there may be material differences in the content, configuration, and climate of the education systems in the two countries, they have one important thing in common: they have identified teachers as key to future societal development and well-being. As such, teachers are treated as professionals, receiving high salaries and high quality training. Finish and Singaporean teachers are some of the best and brightest people in their countries. They are entrusted with their nation's future. There is no culture of artificial administrative control over children's and adolescents' natural learning process. The results are better health among the teachers and better learning experiences for students through greater well-being and superior academic performance.

Training

What Finland and Singapore have been practicing for many years finds strong grounding in the ABC sciences. The ABC framework can be trained. Administrators can be enabled to foster ABC among their teachers. In the same way, teachers can learn how to emphasize ABC support and avoid ABC downers in their interaction with students.

Reeve and a group of ABC scientists wanted to find out how ABC training for teachers would translate into classroom processes and whether that translation had any material effects on student behavior. Over a ten-week period, the researchers followed 20 high school teachers. Ten of them received ABC-based training, while the other ten did not. The results showed that the trained teachers were substantially more ABC-supportive than their untrained colleagues. As we might anticipate, students in the classes of ABC-trained teachers were substantially more engaged in their learning than the students of teachers who were not ABC-trained. A follow-up experimental study led by Jemma Edmunds from the health and life sciences department at Coventry University measured the ABC levels of students taught by both ABC-trained teachers and teachers who were not ABC-trained. The findings confirmed Edmunds' hypothesis: teachers can learn ABC support, which increases the actual ABC levels of their students.

Reeve teamed up with Patricia Hardré from the University of Oklahoma to investigate this phenomenon in supervisor (e.g. school administration) versus subordinate (e.g. teacher) settings and found the same effects as in teacher versus student relationships. ABC-trained supervisors displayed more ABC-supportive behavior, leading to increased work engagement and higher ABC levels in their subordinates.

The Neuroscientific Perspective

Since the turn of the century, neuroscientific research using imaging technology has been able to shed light on the neurochemical and biological processes shaping the relationship between ABC levels and learning outcomes.

The nucleaus accumbens (NAc) is a region in our human brain. It plays a crucial role for learning. What neuroscientists discovered is that the NAc serves as a kind of pleasure center. If we experience something positive, dopamine is released into the NAc, making us feel good. The details of this process are still subject to further research by experimental studies. Scientists such as Alberto del Arco and Francisco Mora from the department of physiology at the Complutense University in Madrid have been exploring the specific role of dopamine in prompting changes to our brain structures (neuroplasticity).

Based on what science has found so far, our prefrontal cortex regulates the activity of the pleasure center and specifically the release of dopamine in the NAc. As we saw in Chapter 3, ABC levels energize the prefrontal cortex to apply our skills persistently and effectively in order to achieve meaningful goals. Roy Wise from the U.S. National Institute on Drug Abuse points out how dopamine in the brain drives goal-directed behavior, including learning. The more a behavior is perceived as pleasurable, the more it gets wired into your brain as a habit. Similarly, if we develop an aversion to something, our brain gets wired to avoid it. In essence, we can become addicted to negative things (like drugs) or positive things (such as learning). And the fact is that humans are born with an in-built addiction to learning, which is part of our survival mechanism. But over-control in education is an important factor in the process of turning an eager, curious, engaged, social, exploring, 3-year-old into a disinterested, disengaged, and anti-social 16-year-old. A lack of ABC affirmation and the excessively controlled content, configuration, and climate in our education systems deflates the prefrontal cortex, which is then hijacked by the amygdala. This causes stress and the release of cortisol in the body instead of dopamine in the NAc. Learning is not perceived as pleasure but as pain. The resulting message wired into the brain is to avoid learning as much as possible through fight-or-flight behavior. Over time, the adorable, pleasant toddler turns into a disheartened, avoidant, delinquent child and adolescent.

The Road Ahead

Modern education has had a 200-year journey. But it is still the same old story. Its pedagogy serves the main purpose of supporting our political and economic systems through control over narrowly defined content, strict configuration, and a toxic climate. There is overwhelming scientific evidence that modern education's system-focused mission of self-preservation through policymaking and administration is ineffective for learning and detrimental to the well-being of both students and teachers.

Education 1.9 was invented to systematically discipline citizens. The transition from Education 1.9 to Education 2.0 in the twentieth century was nothing more than the addition of an economic twist instead of a progressive upgrade. Education 2.0 maintained its focus on what the system needed. The needs of the people have yet to play a role.

What we need today, more than ever, is a forward-looking upgrade of our education to address the challenges of the twenty-first century. The widening gap between who we humans are and how we learn needs to be acknowledged. A revision will require a paradigm shift in focus from the system to the individual. Rethinking modern education would address the following types of questions:

- How can we move from controlling to ABC-supportive pedagogy?
- How can we create the conditions for children to flourish, engage, self-reflect, and innovate?
- What does it take to develop children's life competences and well-being?
- What do we expect the challenges of humankind to be tomorrow so that we can enable our children today to deal with them in the future?
- How can we support, empower, and encourage children to energize their prefrontal cortexes into persistently applying relevant skills in the pursuit of meaningful goals toward creating success for themselves and their communities?

Creating species-appropriate learning environments for our children is neither goodwill nor a fluffy nice-to-have. It is a fundamental, urgent need-to-have. We need to educate our children to the best of our knowledge to help us solve future problems. November 1963 marked the beginning of a new era in the creation of knowledge in education. Oak Elementary School's principal Lenore Jacobsons' letter to Harvard professor Robert Rosenthal and their subsequent discovery of the Pygmalion effect sparked revolutionary work in the educational sciences. Since then, a series of groundbreaking scientific studies have consistently shown that students' learning and well-being is closely related to the quality of social-emotional interactions in classrooms. The science of ABC has contributed several thousand research pieces to the education puzzle. They add up to a clear picture. Teaching styles and materials inspiring Autonomy, Belonging, and Competence in students drives both their academic and social development. Conversely, systematic control over school content, configuration, and climate kills feelings of ABC in people, for example through the undermining effect. Therefore, it is ineffective and harmful.

Almost 50 years have passed since the Rosenthal studies. We are over two decades into the twenty-first century, and yet children and students are still confronted with Education 2.0. What is preventing the conversion of this overwhelming, evidence-based knowledge on best educational practices into Education 2.1?

When Robert Rosenthal published the results of his first studies into the drivers of the Pygmalion effect in 1973, it was the year that Konrad Lorenz won the Nobel prize in physiology. Lorenz has been credited as saying that "at the beginning of a new idea, firstly it is completely ignored, then fiercely attacked and finally, everyone generally accepts it as having been valid right from the start". Harry Harlow's controversial experimental results with primates in the late 1940s are a prime example of this. His findings were ignored by the established scientific community at the time, just as Edward Deci's work was in the early 1970s.

Today, the science of ABC has earned its stripes of credibility with close to 50,000 academic publications. Its findings can be likened to the challenge that Pythagoras, Plato, and Aristotle posed to the notion that the earth was flat, an idea that took over 2,000 years to move from individual ideation to general acceptance. The scientific works of Rosenthal, Harlow, Deci, and the many thousands of ABC researchers out there have been as powerful a rebuttal to ongoing educational practices as the ancient Greek scholars' models were to the flat earth myth. So far, over 50 years of scientific evidence have passed without any noticeable adjustments to modern education. In a recent article on flat earth conspirators, it was suggested that the easiest way to convince them of the sphere model was to have them travel on the same degree of latitude around the globe so that they would arrive at their original starting point. But if policymakers and administrators were invited on an all-expenses-paid trip around the world of education, would that be enough to convince them to adapt modern education to scientifically sound and generally accepted best practices?

The Way Forward

Evolutionary processes take time. The journey of the ABC from a niche idea in the 1970s to mainstream science is a good example. There was a tipping point around the turn of the millennium when the number of scientific studies and publications started increasing rapidly. At present, promoting ABC ideas in modern education still feels like an uphill struggle. Seeds need to be planted, educator by educator! These seeds will grow. Similar to the ABC itself, modern education will reach a tipping point. Education 2.1 will blossom. And at some point in the twenty-first century, everyone will pretend that s/he had recognized the need for an ABC-based paradigm shift in modern education right from its beginnings in the 1970s.

Part III

10. Give and Take

Take what you need and give what you can.

– George Whitman

Evolutionary biologist Mark Pagel has a powerful way of portraying the mechanism that propelled Homo Sapiens to the top of our planet's food chain. In a TED talk, he argued:

> [E]ach of us possesses the most powerful, dangerous and subversive trait that natural selection has ever devised. It is a piece of neural-audio technology for rewiring other people's minds. I am talking about our language. It allows us to implant a thought from our mind directly into someone else's mind and they can do the same with us, without either of us having to perform surgery.

The ABC is the language of human nature. When speaking English, French, Spanish, or Chinese to a person, you speak to the person's head. Addressing a person's ABC means speaking to the person's heart. As individuals, we are meaningless beings on this planet. Collectively, we rule the world through our communication by sending and receiving—that is, sharing information amongst ourselves. The interpretation of this information creates the feelings that drive our behavior. Addressing people's feelings of Autonomy, Belonging, and Competence through communication is the most effective way of energizing their minds and prefrontal cortexes for effective collaboration. This will lead them to engage in the three E's of success. They will create success for themselves and for those around them by persistently applying effective skills in the pursuit of evident goals. In essence, success is a function of people "ABC-ing" each other. Consequently, your proficiency in giving and taking ABC is the foundation of your own success.

Stephen Henderson, the VP at the investment bank I worked for (from Chapter 1), was a great example of the "give and take" mechanism. His communication style of asking for help, time, and expertise as well as giving options boosted my own and my colleagues' ABC. In return, we supported Stephen's ABC with all our resources by giving him the level of control he needed over the process, making him feel part of our team, and allowing him to look competent in front of his superiors. As a result, success was all around us. Stephen rose to the top of the bank. On his way up, he would not get tired of emphasizing how much of his success was related to the great work of the amazing team around him. This message spread internally and throughout the industry. It created a reputation that fueled success for each of us in our individual careers.

Managing ABC levels in yourself and others is a skill that can be learned, like a muscle that can be trained. But where should you start? Should you look after your own ABC levels or take care of other people's ABC first?

The Priority of Taking

American civil rights activist Audre Lorde had a crystal-clear response to this question. According to her, "self-care is not self-indulgence but self-preservation". What can you do with your smartphone when it is out of power? You simply make sure it does not happen. You always carry a charger around with you, and you pay special attention to where a power plug can be located. You would not let your phone's battery run empty, so why would you let this happen to you? How do you maintain a level of energy at which you can properly function? Where are your personal fuel stations? Self-care should be a priority for each of us. Without energy, none of us will be able to contribute in meaningful, positive ways to our own life, let alone the lives of others.

When was the last time you boarded a plane and one of the flight attendants introduced you to the in-flight safety measures?

I have been on countless flights around the world. However remote the location, safety instructions have been more or less standardized around the globe. After a while, you become numb listening to them, as they are being read to you from a little booklet. But in the context of give and take, it is worth paying attention to a specific section of the instructions:

> In case of a loss in cabin pressure, oxygen masks automatically fall from the panel above you. Pull one of the masks toward you and place it firmly over your mouth and nose. *Secure your own mask before assisting others around you.*

What may come across as unethical and egotistical at first actually makes perfect sense when you think it through. If you concentrate on others first, you will run out of oxygen, rendering you unable to help others. How many people will you be able to assist before losing consciousness? On the other hand, if you are up and running, you can help many more people around you who have become dizzy, disoriented, or unconscious.

The first ABC project you should be working on is *you*. Caring for your own ABC levels will generate the energy to power your own success formula. Then, in turn, you will be able to contribute your energy to the creation of success for those around you.

ABC Diagnostics

After deciding to embark on a journey of becoming an ABC practitioner, there are two fundamental diagnostic questions you need to reflect on before implementation. In reference to the formula *Information + Interpretation = Feelings*, you need to ask yourself what you 'interpret' as Autonomy, Belonging, and Competence.

Question 1: What constitutes Autonomy, Belonging, and Competence for you?

In a second step, you need to explore what 'information' inspires your interpretation of Autonomy, Belonging, and Competence as you travel through your daily life.

Question 2: What are the boosters and killers of your Autonomy, Belonging, and Competence in your present life?

I have had extensive, astonishing experiences in asking these questions in my research, teachings, seminars, workshops, and coaching sessions over the last decade. In response, legions of students, business executives, and clients have shared the foundations of their ABCs with me. Let me introduce you to some of the common denominators as well as fancy outliers of their individual reflections.

Autonomy

What do people interpret as Autonomy? The word "freedom" is frequently used to express what autonomy means for them. When drilling down to the key ingredients of freedom, people regularly refer to having options, a choice, or discretion over when, where, and how they do things. Referring to our busy everyday lives, some also point out the freedom of not having to do anything at all. An area that has often been mentioned in the context of autonomy is the field of creativity, ideation, and innovation. When people feel that they have the freedom to come up with novel solutions or contribute new points of view, they have feelings of Autonomy.

What information (circumstances) boost or kill Autonomy in people? Autonomy boosters are life circumstances that give people the freedoms that constitute Autonomy for them. For one of my participants, getting up in the early morning, standing on the balcony, smelling the scent of a cup of coffee in hand, and overlooking the river in front of the house fueled feelings of Autonomy and energized the person for the day ahead. The recent COVID-19 pandemic has forced the business community to rethink how their employees collaborate. The resulting home office policies have been mentioned to me as key factors in increasing employees' feelings of Autonomy when working. Myself, I get a lot of Autonomy out of my running routine. On every run, I can choose the direction, pace, length, and time of my run and change each of them anytime along the way. In one seminar, a person commented on how much Autonomy s/he felt by taking out the garbage. Residing in a multi-apartment complex, s/he got an Autonomy kick out of being able to choose which of the many bins to throw the garbage in.

Traffic jams are omnipresent Autonomy killers. For example, being stuck in traffic on a highway with no way to exit is a draining experience for many people, as it constrains their freedom to move. At work, employees' feelings of Autonomy can be killed by overcontrol, micro-management, and narrow rules, regulations, and guidelines with no bigger picture provided. Another factor that can lead to depleted levels of Autonomy is a lack of resources, for example, limited human resources to implement a business project or a shortfall in financial resources to fulfill personal dreams. One of my clients did not want to leave the house during the day because a very talkative neighbor always involved her in endless conversations and would not let go. Each exchange was a major Autonomy killer for my client who, in her own words, felt "mentally raped" by the neighbor.

Belonging

What do people interpret as Belonging? The feelings most often mentioned to me when elaborating on experiences of Belonging have been "supported", "accepted", or "respected". Given our evolutionary group survival mechanism, it is not surprising that most people refer to these feelings in a group context. Some oft-repeated phrases included: "I trusted my team", "I relied on the support of the others", and "I felt as a recognized part of something much bigger than myself". That is what they feel when they belong.

What information (circumstances) boost/kill Belonging in people? In 2013, I explored the building blocks of Belonging, together with my colleague Geoff Lovell, as part of an international research project. Based on a series of 32 interviews, four core ingredients of Belonging experiences were identified: (1) common concern, that is, pursuing common goals and caring for each other; (2) joint activity, meaning group as well as one-on-one interaction toward a common goal; (3) continuity, highlighting the regular nature of the interaction; and finally (4) time—the hours, days, weeks, months, or years people have known and interacted with each other.

Some examples of settings in which people feel they belong are political parties, biker gangs, or sports team fan clubs. High levels of Belonging energize behavior toward common goals. Belonging boosters such as support, trust, and respect provide the energy for sports teams to win, for churches to survive, and for consumers to buy. Remember the Johnny Walker TV commercial conveying the message that if you buy a bottle, you will have a friend boosting your Belonging?

One of my workshop participants shared with me how much Belonging he got out of his Second Life avatar. Social media have been playing an increasing role in human interactions. To what extent virtual or augmented realities can and will represent equivalents or even replace actual face-to-face interaction remains unknown. How many virtual friends does it take to produce the same level of Belonging as a face-to-face friend?

Second Life is a multi-player online virtual world launched by the San Francisco-based firm Linden Lab in 2003. It mirrors features of real life, and the so-called Residents can customize their avatars to explore the virtual world, interact with other residents, socialize, engage in individual and group activities, and develop, create, and trade virtual property, goods, and services with each other. Second Life has its own virtual currency, the Linden Dollar, which is convertible into real life currency.

One of the participants in my workshop, Brian, told me how much social rejection and exclusion he experienced in his real world environment. He was fired from his position in banking six months prior to the workshop. When that happened, he felt disrespected by his family, let down by his friends, and cold-shouldered by his former colleagues—all of which killed his sense of Belonging. From his point of view, Second Life gave him a second chance and the Belonging he was craving for in real life. As a result, he spent almost all his life, apart from sleep, in the virtual world.

Brian's case is a good example of what kills Belonging in people. I guess most of us can recall a situation in school when two team captains were picked by the gym teacher to select their team members one by one for a game of basketball or a relay race. Who is left at the end of the draw? No captain wants to have the short fat guy or girl on the team. What s/he feels like is the ultimate Belonging killer of social exclusion and rejection. Any form of discrimination—be it race, gender, age, or social class—kills our sense of Belonging. This also applies to excluding citizens who are not vaccinated against COVID from societal activities as well as non-transparent management withholding critical information from company employees.

Finally, the punishment of solitary confinement in prisons shows how significant Belonging is for our human nature. No human being should have to escape into a second virtual life as a result of the hardships that social exclusion and rejections are causing in the real world.

Competence

What do people interpret as Competence? In my interactions with participants, they experienced Competence when they felt they "can contribute", "can overcome challenges", "develop, learn and grow a set of skills". Any form of mastery conveying feelings of "I can do it" was interpreted as Competence.

What information (circumstances) boost/kill Competence in people?

Situational factors that contribute to people's feelings of Competence include when people are "given responsibility", "reaching goals", "learning", "encouraged", "asked for help", "listened to", and "allowed to fail and try again".

A good example of a Competence booster is winning a game in sports. When I interviewed a professional soccer player as part of a research project, he pointed out that "nothing energizes more than winning a match. It boosts your confidence and competence". I had similar comments from business professionals. Their wins involve making the numbers or being promoted. When I consulted with a large German insurance company, one of their salespeople pointed out to me how important the leaderboard in the reception area was to him. Every morning he entered the building, he could see the ranking of his sales numbers compared to his internal competition. "Looking at the leaderboard gives me an extra boost when I come to work in the morning. It transparently shows my competence in contributing to the company".

Helping family and friends is another form of boosting Competence. I imagine we all know a plumber, a carpenter, or an electrician in our social network who helps out family and friends after working hours or on weekends. When I asked my friend Peter why he was spending so much of his leisure time helping people tiling, he said: "I cannot say no to people who ask me for help. It makes me feel so good being able to contribute my tiling skills to making people's kitchens or bathrooms look nice."

Healthcare professionals carry substantial responsibilities for people's lives. Caring for people's health may be the most fundamental form of experiencing Competence in the context of the human survival mechanism. Patients' lives depend on the individual's mastery of the relevant skills. Saving lives can substantially boost your feelings of Competence. But healthcare professionals are also ranked at the top in terms of burnout rates. The human body is complex, and however competent you may feel, at times caretakers can feel overwhelmed and think that they can no longer cope with it.

Feeling overwhelmed and failing are two features of circumstances that kill Competence. When employees are asked to perform too many tasks in too short a period of time, they can feel incompetent. When threatened and downgraded by superiors, Competence can be killed for the long term. In the business world, a lack of opportunities for development and growth can also deplete employees' Competence reservoirs. For example, a middle manager of a European airline company commented to me: "I have been doing this job for 7 years now. There is nothing new for me. I have not had any additional training, education or coaching. I am being reduced to this monotonous job description. I feel incompetent to do anything else. Maybe I need to change jobs."

Fear of failure is another killer of Competence that often surfaces in professional sports. In penalty shootouts in hockey or soccer, the shooter's fear of failure significantly reduces the chances of scoring a goal. Reflecting on the incompetence of not scoring drains the player's energy available to performing the necessary skills to convert. Fulham manager Felix Magath was a great example of how a coach can kill players' feelings of Competence by amplifying their fear of failure through punishment. Magath's behavior conveyed the message of total incompetence to players. They felt like losers and, therefore, lost game after game.

Measuring ABC Levels

Putting a number on outcomes goes way beyond the domain of sports. In fact, most modern successes are expressed and monitored in numbers. The scores, points, and wins in sports are the equivalent of the number of customers, sales, and profits in business, the square meters tiled, and the purchase price of a car in private life. Numbers have become an important tool for modern humans to monitor their progress as a form of success.

SDT researchers have designed a portfolio of measurement tools to diagnose people's ABC levels. Similar to a blood test checking your liver values, blood sugar, or levels of minerals and vitamins in your body, there are tests to measure the level of your mental vitamins. Thanks to science, psychological tests are far less physically intrusive than blood checks.

For example, to measure the level of Autonomy, Belonging, and Competence in a person, SDT research has developed an inventory of measurement tools. Here are some sample questions:

On a scale of 1 (not true at all) to 5 (completely true), please indicate the degree to which the following statement is true for you:

Autonomy question:

I am free to decide for myself how to live my life. 1 2 3 4 5

Belonging question:

I really like the people I interact with. 1 2 3 4 5

Competence question:

I feel capable at what I do. 1 2 3 4 5

Over the last decade, the tools have been adapted to various life domains. That means there are measurement tools available now to specifically measure people's ABC levels at work, at school, in sports, or in the family. These tools are available in most of the common languages.

One question I often receive on ABC measurement is how reliable test results are. Anchored in the physical world, people have doubts that circling a number for mental vitamins in a survey is the same as the detection of the number of red blood cells in a blood sample. And they have a point. In fact, questionnaires can be diluted, for example, by social bias, attitudes, and mood.

Social bias means that people's responses to a question may be influenced by their social context. In that case, a person would not circle the number that applies to how s/he really feels about the people s/he interacts with. Instead, the answer will be based on what s/he thinks the people around her expect her to answer. Attitude is another potential factor in distorting results. For example, optimists tend to score higher than pessimists. The information they receive (the survey question) through their five senses is interpreted in a more positive way, leading to better feelings (higher scores), which in turn lead to higher recorded levels of ABC.

Finally, there is mood. What you will find is that your ABC scores will probably be higher on the day you receive a bonus or a promotion compared to the day your grandmother died.

There are ways to remedy these shortcomings. In scientific studies, these factors become less impactful if you increase the number of participants. You can imagine that if you have several hundred people filling out the surveys, the influence of individual participants suffering from high versus low social bias, positive versus negative attitudes, and good versus bad moods on results is statistically removed.

The benefit of large numbers of participants does not help you when you want to use survey questions to determine your own ABC levels. But time is on your side. What science has found is that people's ABC scores are very stable over time. This means that you can remove the impact of your social bias, attitudes, and mood factors by creating your own statistics. Take the test questions multiple times a day, a week, or a month. In doing so, you can monitor your ABC levels, including the fluctuations and the outliers. Also, you can detect progressive changes in your 'before and after' feelings of Autonomy, Belonging, and Competence when engaging in an ABC-related redesign of your life.

(Re)Designing Your Life

The above sections should have given you some idea of what other people may interpret as Autonomy, Belonging, and Competence

ABC-Diagnostics Matrix	Autonomy	Belonging	Competence
Question 1: **What does it mean for you?**	What does Autonomy mean for you?	What does Belonging mean for you?	What does Competence mean for you?
Question 2a: **What are the top 3 boosters in your life?**	What are the top 3 boosters of Autonomy across your family, social, and work life?	What are the top 3 boosters of Belonging across your family, social, and work life?	What are the top 3 boosters of Competence across your family, social, and work life?
Question 2b: **What are the top 3 killers in your life?**	What are the top 3 killers of Autonomy across your family, social, and work life?	What are the top 3 killers of Belonging across your family, social, and work life?	What are the top 3 killers of Competence across your family, social, and work life?

and what circumstances trigger information that boost or kill A, B, or C respectively. Now it is up you to answer the two diagnostic questions for your own life.

The ABC Diagnostics Matrix below provides a navigation tool for becoming an ABC practitioner. How do you energize yourself to persistently apply effective skills in the pursuit of evident goals? Once you understand what you interpret as Autonomy, Belonging, and Competence in your life, the matrix will help you to identify episodes that either boosted or killed parts or all of your A, B, and C. For example, if appreciation is important for your feeling of Belonging, a pat on the back at work after accomplishing a task may be like a rocket booster for you. On the other hand, not being given any recognition for the same accomplishment could be interpreted as a lack of appreciation and would have the effect of depleting your reservoir of Belonging.

Life domains are interconnected. Experiences of ABC in your family life, your social life, and your work life contribute to the respective reservoirs of Autonomy, Belonging, and Competence, all feeding your overall level of energy to power your individual success formula. You can design your life to optimize your energy level. There are five distinct redesign strategies in your life:

1. Eliminate ABC killers from your life.
2. Diminish the effect of existing ABC killers.
3. Add ABC boosters to your life.
4. Increase the effect of existing ABC boosters.
5. Avoid new ABC killers.

Negativity is part of our human nature. We are all descendants of pessimists who, whenever in doubt, avoided danger rather than aimed for the sky. That is why most of the people I have worked with found it easier to think of negative ABC experiences in their life domains. As a result, redesigning their lives by identifying strategies to eliminate or diminish the effect of ABC killers was their first step in managing their ABC. But what if strategies (1) and (2) cannot be applied in your life? Imagine that you have parents or siblings who kill your ABC at home, or your boss at work is an ABC downer but you can't quit immediately because you desperately need the money. Under such circumstances, you need to turn to strategies (3) and (4), relying on existing ABC boosters or adding new ones to your life. Having a network of ABC 'fuel stations' is a key component of a successful life design. It serves as an insurance policy against sudden ABC killer events such as the death of a close friend or relative. In addition, it helps you to cope with long-term ABC drainage before a solution—such as a new job—has been found. Reflect on what fuel stations you have in your life. Where do you or could you turn to for ABC support?

The cross-subsidization of ABC across life domains is an important feature of ABC management. ABC issues do not necessarily need to be resolved in the same life domain they occur. For example, sports is a common source of ABC from the domain of social life for many people. It can support people's Autonomy by giving them control over their physical activities, Belonging by performing the sport as part of a group, and Competence by conveying a sense of accomplishment. Sports could be considered an all-purpose cure for ABC deficiency. I have seen it help many people compensate for ABC drainage from other life domains such as work.

The more proficient you become in the implementation of Autonomy, Belonging, and Competence as an ABC practitioner, the more you will be able to use the ABC as a prevention tool to avoid creating new ABC-killing circumstances in your life. This is strategy (5). One of the pitfalls of the VUCA world is that it is challenging to assess the impact of your daily decisions on your ABC due to information overflow. The ABC provides a useful tool to scan, arrange, and make sense of your feelings on a regular basis. That way, you can react to new people and circumstances that are likely to negatively impact your ABC and your corresponding energy reservoir. You often do not recognize ABC killers immediately, but you feel them. Learn to listen to your feelings and then use the ABC to analyze them. If your ABC alarm bells are triggered by your diagnostics, you may want to avoid or quit the potential relationship or situation—not because your feelings tell you that something is hard or difficult, but because your subjective interpretation tells you that it could be harmful to your ABC and consequently negatively impact your entire life's energy management.

Life design is a core capability each modern human should have. By applying the ABC of life to yourself, you become the director of your own life's movie. Instead of feeling victimized by circumstances, the ABC will energize you. In turn, this energy will help you create success for yourself and for those around you.

The Art of Giving

There is no objective reality. In fact, there are as many worlds as there are people on our planet. Each of us interprets a piece of information differently, resulting in different feelings. Therefore, giving ABC to other people can be tricky. Even with our best intentions, we can end up harming others' ABC. What may constitute a warm shower of ABC boosting for one person could have the ABC-killing power of an earthquake for another. Or, as the English philosopher and writer Alan Watts put it: "Let me save you from drowning, said the monkey, and guided the fish safely up the tree!". His conclusion from that anecdote: "The road to hell is paved with good intentions!" So however well-intended your way of helping others may be, never assume that other people feel ABC the way you do. Each of us has a very unique version of the ABC Diagnostics Matrix.

An exercise I run with participants to raise their awareness of this point is the 'My ABC is Not Your ABC' activity. Each participant writes their response to Question 1 of the ABC Diagnostics Matrix on three post-its for what A, B, and C mean for them. As a second step, the participants are asked to stick their post-its to a wall under the respective headings of Autonomy, Belonging, and Competence. Assuming we have 20 participants in the room, this will result in 60 post-its of meanings for each of the three feelings. The 'landing' of the exercise is to gather the group in front of the wall of post-its and ask them for their feedback on what they see.

There are always some overlaps among the post-its. For instance, quite a number of them include the word 'creativity' in the Autonomy section. The same applies to 'part of a group' for Belonging and 'accomplishment' for Competence. This is what I would describe as a kind of standard set of responses in Western culture. However, the value of the exercise lies in the non-standard, outlier post-its. For example, participants may be surprised to find the word 'safety' under Autonomy, 'faith' in the Belonging section, or 'self-acceptance' as an expression of Competence. At this point, participants are often flabbergasted when they realize that what constitutes ABC for others may be very different from their own meanings. We all live in our own ABC worlds. In order to give ABC to others, we need to explore and understand their world. The best way to do that is to ask and listen.

If you bluntly ask family members, friends, or work colleagues what Autonomy, Belonging, or Competence mean for them, you will probably overwhelm them or at least receive a few raised eyebrows. A more subtle technique is to listen to their life stories and ask questions about how they felt and why. By listening carefully and asking a few clarifying questions, two to three life stories will be sufficient to get a first handle on a person's ABC meanings. As you begin to understand a person's interpretation of ABC, you can provide them with information that boost their feelings of Autonomy, Belonging, and Competence.

You can ask a person to come up with a new solution to address 'creativity' or you can signal tolerance and patience to give them "flexibility" in the case of boosting their Autonomy. To increase Belonging, you may want to include people in a discussion to make them feel "part of a group" or to let them know your respect for their "faith". To promote feelings of Competence, you could highlight an individual "accomplishment" or recognize the person's self-reflective skills of realizing "self-acceptance".

Perhaps coming up with customized strategies to address individual ABCs is too challenging when you are at the beginning of an ABC practitioner's journey. In that case, there are some standard strategies of giving ABC that work for most people most of the time.

Standard Strategies for Giving

Providing options to people boosts their feelings of Autonomy. Choices energize people. When Stephen Henderson asked us if we could help him on his presentations, each of us had the actual choice to say no without further repercussions. If you want to give people Autonomy, give them options in terms of how, what, or when. Ask your children whether they would rather do the dishes or vacuum the living room when helping with housekeeping; eat broccoli or cauliflower at lunch; go to bed at 8pm tonight and 9pm tomorrow or the other way around. Give your work colleagues the choice of organizing themselves in terms of holiday schedules, finding potential solutions for cost-cutting measures, or selecting between two presentation formats and deadlines.

One word of caution on giving people choices: it takes energy to make decisions. The more options a person is presented with, the more energy it takes to evaluate them and come to a decision. That is why you should not overwhelm people with too many options, as that will cost them more energy than the choices will provide. Two to three options usually hit the sweet spot.

Support is the magic word for inspiring feelings of Belonging. When people feel supported, they flourish. At its very core, support means being interested in the other person, understanding problems and challenges, and offering physical and emotional help. If you want to boost people's Belonging, get to know their children's names, their family situations, or some health challenges they shared with you. Show a continuous interest in them. Are their parents still alive? How are they coping with age? Are they still looking after themselves? People who feel a sense of Belonging in their neighborhoods support each other with their individual skill sets. In my street, we have a carpenter, a roofer, a plumber, and an architect as well as their respective extended professional networks. We all help each other out on our individual home projects. Needless to say, my usual role among all the experts is that of a general assistant carrying stuff from one location to another, maybe gardening, and sometimes negotiating with suppliers of material.

Most people believe it is easy to make others feel competent. They think that by telling them how good, proficient, or sophisticated they are, others will receive a Competence boost. This is not necessarily the case. The devil is in the detail of the communication. Praise is not the same thing as encouraging feelings of Competence. I remember when Jan Frodeno won his first Ironman World Championship in Hawaii, he was asked by a journalist about his future goals: "You have won everything in your sport, Olympic gold medal, Half-Ironman and Ironman world championship. You are the best swimmer, the best cyclist and the best runner in the sport. What are your goals?" The question itself almost puts a ceiling on Frodeno's future career, suggesting that this is it. How can it get any better? Praise puts pressure on people. Your presentation, your school grades, or the meal you cooked were so good. Will you ever be able to achieve the same level again or even better? And what if you don't? Praise can diminish feelings of Competence. Energy is spent on coping with fear of failure instead of focusing on success.

The alternative to praise is encouragement. When people feel encouraged, they see a path of growth and development in front of them. In that case, Competence is not conditional upon overcoming a certain hurdle. Instead, the encouragement message is that your Competence is a part of you. Pinpointing another person's built-in Competence as an ingredient of future successes energizes that person to grow and develop. For example, you could say "This is a good presentation, it looks like you've been developing your skillset in that area", "I really enjoyed your meal again, just like the other times you have been cooking for me", or "It seems like you have been building up your learning skills" to convey that they are on a positive trajectory of realizing their upside potential through continuous improvement.

Frodeno could not have cared less about the journalist's implied ceiling for his career development. Since then, he has won the Ironman Triathlon World Championship three times and improved the Ironman distance world record twice. His motto: "I have been made of all the days you did not see, not the ones you did!"

While options, support, and encouragement respectively provide a high likelihood of inspiring Autonomy, Belonging, and Competence in people, there is another way of creating ABC-boosting circumstances. It could be flagged as the bull's-eye strategy for giving ABC, as it addresses all three mental vitamins at the same time.

Over the last decade, bookstores have seen a remarkable influx of literature on the power of questions as a means to success in life. There are now books on how questions can enable teachers, parents, lovers, therapists, and coaches to better help and support their students, children, relationships, clients, and athletes respectively. The books may be quite different in terms of their content or the life domains they cover. But there is a common thread. A simple question such as "How do you feel about that?" can fuel people's Autonomy by giving them the option to answer. It can also support their sense of Belonging by showing you have an interest in their views and boost their Competence by conveying that they have something to contribute. To conclude, questions are the most powerful standard technique for ABC giving.

When Helping Helps

Benefiting others can take many shapes and forms. Philanthropy, volunteering, or donating blood are just a few examples of activities that protect or enhance other people's well-being. Helping others is more prevalent in our society than you may think. For example, recent statistics suggest that over the last decade, around 26% of Americans and 23% of Europeans have engaged in some kind of volunteering work each year.

Social science research has identified a variety of helper motives. Some people donate money to universities to put their names on lecture halls or libraries. Others contribute cakes to the fundraising activities of a local club because their neighbors do. For Mother Teresa, "a life not lived for others is not a life". Up until 2010, one of the intriguing but unanswered questions in the science of helping was to what extent the motives of helping impacted the experiences of helpers and recipients. SDT founder Richard Ryan and his colleague Netta Weinstein set out to address this question in four pioneering ABC studies.

The researchers used a diary methodology as well as experimental designs to collect data on the dynamics of motives and results. As part of their data collection, they also measured the ABC levels of the helpers and the recipients. All four studies pointed in the same direction: helping increases the ABC levels of the recipient. In turn, it also boosts the helper's ABC if the act of helping is volitional—that is, congruent with one's own self. In contrast, if the helper had external motives, incentives, or rewards for helping—such as fame, career advancement, or competing with colleagues or neighbors—it triggered an undermining effect with no positive impact on helpers' ABC levels. In summary, giving ABC to others boosts the giver's ABC if the act of giving was self-determined and not based on external motives.

The Pitfalls of Giving

Giving ABC can have its pitfalls. The better you get to know a person, the better your understanding will be of what s/he interprets as ABC. But you can never be certain. Therefore, it is important to build a rapport with people on whether your impact on their ABC is what you think it is. Maybe you have been misreading the information they gave you. Or perhaps they felt you did not really mean it when you tried to give them options, support, or encouragement. One way you might fail to connect with people's ABC is by asking questions in the wrong way. For example, your questions may be phrased ineffectively. Questions like "Why did you come home so late last night?" or "Why did you fail to deliver the desired results?" create an atmosphere of fear and pressure, triggering someone's amygdala into fight-or-flight mode. Or you may be failing to listen, for example, because you are looking at your smartphone. Basically, ABC boosting through questions has two components: asking and listening. So if you really mean it, you need to actively listen to a person after asking. Examples of better questions could be "Is everything okay, as you seem to have come home pretty late last night?" or "It seems you did not make it on the delivery. Is there anything we can help you with?". In terms of listening, asking questions of clarification and paraphrasing people's responses to the original question suggest to the ABC recipient that you are tuned into the communication and really mean it.

Manipulation

I have been regularly asked about the potential abuse of the ABC as a tool for manipulation. Humans are very innovative in developing new tools to get what they want, where and when they want it. And like any tool, some humans use tools to gain control over and harm other humans. No doubt, you can apply communication techniques to steer people's behavior in certain directions. For example, given that it draws on people's basic needs and feelings, the ABC is a great tool for "nudging". Nudge theory is a concept in behavioral economics and politics concerning how people can be influenced indirectly ("nudged') to do the right thing. Instead of legislation or enforcement, nudging is designed to motivate people to behave in certain ways, for what economists and politicians consider to be their own good: wearing masks, getting vaccinated, setting up private retirement plans, reducing their CO_2 emissions. But this is not the same as manipulation. Manipulation is when people abuse the ABC for their own self-interest at the expense of others.

Faking ABC-giving can be costly to both the giver and the recipient. Pretending consumes a lot of energy. Givers manipulating people's ABC for their own self-interest do not benefit from the "helping helps" dynamic. Taking advantage of others in the pursuit of selfish goals triggers an undermining effect, depleting the faker's own ABC reservoirs. The sustainability of such behavior depends on the individual manipulator. Psychologically healthy fakers who are aware of and take responsibility for their actions may find it difficult to sustain any kind of intentional manipulation of one or several people around them. They may run into an energy deficit problem of integrating the aspects of faking with their conscience. On the other hand, psychopaths and sociopaths will not suffer from ABC drainage from their faking due to their impaired empathy and remorse. Consequently, they will be able to sustain ABC faking on a continuous basis.

When people become aware of being manipulated by fakers, it will not only destroy that specific relationship; it is likely to have wider implications for the person's trust in others. Some people are scarred for life from such experiences and find it difficult to connect with others. As relationships and interactions build the foundation of ABC generation, victims of ABC fakers can suffer from long-term ABC deficiency, resulting in health issues such as burnout.

Marcus Aurelius once rightly said: "Life is neither good or evil, but only a place for good or evil". We could sum up the challenge of manipulations by deducing that the ABC of life is an effective tool for boosting feelings in people. It is at the discretion of the individual to apply it for doing good or evil.

Implementing Change and Changing Perspective

It is never too late to create success in your life. The US cosmetics entrepreneur Estée Lauder gave the following advice: "Never dream of success, work for it". But what may sound obvious is easier said than done. "People want to change the world, but not themselves," wrote the Russian writer Leo Tolstoy. In fact, very few people have achieved success in their lives by focusing on others. How rational is it to expect different results when you keep doing the same thing over and over again, waiting for circumstances to change? If you want to have something you do not have yet, is it not more effective to change something and do something that you have not done yet?

What do all the ingredients of your success formula—that is, your goals, skills, and persistence—have in common? You! So you are the single most important factor in your success equation. You can try to change the world around you. You can try to ask people, beg them, manipulate them, threaten them, even put a gun to their head. If they do not follow your instructions, you may even pull the trigger and they will still not do it. Alfred Adler, the founder of Adlerian psychology, contends: "There is almost nothing in life you can change, except for yourself. But if you change yourself, almost everything changes around you". Take

Mother Teresa, Steve Jobs, Mahatma Ghandi, Albert Einstein, or Nelson Mandela. They all changed the world by being the change themselves. None of them went out and tried to force people to change. Instead, their own different behavior inspired change in others. So if you want to create success for yourself, have the courage to change yourself. "If the music changes, so does the dance" goes an African proverb. Change your music to the sound of an ABC practitioner to create success for yourself and those around you.

Becoming an ABC Practitioner

Changing your perspective from the outside to the inside can be daunting. Suddenly, you can no longer delegate the responsibility for your life circumstances to others. You are no longer the victim. Now you are in charge. When embarking on your adventure, make sure you develop the three essentials of personal change that will help you along the way: commitment, companion, and composure.

Commitment

Every day I talk to people who tell me that they should move jobs, get divorced, eat healthier, or do more exercise. Every time I meet them, they complain about the same life circumstances without actually having done anything. If you want to change, you first need to make a commitment at the beginning of your journey and stick to it along the way. Turn from a Wanna Doer or Gonna Doer into a Doer. Put your commitments down in writing. Be specific so that you can evaluate and celebrate success. For example, commit to walking three times a week for 30 minutes at a heart rate of 130 for the next six weeks, and keep on documenting it.

Your written commitment and subsequent documentation will give meaning to your journey. And as we have seen in Chapter 3, when we find something meaningful, it fuels our ABC levels, providing more energy than we put in.

Doing requires energy. Oftentimes, I meet people who are so deflated that making a commitment to initiate change is impossible. They have designed their lives in ways that their ABC levels are barely sufficient to keep their heads above water.

Life is a sequence of decisions. This very minute, each of us is at a point in our lives that is the direct result of all the decisions we took. Any future point in your life will be the direct result of your future decisions. Therefore, be aware of the potential implications of your decisions on your future ABC. Most importantly, make a commitment to making sure you create the conditions in your life so that your energy reservoir never runs empty. You need to invest energy in interactions to generate surplus energy out of them. If you do not have any energy left to spend, you need the goodwill and the free giving of others to get you up and running again. Do not end up in that situation!

People who find themselves with their backs against the wall need an initial injection of energy before starting over. In some situations, even medication may be necessary to boost a person's energy level in the short run. However, pills should never be a long-term solution to energy problems. As the ABC journey is taking effect, the pills should be phased out accordingly. An alternative way of kickstarting and maintaining high levels of ABC is finding one or more companions for your journey.

Companion

Change is never linear. Change has its ups and downs. Diagnose your ABC levels before changing. Make potential adjustments to your life design by adding fuel stations and cutting, pausing, or tuning down the most draining relationships before you start. You need to make sure that you have sufficient energy to create the ups and overcome the downs during your journey.

Identifying a companion for personal change can be a powerful source of energy. The person could be a life coach, a mentor, or a close friend. The most important selection criterion for a companion should be trust. There are two dimensions to trust. The first and most obvious one is that you need to trust the person in terms of confidentiality. But secondly, you need to have trust in the person to be able to fuel your ABC levels. For example, when you are down, the wrong companion can kill even more of your ABC out of sympathy. S/he may agree with you on how hopeless and devastating the situation is and put your commitment to change at risk. An effective companion is someone who can light a candle for you even in the darkest of times. S/he may boost your ABC by helping you develop options, by providing support and encouragement, or simply by standing by you.

When I committed to switching my career from being a finance professional to becoming an organizational psychologist, I could not have done it without my companion Geoff Lovell. From the outset of my PhD journey, adjusting from the world of business to academic life had been challenging. A prime example of that was my writing style. Early on, my PhD supervisors asked me to summarize the findings of my literature review in short paragraphs to prepare myself for writing my thesis and future publications. After more than 16 years in investment banking, my writing had become liberal, engaging, and appealing, while academic writing was more on the precise and formal side. Six months into my PhD, I had reached a point where I felt I was never going to make it. My supervisors told me that I was not making any real progress in my writing style or in my adjustment from the world of business to academia. I was about to give up when Geoff came into my life.

I met him during a session in which PhD students present their findings. As I said before, you do not recognize ABC people, you feel them. When I met with Geoff after my presentation, he boosted my Autonomy (by giving me ideas on how to develop my academic writing), my Belonging (by inviting me to consult with him at any time), and my Competence (by suggesting that I seemed to have made quite some progress on my conversion from a businessperson to an academic). A couple of weeks later, I asked Geoff to become my companion—in academic terms, my primary supervisor—on my PhD journey. Fortunately, he agreed. It is very unlikely that I would have completed my PhD without Geoff as my ABC fuel station.

Composure

Life is a marathon and not a sprint. Personal change takes time. Lasting change means wiring the ABC into your brain connections. As mentioned in Chapter 3, the process of neuroplasticity allows for your brain to be rewired throughout your lifespan. You can make a commitment to quit a bad habit such as smoking or adopt a new habit such as starting each day with a short meditation. According to a 2009 study published in the *European Journal of Social Psychology*, it takes between 18 and 254 days for a person to form a new habit. The research also found that it takes on average 66 days to automate new behavior. "Automate" means that the new brain connection is so strong that a person engages in the new behavior automatically (such as not smoking, or meditating).

The large variation in days can be attributed to the habit in question and the person. In general, we can say that changing habits requires composure to go through the many loops of trial and error. American singer and songwriter Portia Nelson wrote the poem "Autobiography in Five Short Chapters", which has become one of the most popular guides for implementing personal change:

Chapter I
I walk down the street.
There is a deep hole in the sidewalk.
I fall in.
I am lost ... I am helpless.
It isn't my fault.
It takes me forever to find a way out.

Chapter II
I walk down the same street.
There is a deep hole in the sidewalk.
I pretend I don't see it.
I fall in again.
I can't believe I am in the same place.
But it isn't my fault.
It still takes a long time to get out.

Chapter III
I walk down the same street.
There is a deep hole in the sidewalk.
I see it is there.
I still fall in ... it's a habit.
My eyes are open.
I know where I am.
It is *my* fault.
I get out immediately.

Chapter IV
I walk down the same street.
There is a deep hole in the sidewalk.
I walk around it.

Chapter V
I walk down another street.

The key take-aways from Nelson's poem are that personal change happens in small steps and takes time. Both require a person's composure to succeed.

If you want to develop the new habit of applying the ABC in your life, moving forward in small steps could mean starting with one mental vitamin at a time. For example, you could start with an initial four-week program by focusing on Autonomy in Week 1, Belonging in Week 2, and Competence in Week 3. Keep a diary each evening on your daily life experiences to monitor progress.

Take Week 4 to review and reconcile before making more specific plans for another four-week cycle. In Week 5, you may want to focus on what factors in your workplace constrain your feelings of Autonomy and develop ideas on potential solutions. In Week 6, the topic could be to further explore your sense of Belonging to your family, partner, children, or parents and explore how you could upgrade it. In Week 7, a focus on Competence may lead you to identify new ideas for physical exercise. Week 8 would be another week of reconciliation and review to draw conclusions and make plans for another cycle.

Let's be clear. You will fall into many holes in your sidewalk journey, again and again. Failure will be part of rewiring your brain for the ABC of life. Never take failure personally. Falling into that hole again is not you;—it is an event on your journey to success. The diary will be a powerful, energizing companion. When you become frustrated and demoralized, the diary will show you your self from yesterday, last week, or last month. It will create transparency on your progress and successes. By flipping back a couple of pages in your diary, you will realize that you have moved on from Chapter I.

The Australian marketing professional Katie from Chapter 2 successfully followed the above approach to lose weight and fulfill her dream of a new lifestyle. Inspired by the TV program Biggest Loser Australia, she made a commitment to lose weight so that she could be like, look like, and feel like the sexy Emma Duncan who had won the show in 2011. Her commitment was strengthened by signing up for a weight loss program in her local club. There, she found a companion in her personal trainer who was creative, supportive, and encouraging—in other words, boosting her ABC. Katie kept her composure. After an initial 15 weeks of losing 52 kilos, she lost another 56 kilos in the following six months. You can see how the first 15 weeks (or 105 days) rewired her brain for "weight loss" success (Katie: "It was very hard in the beginning"). After that, the new behavior was automated and she continued losing weight almost effortlessly (Katie: "At some point, it all felt downhill. Nutrition, exercise, special bootcamp sessions, it was all up to me...it pulled me into a new lifestyle").

Conclusion

As modern humans, we need to reconnect with our human nature. The ABC of life is a powerful tool for enabling individuals, teams, communities, and society to embark on that journey. Giving and taking ABC empowers you to create success for yourself and those around you. Success can mean different things to different people. At its core, it is about persistently applying effective skills in the pursuit of specific, evident goals. The ABC of life is a tool for humankind to ensure its sustainable future as a species. Do not wait for others to use it. Be a Doer!

Part IV

Epilogue: The ABC of Our Future

*We often forget that we are nature. Nature is not something separate
from us. So when we say that we have lost our connection to nature,
we've lost our connection to ourselves.*

– Andy Goldsworthy

No other species on this planet has had more influence on its habitat than modern humans. Some authors have even suggested that in recent centuries, Homo Sapiens has turned into Homo Deus. Our dominance over the planet seems to have reached god-like levels. In reference to geologic times such as the Pleistocene or the Holocene, the term Anthropocene has been coined to describe the overwhelming impact of Anthropos (the Greek word for human) on the world we live in. But what have we used our outstanding role for? On aggregate, we may be healthier, better educated, and—some may argue—better looking. At the same time, we are responsible for the mass extinction of species, environmental pollution, and climate change eroding the very foundations of our survival. In essence, we have used our dominance to trample on everything around us, in turn creating the very conditions for the demise of the human race itself. In the distant future, intelligent living beings on planet Earth may refer to the end of the Anthropocene as the time when Homo Sapiens committed mass suicide. We may take a lot of pride in modern human achievements and the innovations attesting to our superiority. But according to contemporary knowledge, no other form of life in the history of our planet has ever been so self-destructive. In retrospect, the universe may consider humans a sort of cosmic joke. Maybe we have become too smart for our own good. Similar to Icarus who tried to escape from Crete, it seems humans have been trying to escape their humanity. Our innovation and creativity may have promoted a human misconception of having achieved a god-like nature. Icarus fell from the sky and drowned when he came too close to the sun and his wings melted. At this point in time, it looks like the human race will be the cause of its own downfall by continuing to behave like gods instead of realizing that we are part of the nature we have been destroying. Being better-looking in fancy suits and dresses is not going to save us.

The "rule of three" teaches pupils that humans can only survive for three minutes without air, three days without water, and three weeks without food. Our continued misbehavior has increasingly caused the erosion of these three life essentials. You simply cannot have infinite growth on a finite planet. But these are only the most overt symptoms of a more fundamental issue. As humans, we have lost our connection to ourselves. We have lost our grounding. Centuries of so-called progress have increasingly opened up a gap between who we are and what we do. What has certainly progressed is the crippling of three other basic human needs, namely the life essentials of Autonomy, Belonging, and Competence.

For example, modern historians have highlighted the agricultural, industrial, and information revolutions as evidence of Homo Sapiens' superiority. Instead, when taking a closer look, these developments have flipsides that shattered the very foundations of human survival by propelling the undermining of the ABC of life.

Agricultural Revolution

By settling down during the agricultural revolution, humans compromised their Autonomy as they remained rooted in a single location, voluntarily surrendering to a lack of mobility, mono-nutrition, and no escape from adverse weather conditions. Belonging suffered, as farmers started fencing in their properties and becoming more possessive, individualistic, and self-focused. By concentrating on agricultural techniques, their portfolio of skills was reduced to a narrow and limited range of competences.

Industrial Revolution

Factories with more and more sophisticated assembly lines reduced humans to silent and efficient resources in a process of mass production. There was little or no Autonomy in monotonous job environments. Increasing competition between companies and factories and between individuals for jobs drove people apart and killed further layers of Belonging. Factory workers' competence was reduced to a very specific algorithmic task to be performed over and over again. The task had little or no value outside the factories.

Information Revolution

The advent of the information age promised to lead humanity into a land of milk and honey, for example through globalization. Anything, anywhere, anytime was the mantra of endless opportunities. But smartphones, virtual conferences, and information overflow have negatively impacted our Autonomy, Belonging, and Competence. The technology has come to control us. For example, being reachable on our phones for anything, anywhere, at any time of the day kills our Autonomy. Virtual relationships—conferences, communities, or games—fall short of delivering the same kind of trust and amount of energy as face-to-face interactions. This impairs the human sense of Belonging. And finally, constant information overflow and technological disruptions overwhelm our human brains, leading to feelings of helplessness and inadequacy instead of competence.

The Money Revolution

There is another revolution that has catalyzed the erosion of Homo Sapiens' levels of ABC: the invention of money! Much has been written about the history and origins of money. Its ultimate purpose was to use it as a means to facilitate the exchange of goods and services. Money is a very human concept. At one point, people agreed that a piece of paper or a metal coin would be worth something, for example a bag of walnuts. No squirrel would ever trade a bag of walnuts for a metal coin. Humans do. Money is a narrative created by humans.

In recent centuries, this narrative of money has undergone a remarkable metamorphosis. Money has turned from being a *means to an end*, that is the facilitation of trading, into *an end in itself.* It has become the greatest show on earth! Today, making money is a profession. People making lots of money are considered high achievers. Money is considered the mother of motivators for directing human behavior. Money means power. It entertains us on Saturday night gaming shows. At the same time, money can decide whether there is peace or war, life or death. Even though you cannot eat, drink, or breathe money, modern humans have agreed to its role as Homo Sapiens' primary survival mechanism.

The focus on money for the sake of it has accelerated over the last two centuries. When considering the historical trajectory from Adam Smith's groundbreaking eighteenth-century writings on capitalism to Milton Friedman's shareholder value principle in the 1970s, the pursuit of money has become increasingly myopic and ruthless. For example, Smith at least saw the long-term preservation of workers' health as a factor in maximizing profits. But business executives following the Friedman doctrine solely aim to deliver short-term returns for shareholders, percent for percent, at any cost. Workers' health, the extinction of our species, environmental pollution, or climate change have all not played a role in the money world.

Let's use the analogy of a car to put this in perspective. A car needs fuel to go somewhere. In the same way, money fuels a market for exchanging goods and services. The purpose of the car is to get you to a destination. If I proposed to you that the purpose of the car was to produce fuel, you would call me crazy, and rightly so! But that is exactly the trap that modern humans have set for themselves. If we replace the car with markets and the fuel with money, we have subscribed to the insane idea that the purpose of the car is to produce fuel, that is, the purpose of markets is to produce money instead of trading and delivering goods and services. Money has become the destination.

We can add another layer to this thought experiment. Today's cars have two main control mechanisms for drivers: the dashboard and the navigation. The main parameter on dashboards is speed. Navigation provides directions. Speed facilitates the journey, just like money facilitates markets for goods and services. If we substitute goods and services for money as the purpose of the journey, it is like driving a car for speed but without direction. Given the increasing focus on money over the last two centuries, we have been travelling at an increasing speed without knowing where we are going. Recent science seems to indicate that we are all passengers on the same car called planet Earth, heading for a cliff at increasing speed.

Our thought experiment prompts two key questions. How can such obviously irrational behavior be explained? And is there anything we can do to slow the car and change direction?

Psychological Consequences

Remember Kathleen Vohs from chapter 8. She was the brilliant scientist who first investigated the psychological consequences of money in her experiments in 2005. Since then, there has been a stream of scientific studies exploring various aspects of the psychology of money. For example, in a smart study, Paul Piff from the University of California at Berkely investigated the behavior of individuals from a higher social class in 2012. Alain Cohn from the University of Chicago examined dishonesty in banking in 2014. A number of books have also contributed intriguing perspectives to the discussion, including Adrian Furnham and Michael Argyle's *The Psychology of Money* in 2013 and Morgan Housal's recent publication with the same title. They all cover facets of how money drives human behavior. Putting the pieces of a comprehensive review of literature together, the psychology of money provides a clear and alarming picture: our focus on money has been killing us!

The money mantra has eroded our human nature. Its aura promises independence. No more joint problem-solving with other human beings—with money, we can decide single-handedly. No more lengthy negotiations and dissatisfying compromises with fellow humans—money buys us whatever we want, whenever we want it. The research on money conducted by social scientists agrees that it triggers a change in people's thinking, feeling, and acting patterns from "we" to "me and my money". Money replaces other humans as our survival mechanism. Not only do we become more self-focused and remove ourselves from others; we actively wreck social relationships with our anti-social behavior. We think, feel, and act as if we no longer need human ABC. Why bother? We have money! It is much easier to go and buy episodic experiences of Autonomy, Belonging, and Competence on the planet's physical or virtual highstreets. Heels, handbags, headphones, or holidays have become fun substitutes for burdensome, onerous human connections. But the more independent, self-sufficient, and egocentric people become, the shallower their relationship portfolios become. Over time, we have increasingly replaced the natural, sustainable ABC supply of human connections with the artificial, episodic ABC shots of consumption.

Our dependency on money has further escalated our focus on it. The tool originally designed to facilitate human interactions in exchanging life's necessities has turned into a Big Brother determining every aspect of our lives. It kills our natural Autonomy, as money has come to control our everyday actions. Just look at the crucial impact of capital markets on our everyday lives. Our natural Belonging has deteriorated due to the limited quantity and quality of our social interactions. Instead of feeling connected to our local community, we buy artificial Belonging to global brands or celebrities and spend our life on (anti-)social media. And we lose actual Competences. You can pay for services like food supply, plumbing, gardening, or car maintenance, allowing you not to develop the competences yourself. At its peak, human skill portfolios are reduced to the competence of making money.

Unfortunately, the focus on money does not produce the desired effects. Money conveys only a mirage of independence. Instead, we have become more dependent than ever before. Our key problem is that the nature of money is a far riskier companion to rely on than the nature of humans. Money is fugitive, erratic, and does not care. And as social beings, people understand that deep inside themselves. But we are silencing our inner voices by telling ourselves that it is okay, as everybody around us is acting in the same way. We are caught in a vicious circle. Further pursuit of the mirage of independence will only magnify our dependence on money. There will never be enough money in the world to buy sufficient artificial ABC to satisfy our social nature's need for natural, human ABC. This has massive consequences for our behavior.

Resulting Behavior

We have seen how the pursuit of independence leads to an over-reliance on money and a depletion of natural ABC levels. This has a negative double-whammy effect on human behavior. First of all, it triggers the amygdala on a continuous basis for fear of losing the only thing we base our survival on—money! Second, ABC deficiency decreases the energy available to the prefrontal cortex for controlling the amygdala. In summary, the money mantra simultaneously fuels activation of the amygdala and decreases activation of the prefrontal cortex that is keeping the amygdala in check. Given their respective vital functions, the focus on money increases the frequency and extent of irrational fight-or-flight behavior and decreases rational thinking, feeling, and acting. Expressed through the lens of the goals, skills, and persistence success formula, money causes Homo Sapiens to suffer from the three D's of failure. Human goals have become distorted; people apply their skills in destructive ways; and we suffer from a degradation of our persistence.

What that means in practice has been explored by social scientists, for example in the labs led by Roy Baumeister. What they found in their studies on ABC deficiency is a surprisingly accurate description of modern human behavior that has caused humanity's current challenges. In addition to self-focus and anti-social behavior, they discovered in a series of spectacular lab experiments that people's focus on short-term profits far outweighed their concern for long-term consequences. Mass extinctions, environmental pollution, and climate change have been the direct results of Homo Sapiens subscribing to the paradigm of short-term profit maximization at any cost. In addition, the researchers identified another feature of ABC deficiency: overconfidence! When people are low on Autonomy, Belonging, or Competence, their judgment is impaired. As a result, they tend to overplay their hand by taking on risks and developing visions far beyond their capabilities and resources. This sounds strikingly similar to Icarus' downfall.

Let's get real. Homo Deus does not exist. Modern humans' belief in their god-like nature is as much a mirage as the independence promised by money. We are intelligent, creative, tenacious, fallible beings whose survival depends on other humans. But humankind has created an endgame scenario for itself by disregarding the social foundations of its nature, the ABC of life. This has led to a fatal combination of self-interest, a short-term focus on money, and overconfidence. We have to slow down and change direction; set in motion a U-turn back to the future of human survival on this planet. Continuing on our current path means speeding over the cliff ahead of us. So the ultimate question out there is whether the transition from Homo Sapiens to Homo Extinctus can be slowed or stopped, and if so, how?

Do We Need another Revolution?

Have you ever tried to make a U-turn on the highway when going at 100 miles per hour? Probably not, since if you had, you would not be reading these lines. A hefty change in direction at high speed is not a smart thing do. Massive centrifugal forces will spin your car out of control. The subsequent accident is highly likely to have fatal effects. In terms of results, both the erosion of life's essentials and forcing a U-turn of societal misconduct at high speed will be equally suicidal for Homo Sapiens.

Many commentators, scientists, and self-proclaimed experts have promoted the idea of a full and immediate turnaround in terms of how we live together. They insist that after the agricultural, industrial, information, and money revolutions, a sustainability revolution will be needed to save us from our own extinction. There can be no doubt about the fact that humankind needs to change direction to survive. But advertising such change as another "revolution" will not help the mission.

New Communication

Let's come back to Mark Pagel, the professor of evolutionary biology from chapter 10. His quote pointed out, that each human being possesses the most powerful and contagious tool that evolution has ever produced. Through our communication we can wire other people's brains, spread messages, and ignite movements for better and for worse. Through effective conversations, we build connections that allow us to collaborate in complex ways that no other species can. More effective methods of communication enabled Homo Sapiens to prevail over other human species such as Homo Erectus and the Neanderthals and to cement our dominion over the planet. But communication is precisely what has anchored the money narrative in our brains, causing the life-threatening scenario we find ourselves in. The money revolution was created by human communication. This means that it can be changed. Our words can create, change, and destroy worlds. Therefore, we may want to choose our words carefully due to its potential effects. Let's use the power of our communication to generate a new message that will rewire our brains for securing a sustainable future for humankind on this planet.

You cannot solve problems with the same type of communication that created them. Most eras that transformed societies have been labeled as revolutions. The term originates from politics and is associated with sudden and violent upheavals in political systems. What revolutions have in common is an element of what the Austrian political economist Joseph Schumpeter called "creative destruction". Examples include the American Revolution aiming for independence from the British Crown at the end of the eighteenth century or the Russian Revolution that led to the overthrow of the Tsarist regime in 1917. Neither the agricultural, industrial, information, or money revolutions qualify as sudden and violent upheavals or creative destruction. They were, instead, social transformations that took decades and even centuries to unfold. Revolution was simply the term that historians inappropriately gave in hindsight to label these eras in human development.

We are in a different situation today. We are not observing the fish tank from the outside as historians do. We are right in the middle of it. The challenges of mass extinction, environmental pollution, and climate change are ongoing. Designing a new message around disaster, disruption, and revolution is as unsustainable as our current misbehavior on this planet. Such terms are useful in creating short-term awareness and making people more attentive. From a longer-term perspective, such a communication style will trigger societal amygdalas, causing more and more fight-or-flight behavior such as resentment, resistance, paralysis, and ignorance. What we need to get wired into people's minds is an appealing positive vision including action items to achieve it instead of banning or forbidding certain behavior in an attempt to avoid the apocalypse. Diminishing the gap between what we do and who we are cannot be accomplished via a U-turn at full speed. An alternative approach of small but quick and agile steps will lead to both a reduction in the speed at which we are progressing toward the cliff and gradual adjustments to redirect us from our current path. There is no point in throwing the baby out with the bathwater. Capitalism has served us well, for example, as a basis for democracy and for improving our health and education systems. Destroying capitalism is not a prerequisite for a prudent paradigm shift. Let's keep what has worked for us and only fix what is broken. We do not need another episode of Schumpeter's creative destruction. What we need is a gradual transformation back to our nature—a natural evolution, not a revolution. Such a natural evolution requires a new narrative that shifts people's thinking from self-interested, short-term, and overconfident behavior to shared, long-term, and humble action.

New Approaches

Scientific laws are models based on repeated experiments and observations that describe and predict natural phenomena. There is one distinct factor that differentiates the natural sciences from the social sciences. For example, Newton's laws describe and predict the motion of objects and the forces acting upon them. There is no interaction between the physical phenomena and the models illustrating them. The relationship of velocity, mass, momentum, and acceleration has not changed since its formulation. The same is true for gravity, relativity, thermodynamics, electromagnetism, photonics, and quantum mechanics. Whatever the model or formula, it has no impact on the underlying physical phenomena. This is different for the social sciences.

The social sciences study human phenomena. In anthropology, economics, politics, or psychology, research tries to identify patterns of individual and collective human behavior. The models used include culture, supply and demand, social welfare, and personality. The fascinating feature of social frameworks is that they not only describe human behavior; they can also influence the very object they are describing.

A good example is the supply and demand model in economics. On the one hand, it demonstrates the relationship between the price of a specific good or service and the quantity supplied and demanded in a competitive market. In turn, market participants use the model to adapt their price, supply, and demand to the respective situation. It is a circular relationship of people that have subscribed to the narrative of competitive markets based on the model of supply and demand. Inspiring a transformation to more sustainable behavior in modern humans will require new models on which a new narrative can be built.

New Models

Pioneering work on formulating new models as a basis for realigning human behavior with human nature dates back to the early 1990s. John Elkington was the mastermind behind a legendary framework that is known as the triple bottom line. Elkington postulated a new form of adjusted capitalism by introducing the three P's: profits, planet, and people. Instead of maximizing the first P—profits—in isolation, he proposed that market participants take into consideration the impact of their actions on the two other P's: planet and people.

The academic world picked up on Elkington's concept and developed a series of models aimed at integrating the triple bottom line approach with Friedman's shareholder value principle. The "blended value" model in 2003 proposed evaluating business activity on its potential to generate a blend of financial, environmental, and social value. In the same year, the notion of "sustainable value" suggested that sustainability was not a "one-dimensional nuisance". Including social and environmental issues in a company's strategy would benefit their competitive positioning and ultimately create shareholder value. The concept was further expanded on in 2011 when Michael Porter, a Harvard professor and authority on competitive strategy, introduced a new word into the discussion: shared value. The term shifted the debate from the individual firm level to thinking in systems of interrelated companies sharing value chains. Porter's model was taken even further when the concept of "integrated value" was put forward in 2017. The approach identified five global systemic problems—disruption, discontent, destruction, disparity, and disconnection—and presented an integrated plan of actions along five dimensions—continuity, wholeness, restoration, equity, and networking—to drive "positive change in society". The most recent outcome of model ideation in the field has been the concept of stakeholder value, which postulates that the concerns of all parties that have a stake in a business's operations—such as employees, local communities, suppliers, creditors, management, and shareholders—need to be addressed in a balanced way.

Another Chapter

Drawing on the above conceptual developments over the past 25 years, one could conclude that we are well on track to slow down and change direction. Unfortunately, that does not reflect actual reality. In 2018, John Elkington recalled his triple bottom line model. In his assessment, it had served its objective of raising awareness, but by now, it had also become outdated.

The new normal was that businesses were using the PPP for so-called greenwashing—that is, making false claims about their sustainability in order to boost profits. This included donating to charities in environmental and social sectors in compensation for the pollution and psycho-social harm done by companies' operations. In addition, minor tweaks to the concept of the triple bottom line—replacing profits with terms such as prosperity or purpose, for example—had not had the desired effects on business behavior. Elkington therefore decided to twist the message to inspire a new phase of sustainable thinking, feeling, and acting.

Elkington argued that there was only one planet and that therefore businesses should not think of three separate PPP dimensions. The new thinking should no longer allow for an antagonistic relationship between profits on the one side and people and planet on the other. The next stage of the Elkington narrative had only one P, that is maximizing the overlap of the three dimensions. From his perspective, the next phase of slowing down and changing direction could only be accomplished by bringing the profit objective of mighty capitalism in line with benefits for people and planet. His postulate: Let's use business as a force for good. Let's redesign business models by aligning all three—profit, people, and planet—as intermeshed building blocks of companies' competitive advantage. Let sustainable innovation for the benefit of people and planet become the driver of companies' profits.

New Thinking

What is notable about the advent of new models is how their features provide the foundation for new narratives, reminding Homo Sapiens of its nature, that is, surviving in groups fueled by the ABC of life. All models emphasize the multiple facets of human life. Each part needs to contribute its Competence in support of all parts Belonging to the group while preserving its Autonomy. Across the models, the term "group" can span from individuals pooling their skills to ecosystems of companies coordinating their value chains. The common denominator for all of them is the interdependence of the parts. People, planet, profits, finance, environment, society, sharing, integration, and stakeholders are all representations of the same idea of interconnectedness. We are all in this together. Human survival is a group effort. The individual parts need to align, energize, and provide ABC for each other in order for humankind to develop sustainably.

New Narratives

The conceptual work of Elkington and others has not gone unnoticed by politics and business. In 2015, the United Nations put forward a set of 17 sustainable development goals (SDGs) as part of its Agenda 2030:

(1) no poverty
(2) zero hunger
(3) good health and well-being
(4) quality of education
(5) gender equality
(6) clean water and sanitation
(7) affordable and clean energy
(8) decent work and economic growth
(9) industry, innovation, and infrastructure
(10) reducing inequality
(11) sustainable cities and communities
(12) responsible consumption and production
(13) climate action
(14) life below water
(15) life on land
(16) peace, justice, and strong institutions
(17) partnerships for the goals

Two years later, the UN defined specific key performance indicators for each goal to be achieved in the years leading up to 2030. The SDG framework is a classic example of a new narrative inspiring individuals, communities, organizations, and societies to contribute to specific aspects of group survival. It prompts and energizes action through the ABC framework by inviting (Autonomy) individuals, communities, organizations, and societies to commit their heads, hands, and hearts (Competence) to make this world a better place (Belonging).

Similar approaches to new narratives have been launched in the business world. Some of the most impactful ones have joined forces in the Imperative 21 network, a business-led network of currently eight partnering organizations. B Lab, The B Team, Chief Executives for Corporate Purpose (CECP), Conscious Capitalism, Global Impact investing Network (GIIN), Common Future, Just

Capitalism, and Participant collaborate on activities to reset our economic system from shareholder capitalism to stakeholder capitalism. It is another example of a natural, ABC-driven effort. Each partner retains its individual scope of activities (Autonomy) and contributes its respective angle (Competence) to the mission of the network (Belonging), which is to equip leaders with the tools to accelerate their transition to stakeholder capitalism, shift the cultural narrative about the role of business and finance in society, and realign incentives and facilitate a supportive public policy environment. Particularly noteworthy in the context of the interconnectedness of stakeholders is one of the partners' narrative tools. In order to promote the sharing mindset of stakeholder capitalism versus the money mantra's mirage of independence, B Lab (the B stands for benefit) has issued a 'Declaration of Interdependence':

> We envision a global economy that uses business as a force for good. This economy is comprised of a new type of corporation—the B Corporation—which is purpose-driven and creates benefit for all stakeholders, not just shareholders. As B Corporations and leaders of this emerging economy, we believe that
> – We must be the change we seek in the world
> – All business ought to be conducted as if people and place mattered
> – Through their products, practices and profits, businesses should aspire to do no harm and benefit all
> To do so requires that we act with the understanding that we are each dependent upon another and responsible for each other and future generations.

Somewhat surprisingly, these initiatives by political and non-profit organizations like the UN and B Lab have received support from the C-suites of top U.S. companies. In August 2019, 181 CEOs signed and released a Statement on the Purpose of a Corporation in which they committed themselves to leading their companies for the benefit of all stakeholders—customers, employees, suppliers, communities, and shareholders. It remains to be seen whether the statement will actually spur companies to move from just looking good or sounding good to doing good. A serious transformation of business practice is unlikely to happen without new narratives. Company narratives are their mission statements. They are a good place to start when evaluating the state of play in a company's transformation process from shareholder capitalism to stakeholder capitalism. For example, the mission of a traditional company engaging in the typical greenwashing practices may sound something like: "We are the XYZ company. We have the best products and services that are customer-focused and innovative. We support the world's sustainable transformation." The statement is self-focused and overconfident, and furthermore, sustainability appears just as an afterthought. It is unlikely that a business will survive beyond 2030 with such a narrative as part of its marketing and communication. Here is what a company's mission statement may sound like in 2030: "In everything we do, we contribute to the sustainable transformation of our planet. Therefore, our products and services are innovative and sustainable in support of both our customers and our planet. We are XYZ company." The tone of the message is humble, and it is focused on people and the planet. Contributing to people and the planet in their own specific way will be the source of competitive advantage for companies. In turn, this will generate economic benefits such as profit. In essence, any successful future narrative needs to refocus, steering away from the money mantra and towards shared, long-term, humble thinking. But thinking will not be enough. Acting in congruence with your narrative will be the part that will make a difference to future sustainable developments. Publishing a shiny annual report with lots of green content will not help when the CEO is earning 200 times more than the median employee, executives are still serving on committees slowing or stalling economic system change, or goods and services are sourced from other parts of the world instead of locally. Each of us needs to act in the interest of all. Modern humans will need to learn how to act differently in order for humankind to change direction.

Where to Go From Here?

Learning at all levels, from children to executive boards, will play a decisive role in this change in direction. The money narrative has been around for a long time, and it is wired into our brains from the moment we are born. It is so pre-eminent that you cannot miss it. The money mantra is coded into our behavior like an autopilot. So changing direction will mean going into our minds, switching off the autopilot, and exiting the money highway.

As humans, we make mistakes. We take wrong turns and end up on highways that lead us astray. But we also learn from our errors. Collective learning has ensured our survival and our dominion over planet Earth to date. Okay, this time we got lost by speeding out of control on the money highway. Changing direction means getting off that highway—i.e., unlearning the money narrative—and learning about alternative highways.

Doom and gloom scenarios as well as bans and controls will not solve this existential human crisis. Neither despair nor efforts to limit the harm will save us. We need to learn how to put a positive spin on our survival story, energizing people to subscribe to a mission. Which twenty-first-century campaign would you rather be a part of—Disaster 21 or Survival 21? Let's draw inspiration from Antoine de Saint-Exupéry, the French author of *The Little Prince*:

> If you want to build a ship, don't drum up the men to gather wood, divide the work and give orders. Instead, teach them to yearn for the vast and endless sea.

An effective new narrative should remind people of their nature, the ABC of life. The question is not "What can we do?" but "How can we think?". Our thoughts drive our actions. Modern humans who think that we dominate nature may believe that the sun rises because it is 6am, but it is the other way around. Let's consider nature as a partner for our human survival project. Nature is resilient and can get back on track if we give it a chance. Promoting creative, out-of-the-box thinking to come up with novel solutions will boost societal Autonomy. Considering the fascinating, diverse aspects of our nature as collaborators and support factors will boost societal Belonging. Drawing on and applying our vast human portfolio of skills will fuel our societal Competence. Thinking in terms of ABC will energize our actions and make sure we persistently use effective skills in the pursuit of evident goals to overcome this crisis. The result of such a shift in thinking from domination to collaboration will lead to nothing less than a new way of life on earth.

Education will be key for this learning process. Changing direction is not about negating Homo Sapiens' inherent trait of creativity, development, and innovation. It is about teaching and learning how to redirect this ability towards a sustainable human future—in other words, educating people for sustain-ability. A new vision will be needed to provide directions to alternative highways that will lead us to new destinations. The ABC of life can serve as a navigation tool. The Personal Development Goals (PDGs) of Autonomy, Belonging, and Competence could represent a foundation for new narratives driving the change needed to achieve the UN's sustainable development goals.

The ABC of Humankind's Future

Humans survive in groups and will go under as a group. If we want to secure Homo Sapiens' role and existence on planet Earth, we need to create the conditions for sustainable innovation. High levels of ABC ensure that individuals, communities, organizations, and societies pursue evident goals and apply their skills in persistent and effective ways in alignment with our human nature. The resulting success will be the survival of the human species.

There is nothing wrong with the desire to be rich. But being rich on money will not save us. We need to be rich on ABC. Let's use our distinct capacity for communication to boost each other's ABC levels. Let's not wait for others to change their behavior. Each of us can contribute in sharing, long-term, humble ways today to become a role model for others. Albert Einstein once made the prediction that the world will not be destroyed by those who do evil but by those who sit on the sidelines, watching and doing nothing. The ABC of life is an effective tool enabling each of us to change our own life and contribute to the lives of others to overcome humankind's challenges ahead .

Acknowledgements

The foundation of this book was formed by the fascinating academic efforts, resilience, and vision of Edward Deci and Richard Ryan. With their dedication and commitment, they have turned self-determination theory from an academic project into a global movement. Ed and Rich have been living their lives as role models for the principles of this book, inspiring individuals, communities, and societies around the world.

I stumbled across self-determination theory during the literature review I conducted for my dissertation. Geoff Lovell was one of my PhD supervisors. I am sure I am not the only PhD student who on multiple occasions entertained thoughts of throwing in the towel. It was Geoff's energetic encouragement and solution-orientated advice that helped me stay the course and complete the program. He planted seeds that have since grown and from which I have been harvesting throughout my academic career. Without Geoff's indispensable personal and professional support, I would not have earned my PhD and this book would never have been written. According to a well-known proverb, "a friend in need is a friend indeed". That is what Geoff has become for me since he joined my PhD supervisory team.

With respect to the process of publishing this book, I feel deeply indebted to the people who sacrificed their time to review the original manuscript and contribute useful comments and challenging questions as well as compelling endorsements. After submitting the manuscript for publication, Inge van der Bijl was my first contact at Amsterdam University Press. Inge has impressed me with her outstanding professionalism and exceptional expertise, efficiently guiding me through the publication jungle. She made absolutely sure that I would arrive at my final destination – the best published book possible! It was also Inge who enlisted the help of my copyeditor, Gioia Marini. The quality of this book would not be the same without her editorial comments, questions, and suggestions. She really took a deep dive into the content to come up with eye-opening remarks and striking perspectives for revisions. And Eric Guémise led the charge on coming up with the book cover. He is an absolute genius when it comes to design, innovation, and artistry. His inspiring creativity made me think again and again during our brainstorming sessions. I will never stroll through a bookstore again without hearing his voice commenting on the individual book cover designs.

Last but not least, I want to thank from the bottom of my heart those people who encouraged me to write this book. Whenever and wherever I introduced people to the ABC of life – students, workshop participants, families, friends or listeners of my public talks – they asked me to make the ABC principles available to a wider audience in book format. The constant positive feedback and encouragement energized me to the point where I decided to finally sit down with pen and paper to lay out the first structure of this book. I would like in particular to thank my students who attended my classes over the years for their ideas and inspirations generated by in-class and out-of-classroom discussions. As a result, I can honestly say that my learning curve has been at least as steep as theirs. I am incredibly proud of them for making a difference to people's lives by applying the ABC principles to their respective life domains. Finally, I hope that this book will offer new perspectives to their generation for changing their lives and contributing to the lives of others – for the better!

Index